GENDER AND SUSTAINABILITY

Gender and Sustainability

Lessons from Asia
and Latin America

MARÍA LUZ CRUZ-TORRES

AND PAMELA MCELWEE, EDITORS

THE UNIVERSITY OF
ARIZONA PRESS

Tucson

The University of Arizona Press
www.uapress.arizona.edu

ISBN-13: 978-0-8165-3001-4 (cloth)
ISBN-13: 978-0-8165-3795-2 (paper)

Cover design by David Drummond
Cover image: © Bernardo Ertl / istockphoto.com

Publication of this book is made possible in part by the proceeds of a permanent
endowment created with the assistance of a Challenge Grant from the National
Endowment for the Humanities, a federal agency.

Library of Congress Cataloging-in-Publication Data
Gender and sustainability : lessons from Asia and Latin America / María Luz Cruz-Torres
and Pamela McElwee, editors.
    p. cm.
  Includes bibliographical references and index.
  ISBN 978-0-8165-3001-4 (cloth : alk. paper) 1. Rural women—Latin America—Social
conditions. 2. Rural women—Asia—Social conditions. 3. Women in natural resources
management—Latin America. 4. Women in natural resources management—Asia.
5. Women in sustainable development—Latin America. 6. Women in sustainable
development—Asia. 7. Natural resources—Environmental aspects—Latin America.
8. Natural resources—Environmental aspects—Asia. I. Cruz-Torres, María Luz, 1961–
II. McElwee, Pamela D.
  HQ1460.5G45 2012
  305.4098—dc23
                                2012015848

Contents

Acknowledgments

This book would have not been possible without the help and support of many people. Some of the ideas presented in this book were initially discussed in a research cluster titled "The Narrative Prisms of Women and Sustainability," sponsored and funded by the Institute for Humanities Research at Arizona State University (ASU). The institute also awarded us a subvention to help with the costs of preparation of the final manuscript. We are deeply indebted to the institute's director, Dr. Sally Kitsch, for her encouragement, support, and enthusiasm for our project. We are also grateful to all of those who participated in the research cluster, but especially to Angelita Reyes, James Eder, LaDawn Hagland, Rimjhim Aggarwal, and Marcia Nation. We also owe very special thanks to Mary Margaret Fonow for all her support and wisdom throughout the development of this book.

In 2008, we organized a panel on "Gender and Sustainability" for the annual meeting of the American Anthropological Association, held that year in San Francisco, where most of the chapters were presented and many of the authors first met. We express our gratitude to Lisa Gezon and Joan Mencher for being our wonderful discussants at the panel. We would also like to acknowledge all of the authors who contributed to this volume, as well as those who were on the original panel but were unable to contribute papers for this book. We extend a particular thank you to our ASU colleague Amber Wutich, who enthusiastically contributed a chapter, despite not being able to be part of the original panel.

Additional ideas were contributed by attendees at a Faculty of Global Studies colloquium at ASU on gender and sustainability in fall of 2009 as we were fleshing out the introduction, and we thank all those who attended and contributed ideas. We are also very grateful to Gene Anderson, who read a draft of the introduction and provided us with important comments.

Our deepest thanks also go out to our editor at the University of Arizona Press, Allyson Carter, for all her encouragement and enthusiasm for this book, as well as to several anonymous reviewers, who helped us sharpen our analysis considerably.

Special thanks are also due to Leonardo Figueroa and Joshua Sierra, both PhD students in the School of Politics and Global Studies at ASU, who served as research assistants for the project as we were putting together this volume. They organized much of the hard work of formatting chapters, checking references, getting photo credits, and assembling the final manuscript, and we thank them much for their editorial assistance.

Finally, María Luz Cruz-Torres wishes to thank her husband, Carlos Vélez-Ibáñez, and their daughter, Nayely, for all their unconditional help and support during the preparation of this book. Pamela McElwee would like to thank her husband, Chris Duncan, for his support in this and all other endeavors.

List of Acronyms

AUCC	Cotacachi County Assembly for Unity
CITES	Convention on International Trade in Endangered Species
CMI	Coordinadora de Mujeres de Intag (Women's Coordinating Committee of Intag, Ecuador)
CONAMU	Consejo Nacional de la Mujer (National Women's Council, Ecuador)
CRM	coastal resource management
CRMP	Coastal Resource Management Project
CWC	Central Women's Committee of the Maa Maninag Jungle Surakhya Parishad
DAWN	Development Alternatives with Women for a New Era
DECOIN	Ecological Defense and Conservation of Intag
EO	Ecological Ordinance
MLA	member of the Legislative Assembly, India
MMJSP	Maa Maninag Jungle Surakhya Parishad (Mother Maninag Forests Protection Forum)
NGO	nongovernmental organization
US$	United States dollars
VND	Vietnamese Dong
VSS	Van Samrakhan Samities, India (Forest Protection Committee)
WED	women, environment, and development approach
WID	women in development approach

GENDER AND SUSTAINABILITY

CHAPTER ONE

Introduction

Gender and Sustainability

María Luz Cruz-Torres and Pamela McElwee

Scene 1

Early on a Sunday, before her family left for church, Doña Basilia invited me to stop by her house. It was a chilly morning just before springtime began in Cochabamba, Bolivia, and I was relieved to be invited inside for a warm cup of breakfast *maizena* (cornstarch). I had interviewed Doña Basilia twice before and always enjoyed her gentle but mischievous sense of humor. This time I was eager to learn how her family had fared during the long winter dry season. Within a few questions I learned that Doña Basilia had run out of water for bathing and cleaning. With just enough water to cook and wash dishes, the family was growing tense. As I leaned forward, ready to ask how the family was coping during this stressful time, Doña Basilia's husband Don Wálter came home.

I knew Don Wálter well. He was leading a group of men in the fight to improve the community's water access and infrastructure, and he had often explained to me the local politics of water. To my surprise, he pulled up a chair and seemed quite determined to join in on our conversation.

Continuing where I left off, I asked Doña Basilia if she had taken any-thing on credit from a local store. Don Wálter interrupted, "Using credit is absurd. I don't care for it." I was a bit taken aback by his brusque response, but this was consistent with what I knew of this proud family and with what Doña Basilia had told me in the past. I quickly moved on: Would Doña Basilia ask any of her neighbors for help? Again, Don Walter broke in before Doña Basilia had a chance to respond. He said, "We never ask

1

for help. We have had to get by with what we have. [My family] is not going out to beg; I don't care for that. God sends me help . . . we have what we need. We don't beg; I teach this to my children." As Don Wálter spoke, Doña Basilia looked down quietly at her hands. I knew from our prior interviews that Doña Basilia often helped her neighbors and occasionally received help herself. I wondered if perhaps she had kept this part of household management from her husband (from Amber Wutich fieldwork conducted in Cochabamba, Bolivia, in 2004).

Scene 2

On a hot, humid August afternoon, while conducting fieldwork among the Mazatlán shrimp traders of Pacific coastal Mexico, I sat down to converse with Inés and Isabel, two of the founders of their union. It was another slow Monday at the market place, and all shrimp traders were relaxing and amicably talking to one another. I felt that this was a good time to ask the women shrimp traders questions about their work and membership in the union. As I sat down, Inés, who was reading the local newspaper and smoking a cigarette, lifted her head and glimpsed at me. "Los lunes ni las gallinas ponen" (Not even the chickens lay eggs on Mondays), she commented with a smile. While Inés read the newspaper, Isabel rearranged the shrimp in her green plastic buckets, her hands moving in slow motion, as she dug to the bottom and placed the larger shrimp on top.

As I watched, I asked if they felt they were better off now that they have a union. Inés folded the newspaper, placing it on top of one of her ice chests, and responded, "Years ago, we had to go to the lagoons and estuaries to buy the shrimp directly from the fishermen. We worked very hard and many times we were harassed by local authorities and members of the fishing cooperatives. Some of us were arrested and taken to jail. We were selling shrimp walking from house to house in the *colonias* here in Mazatlán. Those were very hard times. We struggled a lot in order for us to be able to sell shrimp here in Mazatlán. We took over this street since we did not have a steady place in which to sell our shrimp. The local authorities tried to relocate us to another place, but we always kept coming back here to our street, the street of the shrimp ladies." Isabel added, "Now we don't have to go around anymore, risking our lives looking for shrimp or finding a place to sell it. Now they [shrimp retailers] bring us the shrimp here" (from María L. Cruz-Torres fieldwork conducted in Sinaloa, Mexico, in 2009).

These two vignettes encapsulate the basic theme of this anthology: women's important and multiple roles in overcoming the challenges of securing livelihoods based on the sustainable use of natural resources. In the case of Doña Basilia in Bolivia, she faced constraints from her husband's disapproval of her role in local charity, problems exacerbated by water shortages that heightened these household and community tensions. But for Isabel and Inés in Mexico, challenges in selling shrimp in a stable marketplace had empowered them to take on stronger roles in both their households and in a cooperative union. These anecdotes illustrate the fact that women's roles vary by time and place, which we demonstrate by case studies in this book from different parts of Latin America and Asia. However, women's struggles to negotiate forces such as global environmental changes, economic development pressures, discrimination and stereotyping about women's roles, and diminishing access to natural resources are a common shared experience. As demonstrated by the story of water access in Bolivia, women must use water on a daily basis to meet the needs of their households, while they often lack the ability to participate in local politics concerning its management and allocation. In other cases, such as the Mazatlán shrimp traders, the struggles women must face in order to be able to gain access to natural resources may in turn empower them, and their communities, in the process. In the chapters that follow, we closely examine the interplay between questions of sustainability, broadly conceived, and women's lives and livelihoods. We strive to understand the complexity of the relationship between gender and sustainability and to bring in the interplay between local and global processes that affect the outcome of the human-environment relationships in Third World countries.

A gender analysis is necessary to understand the roles of households, communities, and even nations in creating long-term resource use strategies that could lead to more sustainable outcomes. By providing detailed case studies grounded in anthropological and ethnographic research, the chapters in this book reveal the multiscale and interconnected dimensions of gender, sustainability, and livelihoods. These case studies include the impact of development of hydroelectric and mining projects on both men and women, the gender division of labor within fisheries and aquaculture industries, women's struggles over access to various environmental resources, the impact of environmental change on women's work, culturally inscribed gender roles in the use of resources such as wild bushmeat, and women's agency and empowerment in trying to find more sustainable ways of living. All of the case studies point out the importance of considering gender when looking for ways to improve the long-term sustainability of natural resources use.

The rest of this introduction examines the history of approaches to the study of gender and sustainability and lays out our proposed theoretical interconnections between these two concepts, particularly as seen through the lenses of livelihoods and globalization. Many authors have already noted that a gender perspective is critical for assessing the human-environment equation. Our goal here is to show how and why gender is becoming even more crucial for understanding how communities and populations face the challenge of achieving a more sustainable way of life, particularly in the face of such significant pressures as globalization and environmental change.

Our Conceptual Framework and Key Terms

Why does gender matter? As this book will highlight, we believe a gender-oriented analysis is crucial for examining the complexity of the interactions of women and men with the environment and for understanding local and global processes impacting people's livelihood strategies. Although gender is usually defined as the socioculturally ascribed roles and responsibilities of men and women and their interaction within a given society, the concept is very fluid and varies much throughout the world. Recent feminist poststructuralist approaches have explored the many additional dimensions of gender, particularly the multiple facets and interactions with other social markers such as power, class, ethnicity, race, sexuality, age, and caste (Verma 2001). It is these many intersections that contribute to make gender a real and lived experience shaping all aspects of life.

The concept of sustainability helps us to understand the effects of environmental change upon people and how they develop short- and long-term responses to deal or cope with these changes. Sustainability is traditionally defined as "the use of environment and resources to meet the needs of the present without compromising the ability of future generations to meet their own needs" (Berkes et al. 2003, p. 3). During the past few decades the notion of sustainability has been gradually broadened beyond simply environmental considerations to include attention to social and economic dimensions and to emphasize its cross-disciplinary nature (Goodland 2002). For example, it is now widely understood that the different dimensions of sustainability overlap; for example, one cannot have environmental sustainability without social sustainability. The chapters in this book examine the links between two or more of these dimensions of sustainability. For example, social sustainability can be understood through attention to social justice and human rights, social networks, reciprocity, and local knowledge, whereas issues regarding livelihood strategies, development projects, neoliberal economic restructuring, labor mobility, and capital penetration are concerned with the economic dimension of sustainability. More recent approaches to sustainability often refer to the idea of "sustainability science" and argue that this is a more holistic, synergetic approach, and one that pays attention to complexity and uncertainty (Clark and Dickson 2003). An emphasis on the role of global processes as drivers of both unsustainable consumption and potentially more sustainable solutions also characterizes this newer literature (Kates et al. 2001; Kates and Parris 2003).

The concept of livelihood also provides us with a useful framework in which to contextualize people's relationship with their environment. Livelihood simply defined refers to the ways in which people make a living, taking into consideration the many factors that shape their choices and alternatives. Ellis (2000, p. 10) provided a more comprehensive definition of livelihood as "the assets (natural, physical, human, financial, and social capital), the activities, and the access to these (mediated by institutions and social relations) that together determine the living gained by the individual or household." This definition takes into account the fact that livelihoods might change over time as a result of changes experienced by individuals or households that in turn would increase or limit access to resources and opportunities (Hapke and Ayyankeril 2004). It also emphasizes the various strategies individuals and households undertake over time in order to deal with uncertainty and vulnerability. The case studies in this book focus primarily on livelihoods that are directly linked to the use of natural resources, such as water, fish, forests, and wild animals. In the majority of the case studies, the access and use of these resources are being transformed or constrained by factors such as development, overexploitation, environmental change, global demand for commodities, and changes in policy and institutions.

As a result of these changes, which are happening at multiple scales and caused by multiple drivers, we need to answer some important questions. What happens to traditional livelihoods when natural resources are degraded and physical environments change? How do people respond to the threats that environmental change pose to their livelihoods? What sectors of the population will be the most vulnerable to these changes? What might be more sustainable pathways for future livelihoods given these changes? Finally, the key question we hope this book answers is: How does analysis of gender and women's roles help us understand the outcomes of the four questions above? The answers that we derive from the case studies are very diverse, but a common theme emerging from all is that gender relations and struggles are intertwined with people's ability to procure and secure sustainable livelihoods. The two cannot be meaningfully separated.

Addressing these questions, particularly from an anthropological perspective and at the local level, requires us to be aware of the drivers of these environmental and livelihoods changes in Asia and Latin America, globalization being chief among them. We therefore pay close attention to the impact of globalization on our themes of gender, livelihoods, and sustainability. Globalization is the current catchword for the flow of people, commodities, capital, images, and ideas that characterizes the contemporary world (Inda and Rosaldo 2002; Gunewardena and Kingsolver 2007). It is now well established that globalization affects women and men differently and that not all women are affected in the same manner, as factors such as class, race, ethnicity, education, and age also structure impacts and responses (Thorin 2001). For example, global structural adjustment programs and other neoliberal policies implemented during the 1980s and 1990s drove numerous changes in the relationships between people and environments in Asia and Latin America, such as the expansion of commodity production for global trade accompanied by the narrowing range of commodities produced, which has had impacts on areas such as land use, labor, food security, and health, particularly for women (Cupples 2004; Resurreccion and Elmhirst 2008). Anthropologists working on globalization agree that our discipline places us in a special and privileged position to study how people experience and respond to these new challenges (Stone et. al. 2000; Inda and Rosaldo 2002; Rothstein 2007).

Points of Departure: Theories of Gender, Environment, and Development

Many of the valuable contributions to the field of gender and sustainability can be traced back to earlier efforts of feminist scholars and activists to mainstream gender into development programs, such as in the pioneering work of Ester Boserup, who argued in *Women's Role in Economic Development* (1970) that women's responsibilities in household economies and hence national development were seriously undervalued. These efforts became an essential component of what came to be known as the women in development (WID) approach, which sought to analyze why development projects often failed to take women into consideration and how these failings had differential social, economic, and cultural impacts (Martine and Villarreal 1997; Momsen 2004). Attention to WID culminated in the first United Nations Conference on Women and Development, which was held in Mexico City in 1975 (Braidotti et al. 1994), with a fourth international conference on women taking place on the twentieth anniversary in Beijing, where the focus had shifted to the idea of *gender*, not just women (Rathgeber 2005).

The WID approach, although considered at the time a groundbreaking path in the field of feminist studies, has been subsequently criticized. First, it failed to consider the intersections between women's productive and reproductive roles. Second, most WID programs demanded women's participation without giving them much back; for example, Melissa Leach noted that "project 'success' has often been secured at women's expense, by appropriating women's labor, unremunerated, in activities which prove not to meet their needs or whose benefits they do not control" (Leach 2007, p. 72). Because WID was premised on putting women into traditional development approaches, rather than challenging these approaches as inappropriate or skewed toward First World countries' interests, WID fell prey to the same critiques of conventional development that began to bubble up in the 1980s (Escobar 1988; Escobar 1995). Finally, WID failed to address the roots of women's subordination and oppression within their particular societies (Howard 1995; Burn 2005). For Third World feminists, the WID approach was too focused on a Western-based development model that failed to make women's empowerment a priority (Sturgeon 1997). Discouraged by this, some decided to form their own organization, DAWN (Development Alternatives with Women for a New Era). DAWN, a nongovernmental organization (NGO) comprised of feminist scholars and activists from countries in Africa, Asia, Latin America, the Caribbean, and the Pacific, was formed during the 1980s, at a time when most Third World countries were battling economic crises and debt that challenged the promotion of equitable development. DAWN sought to advance women's status through cooperation, empowerment, and political mobilization (Burn 2005).

Third World feminists also played a crucial role in urging First World feminists to transform the WID approach into the gender and development approach. Their belief was that unequal gender relations and not women per se should be the focus of development and that the goal should not be to make development better by including women, but to make women's lives better, which might entail the rejection of traditional development altogether (Braidotti et al. 1994). The gender and development approach focused in particular on how power relations at various local, regional, and national levels kept women subordinated and marginalized within economic development and decision-making processes (Burn 2005). This approach's concern with women's empowerment led to the creation and implementation of development projects based on a bottom-up approach to encourage women to become the agents of change in their communities and societies.

As development practice in general slowly became attuned to the important need to understand gender as one component, so too did the world of development begin to more explicitly incorporate environmental concerns (Pearce et al. 1990; Kirkby et al. 1995). The use of the term *sustainable development*, rather than just development, became virtually de rigueur by the early 1990s (Brundtland 1987). With the increasing importance placed on environmental components of development, the trifecta of environment, development, and gender received more attention. Respective oil and fuelwood crises in the First and Third Worlds in the 1970s highlighted these links between environment and development. Because women were the major collectors of fuelwood in the Third World, they were naturally assumed to be both precipitating this crisis and disproportionately impacted by it (Braidotti et al. 1994). This new understanding of the roles and relationship of women with their environment became a central focus of what was to become the women, environment, and development (WED) approach. Rooted in the philosophical ideas of the ecofeminist movement of the 1960s and 1970s and the pioneering work of such figures as Vandana Shiva and Carolyn Merchant, among others, the WED approach sought to understand the relationship between women and nature, with an emphasis on the "links between the oppression of women and the degradation of nature" (Braidotti et al. 1994, p. 7).

Much of the WED/ecofeminist perspective assumed women to be more in tune with nature because of their traditionally ascribed caring and nurturing roles (Shiva 1988). Two major ideas of ecofeminism were that women and nature were both subjected to male domination and that Western science and colonialism were responsible for the environmental degradation and the marginalization of women in Third World countries (Momsen 2004). However, because of ecofeminism's preoccupation with female spirituality and biological characteristics, it has been labeled as essentialist and too simplistic to be able to properly address the complexity of the relationship between women and the environment (Sturgeon 1997; Momsen 2004; Burn 2005). The argument that women's knowledge and action about environmental problems were social artifacts, not biological ones, was a strong one for moving away from the WED approach, which some characterized as a dead-end "trap" (Jackson 1993).

After a much-heated debate about ecofeminism and following feminist scholars' disappointment with the WED approach, a new approach, now known as gender, environment, and development, has emerged (Chua et al. 2000). The transformation stressed the role gender plays in shaping and influencing access to and control over natural resources. The approaches of feminist political ecology have also played an important role in the gender, environment, and development approach since, in the words of Rocheleau et al. (1996, p. 2), it "treats gender as a critical variable in shaping resource access and control, interacting with class, caste, race, culture, and ethnicity to shape processes of ecological change, the struggle of men and women to sustain ecologically viable livelihoods, and the prospects of any community for 'sustainable development'." Feminist political ecology takes as a core precept the idea that gender is one, but not the only, characteristic of socially differentiated resource use, which must be understood as a complex series of negotiations over access and control (Leach 1994; Agarwal 1997; Schroeder 1999).

Although we appreciate the contributions made by the various approaches of women/gender and development to the contemporary field of gender and sustainability, we echo Benería's (2003, p. 1) concerns with development as "an organizing concept." As scholars working in Third World countries, we are fully aware of the many debates and contradictions surrounding the concept of development and its impact upon the communities and peoples in regions such as Asia and Latin America. Our emphasis is then not so much on development per se, as the key word to match with sustainability, but rather on the historical roots and present-day struggles of local people to secure decent livelihoods through their access, use, and exploitation of natural resources. Hence, our attention is primarily turned to livelihoods, rather than development, as has been the approach of most previous works on gender and the environment.

Toward a Framework for the Study of Gender and Sustainability in Local and Global Contexts

The present decade has witnessed the proliferation of studies addressing the interconnections between gender and livelihoods in the developing world (e.g., Brown and Lapuyade 2001; Valdivia and Gilles 2001; Krishna

2004; Niehof 2004; Oberhauser et al. 2004; Venema and Eijk 2004; Bennett 2005; Deere 2005; Fonchingong 2005; Brown 2006; Abbott et al. 2007; Merten and Haller 2007; Rothstein 2007; Turner 2007; Elmhirst 2008; Guhathakurta 2008). From these studies emerges the need to understand the way institutions, social relations, and economic opportunities at multiple scales shape livelihood systems. In particular, these studies have focused our attention on the many gender-based livelihood strategies that households and individuals employ in various geographic, political, and economic contexts, especially in an era of globalization.

For example, most feminist scholars agree that one of the most visible outcomes of economic globalization has been an increase of women's participation in the labor force. Women now constitute the main labor force in nontraditional agricultural exports such as flowers and fruits and vegetables (Thorin 2001). This feminization of labor is partially attributed to socially constructed stereotypes of women as being more patient, docile, and willing to perform repetitive and monotonous tasks or having smaller hands, among other reasons. These stereotypes are used to justify the fact that women's work in agriculture, such as the global cut flower industry, or in maquiladoras, is often poorly paid and lacks social benefits. Women many times face discrimination, sexual harassment, and health hazards in these new occupations (Iglesias Prieto 1985; Mellon 2002; Salzinger 2004). They also lack social protection and are discouraged from unionizing. Given all of these constraints, it is not surprising that a great number of women in Asia and Latin America have opted to pursue livelihoods within the informal economic sector instead (Collins 1995; Fonchingong 2005).

Another important theme that emerges from these studies is the concept of diversification, defined by Ellis and Allison (2005) as a continuous process through which households add, maintain, or drop activities in order to change their livelihood portfolios. Livelihood diversification is crucial in explaining how individuals and households negotiate improvements to their quality of life. In particular, the gender roles associated with diversification provide important clues about the manner in which men and women adapt and respond to challenges posed by the economic crisis and environmental degradation. Many recent studies have looked at such outcomes as the flexibilization and feminization of labor as part of household diversification, whether it is in fisheries, agriculture, offshore data processing centers, transnational factories and maquiladoras, tourism, or the global sex trade (Bolles 1996; Freeman 2000; Pearson 2001; Rowbothan and Linkogle 2001; Naples and Desai 2002; Aguilar and Lacsamana

2004; Burn 2005; Mendez 2005; Neis et al. 2005; Pongsapich 2007; Rothstein 2007; Muñoz 2008; Cabezas 2009).

But these changes in livelihoods cannot be understood merely as a one-way process of global changes pressing down on local existence and constraining choices. Outcomes such as the expansion of women's agency, empowerment, and resistance can also be seen. People can resist and respond to the risks and opportunities imposed by globalization upon their livelihoods, often in innovative and surprising ways, such as in the formation of new institutions, social relationships, and management practices for resources (Reed 2003; Bury 2004; Pongsapich 2007). In traditional communities in Latin America, for instance, strategies or responses to global pressures have included "forming labor unions; promoting health and educational activities; working with activist religious, environmental, and feminist groups and NGOs" (Heyck 2002, p. 20). Feminist scholars have noted the many strategies women in both First and Third World countries use in order to counteract the negative effects of globalization (Naples and Desai 2002; Gunewardena and Kingsolver 2007). For example, one of the most common and effective ways in which women respond to globalization is through collective organization, and women's agency can be enacted in such spaces as local grassroots social movements, NGOs, and transnational feminism (Naples and Desai 2002; Reed 2003).

This book takes what we know about gender, livelihoods, and globalization and positions this knowledge at the intersection of recent attention to sustainability. Despite both areas being important fields of study for some time now, very little literature specifically highlighting the interconnections between gender and sustainability has been published. For example, only three papers specifically on women or gender have been published in the journal *Sustainable Development* since its inception. A recent citation index search of the main environmental social science journals revealed that references to gender or sex or feminism only occurred in 3.9 percent of articles published (Banerjee and Bell 2007). Furthermore, many indicators becoming popular in sustainability approaches, such as ecological footprinting, fail to address gender as something that affects people's lifestyles and consumer choices, as people are aggregated into averages of generic indicators, such as gross domestic product per capita. We are concerned that social sustainability issues, among them livelihoods and gender, may fail to be at the forefront of analysis in these approaches. Thus, this book squarely aims to engage these concepts and link them to broader definitions of sustainability.

Key themes explored throughout the chapters include:

- the potential sustainability of the livelihood diversification and occupational pluralism that has been a result of globalization and has brought women into new roles and new jobs;
- the duality of the private-public spheres that women must occupy, and the roles they must negotiate in each realm, particularly with regard to access to resources and participation in decision-making processes;
- the manner in which women situate their households to sustain both traditional and newly developed livelihoods in light of uncertainty and risk brought about by globalization, the declining availability of natural resources, and climate change;
- the myriad changes in local environments caused by expanded global commodity markets, and how women and communities maneuver around the pressures and unsustainable exploitation often exerted by these global demands;
- the emergence of political activism to resist the challenges posed by global economic, social, and environmental change, and the strategies women have deployed to exert agency, resist local and global threats, and empower themselves.

Structure of the Book

The chapters in the book are organized into three parts, reflecting each chapter's focus on a particular natural resource. The chapters comprising the first part deal with gender and forests.

In Asia and Latin America, women tend to use forests to meet the subsistence needs of their households. They collect wood for fuel, plants for cooking and medicinal purposes, and other forest products for sale, such as seeds, nuts, or flowers, to help supplement the incomes of their families. In contrast, men tend to rely on forests for timber, charcoal, and wild animals, due to perceptions of the labor and time efforts and potential dangers involved in these activities. When major environmental changes such as deforestation occur, it is mostly women who are highly impacted (Agarwal 2001). When forest resources are not available nearby, it means that women must travel longer distances searching for wood and wild plants, reducing their available time to take care of children and perform household tasks. The chapters in this section discuss women's and men's relationships with forests and examine the role women have in decision-making processes regarding policies on access and exploitation of forest resources. The chapters also highlight the many ways in which women engage in resistant practices and collective action to deal with exclusion from forest resources or to protect them, particularly from new threats.

In the first chapter, "Environmentalism and Gender in Intag, Ecuador," Linda D'Amico discusses environmentalism within the contexts of gender relations and globalization in Intag. She examines how the relationship between men and women and their environment is constantly being renegotiated through the call for social rights and in resistance to a proposed transnational copper mine. Her chapter provides alternative and grassroots understandings of environmentalism, documenting how locals (women in particular) have embraced the concept of biodiversity and shaped it according to their own views, values, and needs to mobilize and defend their ecologically sensitive region. She notes that struggles for sustainable futures and alternative development can end up allowing marginalized people, particularly women, to gain more civil and social rights through these struggles.

In the next chapter, "Democratic Spaces across Scales: Women's Inclusion in Community Forestry in Orissa, India," Neera Singh focuses on women's exclusion within community forest management in Orissa and examines a case in which increased roles for women within a local federation of villages led to the transformation of this male-dominated realm. She explores how democratic spaces for women's participation and action emerged across spatial scales, allowing previously immobile women to move away from their proscribed gender roles. She notes that constraints and opportunities for women to participate in public domain vary at different levels of political action and suggests that closer attention to issues of scale and scalar politics can improve interventions to transform power relations.

In the last chapter in this part, "The Gender Dimensions of the Illegal Trade in Wildlife: Local and Global Connections in Vietnam," Pamela McElwee looks at the role of both men and women in the illegal wildlife trade and notes that any attempt to regulate this trade toward more sustainability must take into account gender. Unlike most other chapters that focus most specifically on women, McElwee argues that in the case of forest bushmeat, a gender analysis would focus primarily on the roles of men. She shows there are important cultural notions of masculinity in Vietnam among both the consumers of wild species, such as urban men who desire the prestige of eating in wild-game restaurants, and among the suppliers of wild animals, such as the hunters in remote forested regions who previously used to hunt for family subsistence, but who now primarily hunt for the global trade. As a result of overhunting, local extinctions have occurred, limiting local access to fresh meat and driving many non-professional hunters out of the trade entirely. This has had differential consequences for both women's and men's roles and workloads within households.

Part II deals with gender and water. Access to clean water is a major human right, but in many places who gets access to water is dictated by gender norms. Women are often responsible for making sure their families have sufficient supplies to drink, cook, clean, bathe, irrigate crops, and raise livestock. When deteriorating water quality and scarcity occur, it is often women who are most impacted. The three chapters in this section deal with women's access to water and the effects of environmental change and development upon it.

Amber Wutich's chapter, "Gender, Water Scarcity, and the Management of Sustainability Tradeoffs in Cochabamba, Bolivia," examines how gendered water management norms become blurred in the face of severe water scarcity in a squatter settlement on the outskirts of an urban area. Although women had long been the primary procurers of household water supplies, gender roles shifted as men became actively engaged in the household's struggle to obtain subsistence-level water provision. Yet, outside the household, men's dominance in decision-making was subverted, as women took more responsibility for the enforcement of institutional rules and protection of scarce groundwater resources in the community's water system. The chapter concludes by discussing how sustainability challenges may create new opportunities for women to provide leadership in community decision-making.

In the next chapter, "Gendered Fruit and Vegetable Home Processing Near the US–Mexico Border: Climate Change, Water Scarcity, and Noncapitalist Visions of the Future," Stephanie Buechler focuses on gendered agricultural production and home processing of fruits and vegetables in San Ignacio, a farming community in Sonora, Mexico, near the border with the United States. Her chapter sheds light on environmental and livelihood sustainability under conditions of growing water scarcity and climate change. She reveals that women and men have different visions of the future of small-scale, water-dependent, noncapitalist household production and that changes in this economic sector will have ramifications for community and cross-border social and economic relations. Moreover, the effects of climate change are already being seen, and this has led to increased vulnerability of women and small-scale home enterprises, in particular.

In "Meaningful Waters: Women, Development, and Sustainability along the Bhagirathi Ganges," Georgina Drew focuses on the Indian Himalayas along the primary tributary of the Ganges River, the Bhagirathi.

She argues that notions of sustainability can and should be broadened to include the maintenance of diverse relationships between humans and the nonhuman world. That is, the women highlighted by Drew who are fighting dams upstream from their villages are protesting not just the economic impacts of water scarcity, but loss of cultural relationships and notions of place that influence human behavior. While pointing out the potential for greater inclusion and collaboration between women and groups organizing in defense of the Bhagirathi Ganges, Drew notes that such efforts should be sensitive to women's personal needs, time constraints, social and structural limitations, and goals for involvement.

The last part focuses on gender and fisheries. Although fisheries are one of the most important resources and industries in the world, very little research in terms of women's roles has been published. As Choo et al. (2008, p. 178) note, "gender and fisheries research is a potentially rich field because of its relative novelty and the great diversity of issues and situations." In the Asian and Latin American regions, fisheries tend to be highly gender segregated. For the most part, women are more visible in the marketing and processing of seafood, whereas men tend to fish. However, this is changing as aquaculture takes over traditional fishing activities, and more women enter into this field. The chapters in this section discuss the feminization of labor within the fishing and aquaculture industries, alternative livelihoods for women in fishing families, and women's resistance and unionization to deal with exclusion from fishery resources.

In her chapter "Gender, Sustainability, and Shrimp Farming: Negotiating Risky Business in Vietnam's Mekong Delta," Hong Anh Vu questions whether shrimp aquaculture can be a sustainable livelihood for rural households in coastal Vietnam. She looks at the issues women and men face when engaging in aquaculture, particularly how households negotiate and make decisions regarding their entering into a risky venture such as shrimp farming. She argues that the marked gender division of labor prevalent in shrimp farming, along with cultural proscriptions and taboos, is partly responsible for keeping women at the margin of this activity. She notes that this marginalization has likely increased the economic risks for households as a whole.

In "The Role of Gender in the Reduction of Fishing Effort in the Coastal Philippines," James Eder focuses on alternative coastal zone livelihood programs for resource management in overfished areas of the Philippines. Eder examines the key role of women in establishing new household enterprises that redirect the labor of male household members away from fishing and into more sustainable economic activities. He concludes that efforts of community-based conservation projects, microfinance programs, and others to develop these new sustainable livelihoods need to build on the important role that women play in household economic affairs, otherwise they risk ignoring an important part of household economic structure.

In the last chapter, "Contested Livelihoods: Gender, Fisheries, and Resistance in Northwestern Mexico," Maria L. Cruz-Torres discusses how gender shapes access to control over fishing resources in southern Sinaloa, Mexico. She examines past and present struggles of women in claiming access to the use of the shrimp resources, traditionally allocated to males organized into fishing cooperatives. She also traces the emergence of women's collective action undertaken to assure the continuity of their livelihoods as shrimp traders and how local institutions shape the course of their actions. Using a feminist political ecology framework, this chapter also analyzes the manner in which gender interacts with state policies and local norms of resource allocation to understand the role of women within the Mexican fishing industry.

Final Reflections

We hope this book contributes to a better understanding of the challenges involved in addressing the interconnections between very broad and encompassing concepts such as gender, livelihoods, globalization and sustainability. As could be expected, many creative tensions arise within the process of giving context and meaning to the many dimensions associated with these concepts. However, rather than being seen as an obstacle or excuse, we hope it motivates more anthropologists and scholars in general to actively engage in rethinking how gender and sustainability are inexorably rooted and embedded in the daily lives of millions of people around the world. The final chapter of the book, "Why Gender Matters, Why Women Matter," by Lisa Gezon, lays out the arguments for why gender matters and serves as a call to others to take up this important analysis.

We also hope that the myriad of case studies in this book will show that the social reproduction of households and communities in Asia and Latin America is not only interconnected to culturally constructed notions of gender, but also to local and global processes shaping people's abilities to secure meaningful livelihoods. The fact that in most of the cases it is women who struggle to procure or protect these livelihoods also highlights the need to understand the differential gender impact of global and local economic, political, environmental, and social processes. However, men and women in these two regions are not just passive victims, and this book demonstrates how in many instances they engage, resist, contest, negotiate, and create their own means for dealing with these processes.

If we as anthropologists are truly concerned about how to mitigate human impacts upon the natural resources that would guarantee our survival as a species, then our approach as academics and practitioners should include a careful examination of specific case studies such as those included here. Anthropological ethnographic research provides us with the necessary tools to understand the various strategies and actions people in diverse cultural and geographic settings undertake in order to survive and whether these strategies will be able to lead to a greater balance between the need to sustain and expand human life. Overall, we hope this book contributes to further efforts to understand the complex processes involved in creating and engaging in sustainable livelihoods and equitable gender relations.

References

Abbott, James, Lisa M. Campbell, Clinton J. Hay, Tor F. Naesje, and John Purvis. 2007. Market-resource links and fish vendor livelihoods in the Upper Zambezi River floodplains. *Human Ecology* 35:559–574.

Agarwal, Bina. 1997. Gender, environment, and poverty interlinks: Regional variations and temporal shifts in rural India, 1971–91. *World Development* 25(1):23–52.

Agarwal, Bina. 2001. Participatory exclusions, community forestry, and gender: An analysis for South Asia and a conceptual framework. *World Development* 29(10):1623–1648.

Aguilar, Delia, and Anne Lacsamana, eds. 2004. *Women and globalization*. Amherst: Humanity Books.

Banerjee, Damayanti, and Michael Bell. 2007. Ecogender: Locating gender in environmental social science. *Society and Natural Resources* 20:3–19.

Benería, Lourdes. 2003. *Gender, development, and globalization: Economics as if all people mattered*. New York: Routledge.

Bennett, Elizabeth. 2005. Gender, fisheries and development. *Marine Policy* 29:451–459.

Berkes, Fikret, Johan Colding, and Carl Folke. 2003. Introduction. In *Navigating social-ecological systems: Building resilience for complexity and change*, eds. Fikret Berkes, Johan Colding, and Carl Folke, 1–29. Cambridge: Cambridge University Press.

Bolles, A. Lynn. 1996. *Sister Jamaica: A study of women, work, and households in Kingston*. Lanham, Md.: University Press of America.

Boserup, E. 1970. *Woman's role in economic development*. London: George Allen and Unwin.

Braidotti, Rosa, Ewa Chatkiewicz, Sabine Hausler, and Saskia Wieringa. 1994. *Women, the environment and sustainable development: Towards a theoretical synthesis*. London: Zed Books.

Brown, Alison, ed. 2006. *Contested space: Street trading, public space, and livelihoods in developing cities*. Warwickshire, U.K.: ITDG Publishing.

Brown, Katrina, and Sandrine Lapuyade. 2001. Livelihood from the forest: Gendered visions of social, economic and environmental change in southern Cameroon. *Journal of International Development* 13:1131–1149.

Brundtland, Gro Harlem. 1987. *Our common future*. Oxford: Oxford University Press.

Burn, Shawn. 2005. *Women across cultures: A global perspective*, 2nd ed. New York: McGraw-Hill.

Bury, Jeffrey. 2004. Livelihoods in transition: Transnational gold mining operations and local change in Cajamarca, Peru. *The Geographical Journal* 170(1):78–91.

Cabezas, Amalia. 2009. *Economies of desire: Sex and tourism in Cuba and the Dominican Republic*. Philadelphia, Pa.: Temple University Press.

Choo, Poh Sze, Barbara S. Nowak, Kyoko Kusakabe, and Meryl J. Williams. 2008. Guest editorial: Gender and fisheries. *Development* 51:176–179.

Chua, Peter, Kum-Kum Bhavnani, and John Foran. 2000. Women, culture, development: A new paradigm for development studies? *Ethnic and Racial Studies* 23(5):820–841.

Clark, William C., and Nancy M. Dickson. 2003. Sustainability science: The emerging research program. *Proceedings of the National Academy of Sciences* 100(14):8059–8061.

Collins, Jane. 1995. Transnational labor processes and gender relations: Women in fruit and vegetable production in Chile, Brazil and Mexico. *Journal of Latin American Anthropology* 1(1):178–199.

Cupples, Julie. 2004. Rural development in El Hatillo, Nicaragua: Gender, neo-liberalism and environmental risk. *Singapore Journal of Tropical Geography* 25(3):343–357.

Deere, Carmen. 2005. *The feminization of agriculture? Economic restructuring in rural Latin America*. Occasional paper 1. Geneva: United Nations Research Institute for Social Development.

Ellis, Frank. 2000. *Rural livelihoods and diversity in developing countries*. Oxford: Oxford University Press.

Ellis, Frank, and Edward Allison. 2005. Linking livelihood diversification to natural resources in a poverty reduction context. http://www.uea.ac.uk/polopoly_fs/1.53420!2005 percent20fao percent20div percent20briefing.pdf

Elmhirst, Rebecca. 2008. Multi-local livelihoods, natural resource management and gender in upland Indonesia. In *Gender and natural resource management: Livelihoods, mobility and interventions*, eds. B. Resurreccion and R. Elmhirst, 67–86. Sterling, Va.: Earthscan.

Escobar, Arturo. 1988. Power and visibility: Development and the invention and management of the Third World. *Cultural Anthropology* 3(4):428–443.

Escobar, Arturo. 1995. *Encountering development: The making and unmaking of the Third World.* Princeton, N.J.: Princeton University Press.

Escobar, Arturo, and Wendy Harcourt. 2005. Practices of difference: Introducing women and the politics of place. In *Women and the politics of place,* eds. Wendy Harcourt and Arturo Escobar, 1–17. Bloomfield, Conn.: Kumarian Press.

Fonchingong, Charles. 2005. *Negotiating livelihoods beyond Beijing: The burden of women food vendors in the informal economy of Limbe, Cameroon.* Oxford: Blackwell Publishing.

Forsyth, Timothy. 1996. Science, myth and knowledge: Testing Himalayan environmental degradation in Thailand. *Geoforum* 27(3):375–392.

Freeman, Carla. 2000. *High tech and high heels in the global economy: Women, work and pink collar identities in the Caribbean.* Durham, N.C.: Duke University Press.

Goodland, Robert. 2002. *Sustainability: human, social, economic and environmental.* Washington, DC: The World Bank.

Guhathakurta, Meghna. 2008. Globalization, class and gender relations: The shrimp industry in southwestern Bangladesh. *Development* 51:212–219.

Gunewardena, Nandini, and Ann Kingsolver, eds. 2007. *The gender of globalization: Women navigating cultural and economic marginalities.* Santa Fe, N.M.: School of American Research Press.

Hapke, Holly, and Devan Ayyankeril. 2004. Gender, the work-life course, and livelihood strategies in a South Indian fish market. *Gender, Place and Culture* 11(2):229–256.

Heyck, Denis L. D. 2002. *Surviving globalization in three Latin American communities.* Peterborough, Ontario: Broadview Press.

Howard, Rhoda. 1995. Women's rights and the right to development. In *Women's rights, human rights: International feminist perspectives,* eds. Julie Peters and Andrea Wolper, 301–316. New York: Routledge.

Iglesias Prieto, Norma. 1985. *La flor más bella de la maquiladora.* Mexico City: Secretaría de Educación Pública and Centro de Estudios Fronterizos del Norte de México.

Inda, Jonathan, and Renato Rosaldo. 2002. *The anthropology of globalization: A reader.* Malden, Mass.: Blackwell Publishers.

Jackson, Cecile. 1993. Doing what comes naturally? Women and environment in development. *World Development* 21(12):1947–1963.

Kates, Robert W., and Thomas M. Parris. 2003. Long-term trends and a sustainability transition. *Proceedings of the National Academy of Sciences* 100(14):8062–8067.

Kates, Robert W., William C. Clark, Robert Corell, J. Michael Hall, Carlo C. Jaeger, Ian Lowe, et al. 2001. Environment and development: Sustainability science. *Science* 292(5517):641–642.

Kirkby, John, Phil O'Keefe, and Lloyd Timberlake. 1995. *The Earthscan reader in sustainable development.* London: Earthscan.

Krishna, Sumi, ed. 2004. *Livelihood and gender: Equity in community resource management.* New Delhi: Sage.

Leach, Melissa. 1994. *Rainforest relations: Gender and resource use among the Mende of Gola, Sierra Leone.* Washington, DC: Smithsonian Institute Press.

Leach, Melissa. 2007. Earth Mother myths and other ecofeminist fables: How a strategic notion rose and fell. *Development and Change* 38(1):67–85.

Martine, George, and Marcela Villarreal. 1997. *Gender and sustainability: Reassessing linkages and issues.* Rome: Sustainable Development Department, Food and Agriculture Organization of the United Nations.

Mellon, Cynthia. 2002. *Deceptive beauty: A look at the global flower industry.* Victoria, B.C.: Victoria International Development Education Association.

Mendez, Jennifer. 2005. *From the revolution to the maquiladoras: Gender, labor, and globalization in Nicaragua.* Durham, N.C.: Duke University Press.

Merten, Sonia, and Tobias Haller. 2007. Culture, changing livelihoods, and HIV/AIDS discourse: Reframing the institutionalization of fish-for-sex exchange in the Zambian Kafue Flats. *Culture, Health and Sexuality* 9(1):69–83.

Momsen, Joanne. 2004. *Gender and development.* New York: Routledge.

Muñoz, Carolina B. 2008. *Transnational tortillas: Race, gender, and shop-floor politics in Mexico and the United States.* Ithaca, N.Y.: Cornell University Press.

Naples, Nancy, and Manisha Desai, eds. 2002. *Women's activism and globalization: Linking local struggles and transnational politics.* New York: Routledge.

Neis, Barbara, Marion Binkley, and Siri Gerard, eds. 2005. *Changing tides: Gender, fisheries and globalization.* Halifax, Nova Scotia: Fernwood Publishing.

Niehof, Anke. 2004. The significance of diversification for rural livelihood systems. *Food Policy* 29(4):321–338.

Oberhauser, Anne, Jennifer Mandel, and Holly Hapke. 2004. Gendered livelihoods in diverse global contexts: An introduction. *Gender, Place and Culture* 11(2):205–208.

Pearce, David, Edward Barbier, and Anil Markandya. 1990. *Sustainable development: Economics and environment in the Third World.* Aldershot, England: E. Elgar Publishers.

Pearson, Ruth. 2001. Moving the goalposts: Gender and globalization in the twenty-first century. *Gender and Development* 8(1):10–19.

Pongsapich, Amara. 2007. Women's movements in the globalizing world: The case of Thailand. In *Women and gender equity in development theory and practice: Institutions, resources, and mobilization,* eds. Jane Jaquette and Gale Summerfield, 219–239. Durham, N.C.: Duke University Press.

Rathgeber, Eva. 2005. Gender and development as a fugitive concept. *Revue Canadienne d'Etudes du Developpement* 26:579–591.

Reed, Maureen. 2003. *Taking stands: Gender and the sustainability of rural communities.* Vancouver: University of British Columbia Press.

Resurreccion, Bernadette, and Rebecca Elmhirst, eds. 2008. *Gender and natural resource management: Livelihoods, mobility and interventions.* Sterling, Va.: Earthscan.

Rocheleau, Diane, Barbara Thomas-Slayter, and Esther Wangari, eds. 1996. *Feminist political ecology: Global issues and local experiences.* New York: Routledge.

Rothstein, Francis. 2007. *Globalization in rural Mexico: Three decades of change.* Austin: University of Texas Press.

Rowbothan, Sheila, and Stephanie Linkogle, eds. 2001. *Women resist globalization: Mobilizing for livelihood and rights.* New York: Zed Books.

Salzinger, Leslie. 2004. From gender as object to gender as verb: Rethinking how global restructuring happens. *Critical Sociology* 30:43–62.

Schroeder, Richard. 1999. *Shady practices: Agroforestry and gender politics in The Gambia.* Berkeley: University of California Press.

Shiva, Vandana. 1988. *Staying alive: Women, ecology and development.* London: Zed Books.

Stone, Margaret, Angelique Haugerud, and Peter Little. 2000. Commodities and globalization: Anthropological perspectives. In *Commodities and globalization: Anthropological perspectives,* eds. A. Haugerud, M. Stone, and P. Little, 1–29. New York: Rowman & Littlefield.

Sturgeon, Noel. 1997. *Ecofeminist natures: Race, gender, feminist theory and political action.* New York: Routledge.

Thorin, Maria. 2001. *The gender dimension of globalization: A survey of the literature with a focus on Latin America and the Caribbean.* Santiago, Chile: United Nations Publications.

Turner, Sarah. 2007. Trading old textiles: The selective diversification of highland livelihoods in northern Vietnam. *Human Organization* 66(4):389–404.

Valdivia, Corrine, and Jere Gilles. 2001. Gender and resource management: Households and groups, strategies and transitions. *Agriculture and Human Values* 18:5–9.

Venema, Berhard, and Jelka Eijk. 2004. Livelihood strategies compared: Private initiatives and collective efforts of Wolof women in Senegal. *African Studies* 63(1):51–71.

Verma, Ritu. 2001. *Gender, land, and livelihoods in East Africa.* Ottawa, Ontario: International Development Research Centre.

PART ONE

Gender and Forests

CHAPTER TWO

Environmentalism and Gender in Intag, Ecuador

Linda D'Amico

Intag, a subtropical area situated between the western rainforest and the eastern montane valleys of Ecuador, is a place to think about the ways local and global biodiversity issues are linked. With the threat of mining in the 1990s, local and international environmental, feminist, and indigenous rights activists came together in a shared struggle for socioecological justice. Rural groups developed new political and social organizations to ensure their traditional livelihoods and increase their participation in governance of their rich natural resource base. Residents responded to economic restructuring and the subsequent discovery of metallic mineral deposits in the region by opening political spaces, building on traditional values, and incorporating new kinds of knowledge. Many of Intag's mestizo, Afro-Ecuadorian, and indigenous residents collaborated with each other and outside groups and began implementing sustainable alternatives. However, others were convinced that mining would provide improved standards of living. Social tensions arose as Intag's residents debated future development.

This chapter examines how political ecology evolved as a strategy for Inteños/as to defend their way of life and visions for the future.[1] Specifically, I probe ways that women and men continued to renegotiate relationships with each other and their surroundings through the call for social justice and in resistance to two proposed copper mining projects (Mitsubishi 1995–1997 and Ascendant 2004–2008). Over the past two decades Inteños/as emerged with resilient and ecological identities as they sought to sustain those environments and ecosystems upon which they depend for their livelihoods. I trace the rise of environmentalism in Intag as a path toward a social equity that includes nature, food security, and civic participation alongside the increased mindfulness of biodiversity and local culture. This occurred in the 1990s as the price of copper rose sharply and within the global context of neoliberal reforms. The change in socio-ecological discourse included a rights approach that prioritized food and water security and civic engagement, while being adapted to local realities and co-orchestrated with transnational support.

Collaborative Methods

I've been visiting Intag for more than twenty years. My fieldwork has consisted of participant observation, open-ended interviews, and conversations with hundreds of people. During my sabbatical year (2009–2010), I volunteered for the community newspaper and reported on a variety of events in many communities. I attended scores of meetings and witnessed the ways in which decisions were made. Much of my time included walking on trails and/or riding on buses and in the backs of trucks. In the course of all these processes, I have been fortunate to converse with many people and careful to note gender and power dynamics.

In particular, the social movement and my research were fortified through interculturalism, advocated by indigenous Mayor Auki Tituaña (1996–2009), and through associations with other transnational activists. Interculturalism is an indigenous ideology that stresses the value of diverse epistemologies and the exchange of knowledge sets based upon mutual respect. Like feminism, it is also political in that it advocates for rights and access to equal opportunities for diverse groups. Interculturalism grew out of struggles for indigenous rights and self-determination within Latin America, and it has been widely socialized through bilingual-intercultural education programs in Ecuador and beyond and with support from human rights collaborators (López 1991, 1999; Selverston-Sher 2001; Rappaport 2005).

The nitty-gritty of getting research done in this case was based upon interculturalism as both a theory and practice. Anthropologist Joanne Rappaport described interculturalism as "the selective appropriation of concepts across cultures in the interests of building a pluralistic dialogue among equals" (2005, p. 5). She explained it as a utopian philosophy in which external ideas are appropriated and exchanged in a common sphere of interaction. Ideally, these ideas are reflected through engagement in collaborative endeavors that are mutually advantageous (2005, p. 7). Thus, interculturalism offers a frame for understanding and a strategy for effective cultural pluralism, whereby skills that involve listening, reciprocity, and inclusiveness are valued and practiced. It also lays the scaffolding for gender equity, because by repositioning indigenousness as a valuable force in society, it also opens the door for other kinds of difference to be appreciated. The intersection of feminist (Harcourt 1994; Shiva 1994; Rocheleau et al. 1996; Bhavani et al. 2003; Mohanty 2003), intercultural (Rappaport 2005), and environmental agendas (Escobar 1998; Peet and Watts 2004; Bebbington 2007; Acosta 2009) in northwestern Ecuador brought about inclusive expectations for local rights, including eventually rights for non-human species in this region characterized by mega-diversity.

My objective was to go beyond insider/outsider dichotomies and to expand and reshape knowledge sets. Through my focus on social life in Intag, while exploring collaborative goals that work toward social, economic, and environmental justice, I recognized nested sociopolitical spaces: these extend from farms and forests to villages and parish seats, municipal counties, provincial and national capitals, and across borders. Through the lens of converging local and global interests regarding gender and environmental rights, my research indicates the ways in which complementary discourses can influence and nourish one another. This led to new possibilities for diverse groups to work together, while protecting biodiversity and the ecosystems upon which they depend. These methodologies developed over time, and my collaborators did not hesitate to tap into my skills and knowledge: I wrote and co-authored several funding proposals and contributed articles to the local newspaper, while developing my academic arguments. I also had the good fortune to learn from different perspectives.

Getting outside academic orbits and becoming engaged civically was most important for positioning myself within intercultural and feminist frames of practice. (I lived in the Otavalo [Andean] region from 1989 to 1997 and developed close friendships with leaders in the environmental movement who lived in Intag.) Initially, this meant assisting as a founding member of the first NGO, Defensa Ecológica y Conservación de Intag (Ecological Defense and Conservation of Intag; DECOIN), in 1995. Within this role, as DECOIN organized community workshops to raise awareness of the value of biological diversity and the threat of extractive industries through global restructuring, I urged the prioritizing of women's participation. Most women are on the cutting edge of environmental issues because they mediate natural resource use within daily life. They do this through chores that include washing clothes (without machines), caring for children and elderly family members, cooking, sometimes hauling firewood and water, doing farm work in the fields, harvesting and storing food, tending small domestic animals, and engaging in other household and community work. In 1995, women's participation in public gatherings was unusual except at church, at school meetings, at weekly markets, or on civic holidays. However, by offering transport costs, snacks, and a meal, as well as the opportunity to bring children, these kinds of civic-environmental meetings opened new possibilities for women. But it was not until the formation of the first women's group, Mujer y Medio Ambiente (Women and the Environment), by Sandra Statz and her neighbors in Plaza Gutiérrez, with the aim of providing skills and markets in the elaboration of handicrafts with local materials, did Inteñas really begin participating en force. Handicraft production and participation in ecotourism markets allowed local women more economic autonomy and decision-making in their households.

Ecological and Ethnographic Contexts

Intag is an 1,800 square kilometer subtropical area of Cotacachi County in the province of Imbabura where two of the world's biodiversity hotspots—the Chocó and the Tropical Andes—overlap.[2] Intag borders on the Cotacachi-Capayas Ecological Reserve and contains the largest remaining remnants of Ecuador's western forests, more than 90 percent of which have been removed in the last half-century. Ecologists and biologists underscore the global significance of the biodiversity in Intag cloud forests, where water abounds and unique species flourish (Wilson 1992; Meyers 1997; see figure 2.1).

The history of Inteños/as' demands for social and environmental justice implicates forces and conditions that go well beyond the region. They demonstrate how vertical and horizontal aspects of globalization, or powerful forces from above and below, converge and at times cause conflict. In general, vertical forces have imposed economic and political power that most often benefits a few on top, whereas horizontal forces have to do with popular social movements that include more egalitarian aims (Alvarez et al. 1998; Montoya et al. 2002; Parpart et al. 2002; Postero 2007; Barndt 2008). Inteños/as created initiatives that integrated notions of sustainability into legislation, policy, and daily practices. However, opposition to mining divided many communities because some residents were allured by the promise of quick cash, roads, and other amenities. Out of

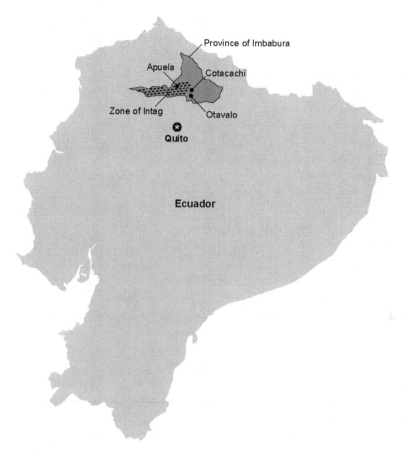

Figure 2.1. Map of Intag, Ecuador, and surrounding locations. Map by
Peonia Vázquez-D'Amico

this conflict emerged spaces for civic participation as well as new models
for understanding access and management of resources.

The situation in Intag is an example of how biodiversity became a
global concern and how cultural plurality and self-determination became
political issues in Ecuador (Whitten 2003; Sawyer 2004; Tsing 2005; West
2006; Bebbington 2007; Kuecker 2007; Escobar 2008). In part due to expanded global advocacy for the environment and women's and indigenous
rights during the 1990s, local, regional, and international groups began
to network with multiethnic groups in Cotacachi County. They put an
innovative theory of action into place based on participatory governance,

scientific knowledge, and building local and global coalitions. In Cotacachi County, interculturalists and feminists, each of whom demanded respect for the rights of vulnerable groups, informed the political ecology of resistance from a rights approach. Rural residents learned they had the right to choose what kind of development they wanted and that nature was an important actor in need of protection if its bounty and their way of life were to continue. These values of equality, respect of difference, exchange for mutual benefit, and solidarity were infused into the struggle for environmental justice.

For most Inteños/as conservation measures were equal to survival because they encountered the direct effects of ecological stress. In particular, Intag women were often the first to deal with the consequences of environmental degradation, including diminished water quality and or scarcity, poor soil fertility, and erosion. Their roles in transmission of cultural values and input in decision-making, particularly at the household level, gave women a vital role in natural resource management and planning for the future. In the 1990s, many Inteñas embraced discourses about biodiversity conservation and shaped it according to their own needs and views. This meant participation in concrete projects to improve their living standards in ways that conserved the environment and their culture. At the same time, they created spaces for their own advancement within national and international campaigns for women's rights and gender equity. At pivotal points in the struggle to keep mining out of the region, women mobilized to defend their way of life. Inteñas recognized that maintaining a salubrious relationship with their surroundings is crucial for future generations. Cultural survival is directly related to environmental quality and sustainability, because their livelihoods are dependent on healthy soil, forests, and watersheds. At a meeting I attended on 14 August 2009, Carmen Proaño, community president of Río Verde, proclaimed, "We can't sell our children's future by letting a mining company come in and contaminate our beautiful river."

Inteños/as value intracommunity relations and depend on mutual assistance through *mingas* (cooperative work parties) to get many household and civic projects completed. Mingas serve as social glue and help keep families and communities together. In order to complete big projects, social cooperation (rather than paid labor) is necessary. As Lupe Sánchez told me, this might take the form of an agricultural minga to plant or harvest a large field. She informed me that her family in Plaza Gutiérrez depends upon the assistance of extended family, affines, and neighbors to get farming tasks completed. Or a minga might transpire after an emergency, such as when a gas tank exploded and the ensuing fire destroyed the house. Neighbors did not hesitate to contribute their labor and other resources to attend to the disaster and construct a new house. Some mingas bring families together to work in a kind of celebratory mode, like when they mill sugar cane into *panela* (raw sugar). Finally, public works are also contingent upon community mingas. These might come in the form of keeping foot and horse trails cleared, or as when electricity came to the region in 2003,[3] and civil work parties gathered to carry the 2,000-pound cement posts to their requisite positions in the rugged landscape. A meal of substance is indispensable to any successful minga, as well as the ability to call the group of people together. Maintaining a network of reciprocal relations is crucial, and women generally have a big hand in provisioning these vital skills, the importance of which cannot be overstated. These values of solidarity, based on mutual interdependence, complement and inform the environmental struggle.

Changing Political Economy in Intag

Ethnohistorical references mention Intag as an important region for inter-zonal and/or microvertical trade with various native groups in the adjacent inter-Andean valleys of Cotacachi and Otavalo. Intag's elevation at about 1,800 meters above sea level and its subtropical climate allowed for the agricultural production of sisal (important in the manufacture of sacks and rope for global shipping) and cotton. In addition, there was some trade from the extraction of minerals, including salt and gold (Murra 1972; Salomon 1981; Espinoza 1988). Contemporary residents identify burial mounds where gold figurines have been found, suggesting a complex prehistoric society. The topography, comprised of the steep Andean foothills, posed difficulties for travel. However, by the early twentieth century Intag became attractive to *colonos* (homesteaders) as well as the landed elite for sugar production.

By the turn of the twentieth century, demographic pressures in the sierra[4] and the allure of lucrative profits from the manufacture of alcohol from sugar cane motivated colonos to migrate into the rugged and sparsely inhabited lands. Census records indicate that the population grew during the first half of the twentieth century. Muleteers extracted wood and transported sisal, bootleg alcohol, raw sugar, beans, cattle, tropical fruits, and other agricultural products to markets and distributors in Otavalo, Cotacachi, Ibarra, and Quito. Residents recall the 1960s as an era prior to the appearance of motorized vehicles when small-scale farming contributed to bustling commerce. However, as public services did not grow to meet demographic demands and when the bottom fell out of global markets for sisal because of plastic substitution, emigration became a common strategy for family survival and advancement.

Intag is the remote and less populated western and subtropical region of Cantón (county) Cotacachi. The county is divided into the urban zone located in the Andean region on the eastern flanks of Mount Cotacachi (4,500 meters), where two-thirds of the (mostly) indigenous and mestizo population lives. The Andean region contrasts greatly with the subtropical Intag region (extending from approximately 200 to 2,300 meters in elevation), where a multiethnic population lives, including mestizo, African-Ecuadorian, and indigenous people, alongside a handful of expatriates. The 2001 census documented approximately 15,000 residents.

Each parish is the seat of local government, where residents have erratic electricity and telephone services. Primary school education is available in all parishes, and secondary schools in four parish seats. However, in most cases educational quality is compromised by a dearth of didactical materials and qualified teachers, in addition to high rates of absenteeism on the part of teachers. The region depends upon two unpaved roads for human and commercial transport, but travel over these roads is, at best, slow (it takes two and a half hours to travel sixty kilometers) and, at worst, beset by intermittent landslides that curtail transport during the rainy season from November to April. Small businesses operate in parish seats, each of which also has a Catholic church.

Intag includes more than ninety hamlets as well as isolated farms, some of these connected by footpaths and/or secondary roads that are only passable with four-wheel drive vehicles or on horseback. Most Inteños/as make their living through subsistence agriculture and cattle raising. According to the 2001 census, poverty and child malnutrition exist at rates above 60 percent (INFOPLAN 2001 in Segarra 2007).

Under pressure from international financial institutions, the government of Ecuador began to restructure the economy in the 1980s. This included political decentralization, reduction of the public sector, and deregulation (Kuecker 2007; Escobar 2008). The World Bank and the International Monetary Fund promoted neoliberal reforms in order to stimulate foreign investment and development. These institutions also encouraged the government of Ecuador to legislate new mining laws that deregulated the mining industry. In addition, the World Bank loaned the government of Ecuador US$14 million to create a geochemical database that provided private investors information about mineral deposits to stimulate exploration. By the 1990s, Bitshimetals of Japan, a subsidiary of Mitsubishi Corporation, was granted a mining concession. This concession was located in Intag in the community of Junín, a hamlet located on the slopes of the Cordillera Toisán, a buffer zone to the Cotacachi-Cayapas National Reserve.

The Rise of Environmentalism in Intag

Intag's inhabitants unexpectedly found themselves at a global crossroads in the 1990s. Giovanni Paz, a "green" Catholic priest who practiced liberation theology and spoke of nature as God's precious house, first alerted Inteños/as to the threat of mining. Alongside Cuban-American expatriate Carlos Zorrilla and other concerned residents, Paz created the NGO DECOIN in the town of Apuela in January 1995. From its inception, DECOIN's priority has been to raise ecological awareness, promote conservation, and protect community and environmental rights. With dynamic leadership from Zorrilla, an Intag resident for more than thirty years, Silvia Quilumbango, an agricultural engineer who married and settled in Peñaherrera, Paz, and many others, DECOIN developed transnational alliances on multiple scales to tackle complex political-ecological issues. These horizontal connections to regional, national, and international organizations have proven to be crucial networks of exchange, support, and mobilization. Moreover, DECOIN paved the way for scores of other groups to reorganize civil society toward sustainability and improved standards of living.

Of equal importance, in 1996 indigenous economist Auki Tituaña was elected as municipal mayor. (In Ecuador, municipalities include entire counties.) Tituaña's charismatic leadership strengthened democratic local governance through public administration reforms.[5] His first act as mayor was to call for the formation of citizens' assemblies where residents debated their problems, assets, organizational structures, and visions for the future. From these debates emerged a civic organization, the Asamblea de Unidad Cantonal de Cotacachi (Assembly for County Unity; AUCC), to "promote spaces for social justice, respect for Mother Earth, and gender equality." AUCC evolved as a democratic body to set policies for political authorities to carry out. The Comité de Desarollo y Gestión (Committee for Development and Management) acts as a board of directors for the AUCC and includes a representative of each of the assembly's committees, plus the mayor, to debate pressing issues.

Initially, the three main goals of AUCC involved elaborating a plan for: (1) integrated development to incorporate both the Andean and Intag regions; (2) participatory plans to improve the quality of life for all the people of the county; and (3) the promotion of self-determination, self-management, and interculturalism. The committees gave impetus to trans-regional coordination and participation, including the less populated and what heretofore had been isolated Intag communities. The AUCC also received generous funding from international NGOs and the Diputación de Barcelona (the political authority of Barcelona, Spain), which enabled domestic NGOs to impact social life directly.

Tituaña's political model provided the space for self-reflection and increased participation and coalition-building. Intag's residents discussed issues concerning poverty, ecological degradation, and inequalities in the region and synthesized their resolutions into policy proposals. These political activities occurred when Inteños/as were considering whether their cultural values were reconcilable with the proposed mining project in Junín. The fact that Inteños/as held key positions on AUCC's environmental and other committees, including Gladis Vallejos as representative of the Women and Family Committee and Silvia Quilumbango as alternate (and who was also on the board of DECOIN), was important. These two women were recognized leaders with credible knowledge about the impacts of an open pit copper mine and at the forefront of alternative approaches to development. In addition, Patricia Espinoza's leadership as the first president of AUCC ensured a more inclusive approach to the county's development.

Mayor Tituaña promoted intercultural processes among multiethnic constituents in their participation in parish and county assemblies, which facilitated the development of their skills in democratic local governance. As Peñaherrera resident Sonia Córdova, a mestiza, said at an event paying homage to Tituaña's works near the end of his administration on 14 July 2009, "We've learned to be proud of who we are. We're campesinos/farmers, and our work is important. Now, thanks to Auki, we are proud of our indigenous roots. Through interculturalism we're all brothers and sisters struggling for our development the way we want. We know that for social change, we have to be united and do things from the ground up."

Intercultural dexterities also proved invaluable for Inteños/as as they increasingly interacted and negotiated with outside groups. Inteños/as incorporated new kinds of knowledge and ways of expressing and accessing information, while initiating useful dialogues about citizens' rights (including human, women's, and environmental rights) and responsibilities. Interculturalism provided the theoretical framework as groups created platforms for airing their views, collaborating, and developing inclusive and sustainable agendas for Cotacachi County, including the region of Intag. As concerns about environmental and indigenous rights grew transnationally during the 1990s, Inteños/as broadened their social networks, which created more spaces for intercultural experiences and brought financial, intellectual, and moral support.

During this same period and based on priorities articulated during the Fourth World Conference on Women (Beijing in 1995), regional, national, and international groups worked to raise social awareness of women's rights and promote legal reform in Ecuador. The Consejo Nacional de la Mujer (Women's National Advisory Council; CONAMU) was created by Ecuadorian women in 1997, with three representatives from government and three from national women's organizations, to advocate for gender equity and integrate action plans for this end into national and regional development plans. With constitutional reforms, by 1998 the Law of Quotas determined that at least 30 percent of political candidates must be women to help ensure women's rights are considered (Del Campo and Magdaleno 2008). CONAMU developed regional and local networks to disseminate information about legislation passed in 1995 to protect women from violence and expanded in Ley 103 in 2005 through the Law Against Domestic Violence. In coordination with CONAMU, the government established a National Plan for Equal Opportunities 1996–2000 that took a human rights approach for women's rights (Del Campo and Magdaleno 2008, p. 290).

During this period, various Spanish NGOs (Ayuda en Acción and Xarxa) with their local affiliates organized workshops in Intag specifically aimed to improve women's leadership and organizing skills and to familiarize them with their rights. Local involvement was in part a response to the intensified neoliberal reforms that adversely impacted communities as fewer services were offered by the national government. Residents were eager for economic alternatives, particularly after dollarization of their currency in 2000 and the value of their agricultural products decreased due to the flooding of their markets with foreign competition. Tituaña's decentralized model of government offered Inteños/as multiple opportunities to become civically involved. For example, Gladis Vallejos, a member of the Comité de Desarollo y Gestión from Peñaherrera, in coordination with Ayuda en Acción and AUCC initiated a series of workshops in the region to address the importance of women's roles in society.

In 1998, Acción Ecológica (Ecological Action), a Quito-based NGO, arranged a field trip for a delegation of Inteños/as to visit an open pit mine in Oroya, Peru. They targeted women, in particular, to learn about environmental and social impacts of extractive industries (Martínez-Alier 2002, p. 62). Women did their own research and were impacted by the field trip. Silvia Vetancourt went on the trip and commented, "The open pit mine cut a line through the town: on one side was the mine which left nothing alive and on the other side was filth, poverty, and social delinquency. In the middle of town was a lake, which previously had served residents for drinking, bathing, and washing. Since the mine, the lake is polluted and unsuitable for human use. Seeing this scared us. All the schools, health centers, and other things the company promised never materialized. We returned to Intag resolved not to be blinded by false promises and lose the natural wealth we depend on."

As the result of access to more information, many Inteños/as considered the proposal for open pit copper mining in primary forests as a path to socioecological disaster. The proposal also drew attention from biologists, environmental organizations, and human rights activists from around the world. In 1997, renowned Harvard entomologist E. O. Wilson wrote a letter for DECOIN in defense of the protection and conservation of Intag forests to be used in court proceedings.[6] After a global letter-writing campaign to protest the infringement on environmental rights, alongside local demands to have access to the environmental impact study and prior community consultation, Bitshimetals pulled out.

As civil society expanded self-government under the leadership of Tituaña, Inteños/as reconsidered their environmental priorities. In 1997 and 1998, the AUCC's Environmental Committee proposed a resolution to declare Cotacachi an Ecological County. After input from all constituent assembly committees in all parishes and technical assistance from NGOs, including leadership from DECOIN, the municipal council passed an Ecological Ordinance (EO) on 11 September 2000.

The EO was in large part a direct response to the threat of open pit copper mining. It declared "as a priority interest, the conservation and sustainable management of native forests and biodiversity of the county" (EO 2000, p. 3). The EO called for the creation of "Municipal Ecological Reserves to protect fragile ecosystems, including areas with rich biodiversity, areas with endangered species, areas with potential for tourism, areas rich in hydrological resources, in response to community requests . . . and when [reserves are] established on public land, should be managed by the communities in a sustainable way" (EO 2000, p. 4). In addition, the EO served as a legal tool and a cultural construct to restrain environmental degradation and introduce incentives for sustainable resource use. Local communities identified water security as a priority: "In communities or populated centers that suffer from water scarcity because of contamination due to unsatisfactory watershed management, the Municipality will declare the watershed sources as areas of public interest and proceed to expropriate them with the purpose to secure their conservation and protection, and to guarantee the quality of water for human consumption" (EO 2000, p. 5).

The EO outlined a community vision that integrates biodiversity protection with sustainable development as the means to improve the economic circumstances and quality of life of county residents. At the same time, it framed increased civic participation as the pathway to an integrated approach to environmental sustainability, forest conservation, and collective socioeconomic transformation.

The EO raised local awareness of the value of environmental resources and, by returning authority to local governments, offered a model for decentralization. The EO prioritized alternative development, including community-based ecotourism, agroecology, local handicraft projects, environmental education, and the creation of community-managed and -owned protected forests and water catchments. These initiatives engaged civil society in ways that continued to enhance participation, social justice, and local empowerment. The EO articulated a plan where stakeholders' input was crucial. Their charge was to "create and administer social and economic incentives to help form sustainable models of natural resource use and environmental awareness" (EO 2000, p. 2). Moreover, it drew further national and global attention to Intag, which helped to increase transnational funding for sustainable projects and habitat conservation.

Support from and alliances with national and international NGOs incorporated diverse intellectual and financial resources into the struggle for social justice in Intag.[7] This overlapping of geographic scales, values, and priorities brought together disparate frames of reference to bridge local and global social capital. The mining threat, alongside the AUCC, spurred grassroots organization, leadership development and planning, political mobilization, and the building of coalitions.

Concurrently, because of the lack of media outlets in Intag, concerned residents came together in 2000 and launched a nonprofit community newspaper. *Periódico Intag* emerged as a print forum for local debate and a medium to disseminate local, scientific, and other kinds of knowledge. Under the leadership of editor and historian Mary Ellen Fieweger and cofounder José Rivera, the staff had three major objectives: (1) to offer a space for residents to share news, opinions, and analysis with their neighbors; (2) to keep readers informed of projects proposed and implemented by governmental and nongovernmental entities; and (3) to provide information on topics related to the natural environment. Moreover, part of its mission is to train and employ local reporters to communicate Inteño/a perspectives and analyses and to increase literacy in the region.

The bimonthly editions of *Periódico Intag* have been crucial in constructing shared visions of a green and sustainable local identity for the region (Anderson 1991; D'Amico 2012). The newspaper reported on realities of life in Intag by appealing to egalitarian and environmental values. By emphasizing a sense of belonging in the collective struggle for social and environmental justice, *Periódico Intag* contributed to citizen expectations with regard to civic duties and mediated the political-ecological dialogue by interfacing scientific knowledge with anticipation for socioecological justice. Recent research indicated that local governance is a decisive factor for biodiversity conservation (Ribot 2008), and this requires an informed citizenry. The impact of *Periódico Intag* in disseminating information and building regional identity was important on various levels. The online editions in Spanish, English, and German also helped to keep the transnational environmental community informed.

Gender and Sustainability

"We can thank the mining companies for opening our eyes to the fact that we are true fighters and leaders, committed to giving our lives in defense of our rights," declared Piedad Fuel from the community of Barcelona in the parish of García Moreno (Fieweger 2007, p. 7). Fuel's sentiments are echoed by many other Inteños/as, but these views do not diminish the fact that at times organizational processes and intracommunity struggles were acrimonious due to oppositional views on development.

At the onset of the political and environmental struggle, gender roles were primarily constructed within cultural norms that generally confined women to domestic and farming activities. Attending a meeting in Apuela, the regional capital, was a huge time commitment. But these meetings were like seminars in continuing education. Many attendees became leaders who pressed for socioecological justice. At the same time, local meetings were linked to global concerns and often supported by international organizations. Success, however, was based on Inteños/as' figuring out how to implement and evaluate projects within their cultural values.

As an example, when the Mujer y Medio Ambiente formed in Plaza Gutiérrez in 1997, their goal was to generate income in ways that did not adversely affect their way of life or the environment. According to local resident Julia Guerrero, members wanted to draw attention to the fact that "We are women who work with natural elements. We get our dyes from plants, and our thread comes from *cabuya* [sisal], which grows all around us. We named our group Women and the Environment to show that we can make things without cutting down the forests." At first, their only market was at the ecolodge and forest reserve La Florida, where some of them also worked on occasion as cooks and housekeepers. Productive activities infused much needed cash into their households, while promoting economic independence and exposing them to intercultural values. Such cultural interchanges included the recognition by Inteñas that tourists and/or foreign students valued the biodiversity in Intag forests and that higher education was available and salient for women and men. Many young US, European, Japanese, and Australian women participated in international exchanges (more so than men), modeled new kinds of interactions with Inteños/as, and held them in high regard.

However, for some of the local women, membership in Mujer y Medio Ambiente was not easy. Within the organization, they were required to attend monthly meetings to discuss dying techniques, design, quality control, orders, payment, and other matters. These activities required that participants be absent from their homes. At first, some partners or husbands were not supportive. Getting from one place to another in Intag often involves movement on foot or horseback. Particularly in the rainy season, saddling up a horse with small children and/or navigating the steep and muddy trails makes mobility slow at best. According to one member, "Our husbands wondered what we were doing out of the house, and in some instances were reluctant to give us permission." Upon returning home, a few women were even abused because they were "late" or their partners were suspicious of their activities.

By 2010, however, Mujer y Medio Ambiente members I met with were gone most of the day for their monthly meetings. "Our work is appreciated and we bring in much needed revenue to help our children go to school," was the refrain I heard from several women. "In addition, we now have a support system and won't tolerate abuse. We know our rights," Silvia Vetancourt, the president of the group, declared. Norma Bolaños, director of the group, stated, "Our husbands value our work and even help us with chores when we have a large order with a deadline." It is not unusual for men to assist in household chores when there is a large order to complete (see figure 2.2).

As civil society organizations continued to expand, equity issues became part of institutional discourse. In 2001, AUCC offered workshops about the meaning of citizenship and leadership. For six months, thirty

Figure 2.2. Inteñas completing a sisal handicraft order for Japan, October 2009. Photo by the author

women from various communities met on a regular basis to analyze women's issues. In 2002, they came up with the resolution to form a regional organization and came together to elect the board of directors for the Coordinadora de Mujeres de Intag (the Women's Coordinating Committee of Intag; CMI), an umbrella organization for all the community women's groups in Intag. In 2010 CMI included ten groups. The main objectives were to strengthen the participation, empowerment, and autonomy of Inteñas and to construct equitable relationships between women and men in order to enrich democratic and intercultural processes and better the quality of life (Segarra 2007, p. 16).

With support from the Diputación de Barcelona, Ayuda en Acción, and Xarxa, the CMI aspired to improve the quality of families' lives through integrated and sustainable development. It brought the different groups together at least once every other year to formulate strategies for ongoing workshops and to exchange experiences. At the 2010 CMI Assembly, the coordinator outlined the importance of collective activities for cultivating networks that fit within local values based on reciprocity and protection of natural resources. While coordinating with national and international organizations, CMI worked directly with local groups and sponsored workshops that focused on gender equality, domestic abuse, sustainable development, income-generating activities, business management, and reproductive health. CMI also funneled technical assistance and outside funds into local projects.

For example, the community of El Rosal (in the parish of García Moreno and near Junín) promoted the production and marketing of aloe soaps, shampoos, and creams. They also initiated an ecotourism project, where visitors stayed in their homes to learn about fair trade, aloe production, and biodiversity issues. Other women's groups organized in different communities to initiate projects for income generation that included the production of herbal remedies, banana and yucca flour, community ecotourism, lufa products, sisal handicrafts, and other activities. The status and income that groups and their members received from local and global projects gave them leverage in community and household decisions. At the same time, representative leaders participated in regional, national, and international forums concerning gender and the environment and reported back.

In some instances these organizations were aligned with university students and other groups that came from Quito or abroad. For example, the Mujer y Medio Ambiente women's group specialized in offering homestay experiences to foreign students and ecotourists. In addition to providing extra household income, these stays opened intercultural opportunities that imparted widening cultural expectations, particularly with regard to girls' and women's advanced education and economic security. Through such cultural exchanges, participants were also compelled to upgrade and maintain basic services in their homes, which improved the quality of their families' lives as well. The majority of members utilized the extra income to better their families' diet and to send children, and girls in particular, to secondary school.

Numerous Intag men and women also grow coffee on their farms. Since the late 1990s many have participated in the Asociación Agroartesanal de Caficultores Río Intag (Río Intag Agroartesanal Coffee Growers Association), a regional fair-trade coffee growers' association. According to their website, the association formed in 1998 as a response to "multiple and growing environmental problems originating from pressure by transnational mining interests, deforestation, and inappropriate farming methods." Presently there are more than 400 families who belong to the coffee growers association, who have received training and access to fair-trade markets in Japan, Germany, and Ecuador. Farmers from Intag are producing shade-grown, organic coffee that is interspersed within forests or other crops. This contrasts with monocrop coffee plantations that wipe out local biodiversity. Most importantly, in addition to improving the grade and roasting of locally grown coffee, coop members receive augmented revenue. Because visitors wanted to interact directly with fair-trade coffee growers in cloud forests, farmers in the association also created an ecotourism project for extra income.

Despite the passage of the EO, struggles concerning alternative development and self-determination have continued in Intag. In August 2002, the Ministry of Energy and Mines auctioned off 7,000 hectares of subsoil rights in Junín. In May 2003, the municipality of Cotacachi, including six parish governments in Intag, dozens of communities, and twenty-four NGOs requested a restraining order from the courts, arguing the illegality of the mining concession due to the region's status as an Ecological County. The judge who heard the case at the county level decided in favor of Cotacachi plaintiffs. As a result, the concessionaire appealed the decision, and two of the three appeals court judges who heard the case voted in favor of community rights. However, due to lack of unanimity the case automatically went to the full nine-judge Constitutional Tribunal panel; five of the nine judges ruled against the municipality and communities.

In December 2003, the concession was sold to Ascendant Exploration, a Canadian company. Mayor Tituaña wrote to voice his concerns about lack of prior community consultation and legally required municipal approval. Ascendant hired a consultant to win over indigenous and local communities, and the consultant attempted to purchase favor from the Union of Peasant and Indigenous Organizations of Cotacachi.[8] In 2004, Ascendant sued the editor of *Periódico Intag* for libel, alleging US$1 million in damages (the lawsuit was later thrown out of court). It was the first in a series of lawsuits against some forty community leaders and residents in an attempt to intimidate. The executive director of DECOIN had his life threatened, and the company allegedly hired police to harass his family and threaten his safety. As conflict escalated, most Inteños/as continued to oppose mining and created and collaborated with NGOs and each other in civil and political life to promote the precepts of the EO.

However, Ascendant had some support in Junín, especially among young people in need of jobs in a place where the daily wage was at best US$5 a day. After her husband was killed in an altercation with pro-miners in the early 1990s, Charo Piedra, a leader in Junín, commented how she and other women were challenged to maintain social harmony and conventions within their families and community. This was not easy. She added that even with the first exploratory mining activities in 1996, farmers in Junín identified adverse effects to water quality in the streams they depended upon for drinking, cooking, washing clothes, bathing, and watering animals. (Most Intag households, hamlets, and small communities rely on primary water sources, which they tap with hoses that run directly to their homes.) As a farmer and general manager of the community ecotourism project in Junín, Piedra pointed out the appeal of managing and owning their watershed reserve, "Water is life, and if we don't take care of its source, everything will end. If we want water in the future, we can't log. We have to protect our forests." The bamboo tourist cabin she manages with other community members was built in 1999 with cooperation from DECOIN and financial support from the German NGO GEO-Retten. Junín residents also oversee the 1,500-hectare community forest reserve as part of their community ecotourism project, where they guide scientists, students, and other visitors to explore the phenomenal biodiversity, magnificent landscapes, and waterfalls.

The director of the British NGO Rainforest Concern, already active in Ecuador, had heard of DECOIN and approached the director in the early 2000s to inquire about land conservation projects in Intag. In line with the EO, Inteños/as identified water security as a priority to ensure water use for home and farm activities, especially during the dry season (June to October). With funds from donors in the United Kingdom, DECOIN began purchasing watershed reserves for communities to own, manage, and protect. Community members built on traditional values of mutual assistance and cooperation to come up with models for environmental governance to oversee their hydrological reserves.

According to the coordinator for the watershed project, Armando Almeida, it is common knowledge that "If we aren't good forest stewards, water dries up." He added that many Inteños/as have already observed climate change as the result of deforestation in the form of diminished rainfall and longer summers. After the first project, other communities also solicited DECOIN's financial and technical support in order to survey, purchase, and protect their watersheds. Intag women particularly championed these reserves because they realized that public health is contingent upon water security. Through community mingas, women and men managed, reforested, and conserved forests that safeguarded fresh water for future generations.

Even with the engagement of many Inteños/as in sustainable alternatives and participation in more than twenty NGOs, Ascendant Corporation continued pouring resources into a public relations campaign from 2004 to 2006. However, the coalition of anti-mining groups grew despite Ascendant's alleged attempts to sabotage their organizations and buy off community leaders. The company did sway some Inteños through the illegal purchase of homesteads[9] at ten times the market value. Despite the fact that Ecuadorian law mandated prior consultation with communities before exploration, Ascendant kept trying to bully its way in. At local assemblies, Inteños/as, including parish governmental authorities, repeatedly rejected the proposal for mining development in favor of sustainable development based upon conservation. The framework of the EO proved effective in setting the sociopolitical stage for the kind of development the majority of Inteños/as wanted.

Frustrated by Ascendant's failure to respect their rights, on 12 and 13 July 2006 more than 500 Inteños/as organized and participated in an anti-mining march to Cotacachi and Quito, where leaders met with municipal authorities and the Minister of Energy and Mines. These authorities were sympathetic to Inteños/as' demands and agreed to investigate the legality of Ascendant's conduct, but no action was taken.

On 2 December 2006, Ascendant tried to force entrance into communities to set up the mining camp. The anti-mining coalition gathered on the road and blocked entrance to the mining concessions. Piedra commented, "It was the women who put our bodies on the line and stood up to the paramilitaries that Ascendant hired. We wouldn't let those thugs pass." As shots were fired and tear gas released, a female German volunteer for *Periódico Intag* captured the aggression on camera, and photos appeared in national and international media. Ecuadorians and others had to reconsider some of the negative social, cultural, and ecological costs of mineral extraction. As Marcía Ramirez, secretary of the Intag Development Committee and resident of Junín, explained to a reporter for *The Tyee* of Canada, "It isn't fair that a foreign company can come here and contract people who attack us for defending our rights, for wanting to live in a healthy environment, for defending our land and our water" (Moore 2009).

Concluding Remarks

This chapter has examined ways that unequal encounters and frictions led to new models, where Intag's women and men participated to defend their livelihoods and ways of life. They engaged in social, economic, and political processes that fueled grassroots environmentalism and their own empowerment. Within this context, where they revalued their traditions that linked them to their surroundings, Inteños/as began to construct a more inclusive plan for sustainable development. The EO mapped out shared goals, where human and environmental rights complemented each other for a sustained future. The EO drew global attention to what was at risk and built social networks within Intag, Cotacachi, Ecuador, and beyond. As Inteños/as formed coalitions within their communities and county (which included expatriates with English skills) and across regional and national boundaries, they constructed intercultural spaces to debate and formulate new ways to articulate their autonomy and solidarities.

These nested collectivities were fertile grounds where Inteños/as' voices gave shape to local governance and control of their resources. First, they reshaped the political dialogue in an inclusive way that directly took into consideration the realities of their lives. This raised their political consciousness within new gender and environmental lexicons, where public and private spheres were not mutually exclusive and where human and natural spheres were linked. In some cases household relations were also rearranged as women moved to the frontline of income generation and the protection of precious resources. This is a lesson in how power relations were decentered through give and take, due to new opportunities and learning from difference and mutual respect. In this case, heretofore marginality became front and center, where the confluence of forces and interests brought together ideas of science, social science, and local empowerment. Through collaboration with outsiders and direct participation, Inteños/as stood up and spoke to vertical structures of power and demanded and created respect for their human and environmental rights. They opened ways to defend the vital resources integral to the well-being and health of their families. Their quest through the EO and other activities is nothing less than an attempt to revamp political and economic systems in order to perpetuate environmental and social justice.

In this case, intercultural, feminist, and environmental ideas coalesced in ways that put the needs of human beings and other species before economic gain. These ideas offered possibilities to transcend gender, ethnic, class, and species boundaries. The converging and cross-fertilizing of polyphonic scripts began to reshape theory and/or decolonize ideas from the ground up as the means to map out ways societies and economies can function more equitably. By acknowledging local savvy in the production of knowledge and recognizing its value, this study represents purposeful practices that are a force for solidarity, empowerment, and change. These circles of overlapping local and global interests linked to socioecological responsibility are exemplified by the banner of the Intag Women's Assembly (3 October 2009):

Our Dreams
We dream of Intag as a zone where freedom and self-determination reign,
where each member of the population can make her/his own decisions,
a zone where the principle of mutual respect among people and
with nature is the basic premise by which we live:
A zone free from mining.

Notes

1. I refer to both genders in the plural as Inteños/as, to recognize the visibility of Inteñas.

2. According to biologist Norman Meyers, "Much of the world's biodiversity is located in small areas of the planet. As much as 20 percent of the plant species and a still higher proportion of animal species are confined to 0.5 percent of Earth's land surface. These species are endemic to their areas, so if the local habitats are eliminated, these species will suffer extinction. The areas in question are indeed threatened with imminent habitat destruction. It is the two attributes together that cause the areas to be designated 'hotspot'" (1997, p. 125).

3. Electricity came to parish seats more than fifteen years ago and to communities over the twelve-year period Mayor Auki Tituaña was in office, funded by municipalities in Spain.

4. According to Weaver (2000, p. 70), Ecuador's population nearly tripled from 1850 to 1930, growing from 816,000 to 2,160,000.

5. Cotacachi County was recognized by the United Nations and Dubai, United Arab Emirates, for Best Practices in 2000; by the InterAmerican Forum for the Rights of Children and Youth via the Dreamer Prize in 2001; and by United Nations Educational, Scientific, and Cultural Organization for democratic work and intercultural dialogue via the Cities for Peace Prize in 2002.

6. In a letter written to Carlos Zorrilla 10 October 1997 (http://www.intagcloud forest.com/wilson.htm), Wilson stated:

> As I pointed out in my 1992 book *The Diversity of Life*, the forests of western Ecuador are among the hottest of hotspots in the world, meaning that they are among the most endangered ecosystems—down to 10 percent their original extent, mostly destroyed in the past forty years—and also contain exceptionally large numbers of plant and animal species found nowhere else in the world.
>
> The extraordinary value of Ecuadorian western forests, including the largest remaining remnant that includes Intag is well known to biologists around the world and often cited in the scientific literature. After studying the database provided me by Conservation International, the rich biodiversity in remnant forests, and the potential value of their flora and fauna to these endangered habitats should be given the very highest priority in conservation worldwide. Their potential in new medicinal, and other products, their scientific importance, and their symbolic value as a natural resource are beyond measure.
>
> I am also alarmed by the poor reputation that Mitsubishi Corporation (of which the Bitshimetals Exploratory Corporation is a subsidiary) has for irresponsible natural resource extraction. It has been under a worldwide boycott since 1989 for its poor record in the timber industry, and for ignoring criticism of its extraction practices. From all this information together, I strongly support your lawsuit to protect the Intag forest.

7. The following is a list of NGOs, Foundations and governments that have funded projects in Intag (and I do not pretend to include all): Rainforest Concern, GEO-Retten, Ayuda en Acción, Pro Derechos Ciudadanos, Río Intag Agroartesanal Coffee Growers Association, Friends of the Earth Canada, Friends of the Earth Sweden, Swedish Government, United Nations, Manos Unidas, US Agency for International Development, Programa de Apoyo a la Gestión Desentralizado de los Recursos Naturales (European Union), French Electrician Syndicate, Cuba Solar, Engineers without Borders, Sloth Club (Japan), Comité de Derechos Económicos y Sociales (Ecuador), Acción Ecológica, DECOIN, Commissión Ecumenica de Derechos Humanos (Ecuador), Minewatch Canada, Atlanta Botanical Gardens, Lindbergh Foundation, Threshold Foundation, Diputación de Barcelona, Generalitat de Catalunya, Consum Xarxa Solidari, Xarxa, Manduricaos Solidario, Talleres Gran Valle, Greengrants Fund, Fundación Zoobreviven, Ministry of Foreign Affairs of Finland, and World Wildlife Fund Finland, among others.

8. See *Periódico Intag* 2006 for full reference.

9. These kinds of lands granted by the Institute for Land Reforms or the Institute for Agrarian Development to homesteaders does not permit the sale to foreign entities.

References

Acosta, Alberto. 2009. La maldición de la abundancia: un riesgo para la democracia. In *La Tendencia—revista de análisis político*. No. 9 mar/abr. Quito: FES-ILDIS.

Alvarez, Sonia E., Evelina Dagnino, and Arturo Escobar, eds. 1998. *Cultures of politics, politics of cultures: Re-visioning Latin American social movements*. Boulder, Colo.: Westview Press.

Anderson, Benedict. 1991. *Imagined communities*, rev. ed. New York: Verso.

Barndt, Deborah. 2008. *Tangled routes: Women, work, and globalization on the tomato trail*. Lanham, Md.: Rowman & Littlefield.

Bebbington, Anthony. 2007. New states, new NGOs? Crises and transitions among rural development NGOs in the Andean region. *World Development* 25(11):1755–1765.

Bhavani, Kum-Kum, John Foran, and Priva Kurian, eds. 2003. *Feminist futures: Re-imagining women, culture and development*. London: Zed Books.

D'Amico, Linda. 2012. "El agua es vida/ Water is life": The formation of ecological identities and community watersheds in Intag, Ecuador. In *Water, cultural diversity, and global environmental change: Emerging trends, sustainable futures?* ed. Barbara Rose Johnston, Lisa Hiwaski, Irene Klauer, Ameyali Ramos Castillo, and V. Strang. Paris/Jakarta: United Nations Educational, Scientific, and Cultural Organization/Springer.

Del Campo, Esther, and Evelyn Magdaleno. 2008. Avances legislativos de acción positive en Bolivia, Ecuador y Perú. In *Mujeres y escenarios ciudadanos*, ed. Mercedes Prieto. Quito: Facultad Latinoamericana de Ciencias Sociales.

Ecological Ordinance (Ordenaza Ecológica). 2000. Cotacachi: Imbabura.

Escobar, Arturo. 1998. Whose knowledge, whose nature? Biodiversity, conservation and the political ecology of social movements. *Journal of Political Ecology* 5:53–82.

Escobar, Arturo. 2008. *Territories of difference*. Durham, N.C.: Duke University Press.

Escobar, Arturo, and Susan Paulson. 2005. The emergence of collective ethnic identities and alternative political ecologies in the Colombian Pacific Rainforest. In *Political ecology across spaces, scales and social groups*, ed. Susan Paulson and Lisa Gerson, 257–278. New Brunswick, N.J.: Rutgers University Press.

Espinoza Soriano, Waldemar. 1988. *Ethnohistoria Ecuatoriana*. Quito: Abya-Yala.

Fieweger, Mary Ellen, ed. 2007. *Mujeres líderes en el desarrollo de la zona de Intag, canton Cotacachi*. Cotacachi: Asamblea de Unidad Cantonal de Cotacachi.

Harcourt, Wendy, ed. 1994. *Feminist perspectives on sustainable development*. London: Zed Books.

Kuecker, Glenn. 2007. Fighting for the forests. *Latin American Perspectives* 153:94–107.

López, Luis Enrique. 1991. *La Educación en áreas indígenas de América Latina: Apreciaciones comparativas desde la educación bilingüe intercultural*. Guatemala City: Centro de Estudios de Cultura Maya.

López, Luis Enrique. 1999. El lenguaje en el desarrollo de los conocimientos e ámbitos escolares urbanos con diversidad cultural. In *Interculturalidad y calidad de los aprendizajes en ámbitos escolares urbanos*, ed. Nora Mengoa. La Paz: CBIAE.

Martínez-Alier, Joan. 2002. *The environmentalism of the poor: A study of ecological conflicts and valuation*. Northampton, Mass.: Edward Elgar.

Meyers, Norman. 1997. The rich diversity of biodiversity issues. In *Biodiversity II: Understanding and protecting our biological resources*, eds. M. Reaka-Kydla, Don Wilson, and E. O. Wilson. Washington, DC: Joseph Henry Press.

Mohanty, Chandra. 2003. *Feminism without borders: Decolonizing theory, practicing solidarity*. Durham, N.C.: Duke University Press.

Montoya, Rosario, Lessie Jo Frazier, and Janise Hurtig, ed. 2002. *Gender's place: Feminist anthropologies of Latin America*. New York: Palgrave Press.

Moore, Jennifer. 2009. Canadian mining firm financed violence in Ecuador: lawsuit. *The Tyee*, 5 March. http://thetyee.ca/News/2009/03/03/CanMining/

Murra, John. 1972. El 'control vertical' de un máximo de pisos ecológicos en la economía de las sociedades andinas. In *Visita de la Provincia de León de Huánuco en 1562*, Vol. 2, ed. J. V. Murra, 427–476. Huánuco, Peru: Universidad Nacional Hermilio Valdizán.

Parpart, J., Shirin Rai, and Kathleen Stand. 2002. *Rethinking empowerment: Gender and development in a global/local world*. New York: Routledge.

Peet, Richard, and Michael Watts. 2004. *Liberation ecologies, environment, development, social movements*, 2nd ed. New York: Routledge.

Postero, Nancy. 2007. *Now we are citizens: Indigenous politics in postmulticultural Bolivia*. Stanford, Calif.: Stanford University Press.

Rappaport, Joanne. 2005. *Intercultural utopias: Public intellectuals*. Durham, N.C.: Duke University Press.

Ribot, Jesse. 2008. *Building local democracy through natural resource intervention*. Washington, DC: World Resources Institute.

Rocheleau, Diane, Barbara Thomas-Slayter, and Esther Wangari. 1996. *Feminist political ecology: Global issues and local experiences*. New York: Routledge.

Salomon, Frank. 1981. Weavers of Otavalo. In *Cultural transformations and ethnicity in modern Ecuador*, ed. N. Whitten. Champagne-Urbana: University of Illinois Press.

Sawyer, Susana. 2004. *Crude chronicles: Indigenous politics, multinational oil, and neoliberalism in Ecuador*. Durham, N.C.: Duke University Press.

Segarra, Edith, ed. 2007. *Plan de vida de las mujeres de Intag*. Cotacachi: Asamblea de Unidad Cantonal.

Selverston-Sher, Melina. 2001. *Ethnopolitics in Ecuador*. Miami, Fla.: North-South Center Press.

Shiva, Vandana. 1994. Development, ecology, and women. In *Ecology: Key concepts in critical theory*, ed. Carolyn Merchant. Atlantic Highlands, N.J.: Humanities.

Tsing, Anna. 2005. *Friction: An ethnography of global connection*. Princeton, N.J.: Princeton University Press.

Weaver, Fredrick Stirton. 2000. *Latin America in the world economy*. Boulder, Colo.: Westview Press.

West, Paige. 2006. *Conservation is our government now: The politics of ecology in Papua New Guinea*. Durham, N.C.: Duke University Press.

Whitten, Norman E. 2003. *Millennial Ecuador: Critical essays on cultural transformations and social dynamics*. Iowa City: University of Iowa Press.

Wilson, Edward O. 1992. *The diversity of life*. New York: Norton.

CHAPTER THREE

Democratic Spaces across Scales

Women's Inclusion in Community Forestry in Orissa, India

Neera M. Singh

On 10 November 2004, a few days before Diwali, the Indian festival of lights, the rural town of Ranpur in Orissa is taken over by women. The mundane main street comes alive with a riot of colors as more than 1,500 women attired in saris of different hues and shades march through. Women from about 200 villages rally for their long-standing demand of a government purchase center (known as *phadies*) for the collection of *kendu* leaves from the women collectors.[1] Many of them have walked several miles to come here. With babies on their hips and placards in their hands, they enthusiastically chant slogans and march through the street. Such large gatherings are rare, except when political parties herd people in trucks for rallies. A policeman comments, "How the hell did you get so many women [here]?"

On 9 March 2005, women from Ranpur are staging a sit-in demonstration (*dharna*) in front of the State Legislative Assembly in Bhubaneswar. Their demand for kendu leaf phadies has now brought them to the capital city. For ten days, nineteen women face strong sun and frequent rains in their make-shift camp. For some of them, this is the first time that they have stepped outside their local community, but they are learning fast how to be political actors in newly discovered spaces.

In June 2005, in a village in Ranpur, I am interviewing a woman leader who participated in the dharna in Bhubaneswar. I ask her why women do not participate in forest management meetings in her village. She says, "How can we? We are not invited." She contrasts her experience in the capital city with that in her own village, "In a place that is strange to us, we have voiced our concerns. This is our home, our own place, and our own people. Can we not speak here?" I prod, "So, why don't you?" She retorts, "How can I? If I do, they [the men] will say this woman has become very outspoken."

These three ethnographic moments partially represent women's organizing, action, and inaction at different spatial scales in the forested landscapes of Orissa and frame the discussion in this chapter. I use a case of women's organizing for forest-based livelihoods to illustrate how women are sometimes able to use democratic spaces at higher spatial scales to overcome constraints to their participation at the local level.

In forested landscapes of developing countries and subsistence economies, rural women depend critically on forest resources but tend to be excluded from their governance and decision-making (Agarwal 1997; Colfer 2004). As a result, the special ecological knowledge that women have from their lived practices and interaction with local forests remains poorly deployed in forest management. Despite recent shifts toward decentralized community-based forest governance arrangements (Agrawal et al. 2008), women's marginalization in forest decision-making continues (Agarwal 2001; Sarin et al. 2003; Colfer 2004). The idea that local communities can be good stewards of local resources derives traction from idealized notions of communities as homogeneous units characterized by stability and harmony (Guijt and Shah 1998); hence unequal local power relations and structural constraints to equity tend to be downplayed (Mohan and Stokke 2000). Even though the essentialization of notions of community and participation has come under scrutiny (Brosius et al. 1998; Agrawal and Gibson 1999; Cooke and Kothari 2001; Flint et al. 2008), the problem of social exclusion and elite dominance persists due to the difficulty of transforming strongly entrenched power relations (Colfer 2004).

In the Indian state of Orissa, several thousand villages are protecting state-owned forests through community-based arrangements. In contrast to the state-led devolution through Joint Forest Management, these community forestry initiatives represent democratic assertion from below, through which citizens assert greater control over decisions that affect their lives. At one level, they further democracy by seeking to alter state-citizen relations and interactions in the realm of forest governance. But at another level, they are rooted in traditional local institutions within which certain groups of people, particularly women, *dalits*, and *adivasis*,[2] are marginalized. But these traditional institutions are not static and they continually interact with other processes of social change and formal institutions of democracy. This chapter discusses a case of a community forestry federation in which women used space for participation at higher spatial scales to overcome constraints to their participation at the community level. Drawing on multisited ethnography (Marcus 1998), I illustrate how power relations manifest differently at different scales and marginalized people can gain voice and visibility by traversing through levels and organizing where power relations are less strongly entrenched. I also suggest that focus on the "environment" might offer an apolitical ground from which women can enter into more political domains and transform gender relations in families and communities.

Conceptual Framework:
Democracy, Space, and Scale

Beyond voting rights, democracy is a way of life and implies control by citizens over their collective affairs and equality between citizens in the exercise of that control (Beetham 1999). Given the historic exclusion of local people from forest governance, forestry reform advocates tend to focus on transforming state-citizen relations and pay inadequate attention to citizen-citizen relations and power differentials within communities.

Ideals of equality demand not only equal political rights, but also social conditions that support equal opportunity to speak and be heard (Young 2000). In social contexts such as those in Orissa, strong social stratification and power inequalities get in the way of inclusion and political equality. All voices are not equal: Some utterances are more important than others, and some voices are perpetually silenced. It thus becomes important to assess how power relations are altered so that women can gain more voice and become equal citizens. It is also important to view citizenship as not just a status but also a practice (Oldfield 1990) and to be attentive to structures that define the parameters of citizenship as well as to individual agency that shapes what it is to act as a citizen (Lister 1997). Often it is the local rather than the national that is the arena for citizenship struggles and expression of human agency (Lister 1997, p. 34), and we need to consider citizenship as a "multilayered construct applicable simultaneously to people's membership in sub-, cross-, and supra-national collectivities and in nation-states" (Yuval-Davis 1999).

Recent feminist scholarship has drawn attention to different locales and spatial scales as sites of political action and engagement (Harcourt and Escobar 2005). Cornwall (2004) encouraged us to analyze arenas of democratic participation in spatial terms. Drawing on Lefebvre (1991), she used space as "a concept rich with metaphor as well as a literal descriptor of arenas where people gather, which are bounded in time as well as dimension" (Cornwall 2004, p. 1). She urged us to analyze how particular sites come to be populated, appropriated or designated by particular actors in ways that enable or disable social transformation and to pay attention to the relations of power that permeate any site for public engagement.

In my analysis, I draw from recent work on the concepts of scale and scalar politics in geography and beyond. This work emphasizes that there is nothing ontologically given about scale; rather, scale is socially constructed, contested, and reconfigured (Marston 2000; Brenner 2001; Brown and Purcell 2005). Further, the boundaries between home and locality, urban and regional, national and global scales are blurred and "established through the geographical structure of social interactions" (Smith 1993). While there has been an explosion of literature on the politics of scale, there has been relatively little exploration of how power relations at different scales are experienced by people inhabiting or traversing these scales. How does democratic space differ across scales? Are there some scales that are more amenable to democratic organizing and expression of marginalized voices than others? How can marginalized people, such as women, use movement through scales to gain political skills, voice, and visibility and circumvent power relations? I use ideas of democracy, democratic spaces, and their expression at different spatial scales as analytical lenses to analyze women's organizing and action within community forestry in Orissa.

The Setting: Community Forestry in Orissa

In Orissa, 8,000 to 10,000 villages independently protect about 15–20 percent of the state-owned forests through community-based arrangements (Kant et al. 1991; Conroy et al. 2001; Singh 2002). Orissa is one of the most forest-rich states in mainland India. It also happens to be the most economically underdeveloped. Almost 40 percent of Orissa's geographical area is legally categorized as forests, with actual forest cover around 23 percent. A majority of the rural population lives in forested landscapes and depends on forests and marginal lands for subsistence and livelihood needs. Women in poor households especially depend on forests for fuel and a variety of forest products to supplement food and household income.

This dependence has led villages to invest in devising elaborate patrolling and management arrangements even in the absence of formal legal rights. Some villages started protecting forests as early as the 1930s, whereas the majority started in the mid-1980s.

These forest protecting villages have come together as federations at different spatial scales to assert their rights over forests that they protect, improve collective bargaining positions, resolve conflicts, and learn from each other (Singh 2002). In many cases, clusters of villages came together to collaboratively protect a patch of forest or to better coordinate their respective forest protection efforts in view of shared forest resources. These self-emergent federating efforts were later extended to higher scales by NGOs, local influential individuals, or forest bureaucrats. In the early 1990s, some NGOs facilitated district-level federations. A state-level federation called Orissa Jungle Manch was formed in 1999. As of 2009, there are twenty-five district federations and other local-scale federations in Orissa. However, these community forestry groups that rely on traditional authority structures are not necessarily very democratic internally.

Various studies indicate that women face hardship in the initial years of forest protection or bear a disproportionate burden for conservation. They have to walk longer distances to gather fuel or get humiliated by local forest guards who patrol local forests (Sarin et al. 1998; Agarwal 2001; Singh 2001). Some of these problems ease as forests regenerate and access to forest is gradually restored, but women's exclusion from forest decision-making continues. This exclusion has implications for women's access to forests and forest-based livelihoods, as well as for forest management and sustainability. Women are not only excluded at the community level, but also in federations at higher spatial scales. Although most community forestry federations are male dominated, I discuss here the case of one federation, Maa Maninag Jungle Surakhya Parishad (MMJSP),[3] in which space for women led to transformation in the erstwhile male-dominated federation and put women's forest-based livelihood concerns on the advocacy agenda of the federation.

Maa Maninag Jungle Surakhya Parishad

MMJSP is a federation of forest protecting villages in Ranpur block of Nayagarh district in Orissa. MMJSP was formed in 1997 with an initial membership of 85 villages. In 2007, its membership stood at 187 forest-protecting communities clustered into eighteen groups, based on historic social, cultural, and shared resource related ties, with membership ranging from four to fourteen villages in each group. Ranpur block is a drought-prone area, and forest-based livelihoods play a critical role in the lives of the poor, especially of adivasis and dalits. The total geographical area of the block is about 142 square miles, and almost 35 percent of the geographic area is recorded as forest. Almost 39 percent of the households in the block are landless. Landlessness is especially pronounced among adivasis and dalits, at around 70 percent. For the landless, dependence on forests is especially high. Of the 271 village settlements, 187 are involved in conserving forests. A few villages began protecting forests in the 1960s, whereas most others started in the 1980s. These initiatives were prompted by local dependence on forests for products and services.

Methodology

Fieldwork for this research in Ranpur was conducted over several months between 2004 and 2007, when I lived and worked in Orissa (see figure 3.1). My extended presence allowed long-term participant engagement in local processes and events that I was studying. I participated in numerous meetings at different scales of analysis during the three years. Further, I draw on insights from my long-term work with Vasundhara, a Bhubaneswar-based NGO working on forest conservation and livelihood issues that was involved in the formation of MMJSP. In 1991, I founded an NGO, Vasundhara (which means "Mother Earth" in Hindi and Sanskrit) to work on forest conservation and local livelihood issues in Orissa. Vasundhara was involved in facilitating the formation of MMJSP. Through my work with Vasundhara, I was closely associated with MMJSP from its inception. In the tradition of radical objectivity, I embraced my bias and both the burden and advantages of my positionality and past association with MMJSP.

My methods included conversational interviews with village men and women and leaders of MMJSP, study of records of meetings of MMJSP and of women's group meetings, participant observation of meetings, focus group discussions, and interviews with NGO staff. I also analyzed records of MMJSP meetings from 1997 to 2007 to trace its transformation over the years. Three focus groups were conducted with women in village settings to understand constraints to their participation. To understand women's inclusion at the community level, I conducted a detailed study of forest decision-making processes in six villages and in two clusters of villages. In the following sections, I discuss the constraints to women's participation

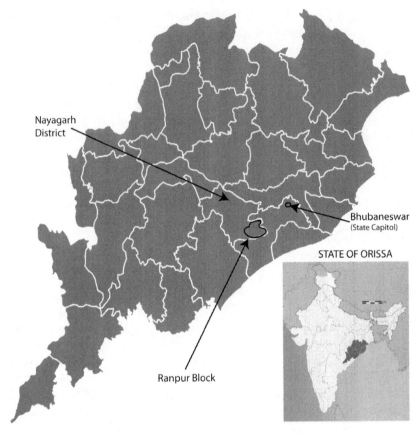

Figure 3.1. Map of Ranpur and Orissa, India. Map by Pamela McElwee

at the community level and how opening of space at the block level impacted spaces at other scales.

Restricted Space at the Community Level: How Can We Go Uninvited?

In Ranpur, as is typical in coastal Orissa, patriarchy is strong and women tend to be excluded from community decision-making, including community forestry. According to a survey conducted by Vasundhara and MMJSP in 2005, in the 111 villages involved in forest protection, only 23 villages had women representatives on the forest protection committees, and only 7 percent of the officeholders in these committees were women. Representation of dalits and adivasis was equally low at 7 and 16 percent, respectively. Women's actual presence and participation in the committee meetings tends to be minimal.

At the village level, women face strong social and cultural taboos that restrict their participation in the public sphere. Women's nonparticipation in community decision-making is mostly attributed to culture and accepted as the way things are done locally. Some of the common remarks that recurred in my interviews include the comment that a "Village story [situation] is different than a city's," or a male leader's comments that "We are not so modern that we will involve women." Women also talked about cultural taboos: "Someone is a father-in-law or uncle-in-law, how can we go and sit with them. . . . Won't we feel shy? Men will say, how immodest she has become, she is coming and sitting with us. We have to take care of our honor." Women also pointed out constraints related to confidence: "If we go once, we will get the courage, [but] we have never gone. That is why we feel shy. How can someone who has never opened her mouth speak? Once she speaks up, then she can."

In many villages, women have been included in recent years due to an institutional provision for women's representation on the Joint Forest Management committees, called the Van Samrakhan Samities (VSS). The law stipulated that there should be at least three women on the executive committee of the VSS. However, often the women included as members of the VSS are not aware of their appointment (cf. Agarwal 2001). Women are thus only notionally present and hardly attend VSS meetings. In a focus group, one woman said, "Men decide [when they will meet]. They fix a time and meet." Another added, "[Men] never inform or invite us. We could go if they invited us. How can we go uninvited?" On whether they were informed about the decisions taken at these meetings, women wryly added, "We do not ask, and they don't tell. Maybe they inform other men, but we don't get to know." In many cases, the minutes of the meetings are sent to women for their signatures and they are expected to sign without bothering to read them.

As is widely noted in the literature, meetings are often scheduled without taking into account women's time availability or convenience, such as being held in late evening hours in the village temple premises, even though women's entry to temples is restricted.[4] Time- and space-related constraints keep women as well as dalits out of community decision–making forums. The case of Das Mauja Jungle Surakhya Samiti (Ten Village Forest Protection Committee) illustrates this. This committee has been protecting a contiguous patch of forest for more than twenty-five years. An executive committee of twenty people, two representatives from each village, meets every Sunday evening to coordinate forest management. The meetings continue until late at night, and women cannot attend them due to cultural taboos. Men do not feel the need to change the meeting venue or time to accommodate women's needs. Although this committee was traditionally all male, since 2005 three women have been included in the VSS as per Joint Forest Management norms. Even though a VSS has been formed, for all practical purposes the informal committee continues to function, and women are only invited to attend when someone from the Forest Department or NGOs come to the meeting. Otherwise, men simply get the women members' signatures on the proceedings. Many villages in Ranpur also organize an annual feast to celebrate community forestry and to involve village youth in forest protection. In these community feasts, women cannot join in and surplus food is sent home for them when the party is over. Women's absence from these formal spaces of community forestry is at odds with their otherwise active role in forest management.

Space for Women at the Federation Scale

Marginalization of women is further accentuated at higher spatial scales within community forestry federations. Leaders from the village level, who tend to be male, are usually tapped to become members of the federations. Like other federations, MMJSP was initially male dominated; there were no women present at the initial meetings that led to the formation of MMJSP. Male leaders also resisted creating space for women within the MMJSP governance structure. At one of the initial meetings of MMJSP in 1997 that I attended, I remember very clearly the vehement opposition to my suggestion that the MMJSP's male leaders consider women's representation in their governance bodies. They were appalled at this suggestion, and their immediate response was, "But women are the destroyers of the forest [as gatherers of fuel and fodder]. How can we include them? No forest will remain if we involve women and dalits." Gently, my colleagues at Vasundhara and I persisted in our efforts to convince them. After the meeting was over, the men discussed this until late in the night. The next morning, one of the leaders informed us, "We have decided that we will keep women. If we don't, it will not look nice." This federation has since come a long way from that time when the men created space for women only to appear progressive (Singh 2007).

In 1997, the first year of MMJSP's existence, no women attended any of the eight meetings held during the year. The following year, a couple of higher-caste women started attending MMJSP meetings. The problem of women's involvement was discussed at a meeting in May 1999, and it was decided to form a task force to address the problem. The facilitating NGO, Vasundhara, played an important role in this. As a Vasundhara field staff member said, "This was a sensitive issue. We were committed to bringing women in, but did not want it to be seen as an external imposition. While we respected their autonomy as a people's organization, we also wanted to see more women and other marginalized sections included. So, we kept raising the issue."

This task force met for the first time in July 1999, with only one woman in attendance, and decided to organize local meetings to discuss strategies for involving women. In these local meetings, women suggested that they fix a time for regular women's meetings at the block level. On 26 September 1999, the first women's meeting was convened. At this meeting, participants decided to form a Central Women's Committee (CWC) and to meet every month on the eighteenth. (Women refer to these meetings as *mahila* meetings [women's meetings] or simply as *athraha tarikh* meetings.[5]) At the initial meeting in which CWC was formed, only seven of the twenty-five participants were women. However, gradually, women started coming to the monthly meetings and began asserting themselves within the federation.

Space for Women through Meetings

The athraha tarikh meetings serve as an open space for women to discuss their problems, meet other women, and learn from each other. Since 2000, a tribal woman has presided over these meetings. This was a marked improvement from the initial stage, when it was male federation leaders who facilitated women's meetings and encouraged them to speak up. The male leaders continue to attend these meetings, but are often patronizing and want to project the women's group as their project. While this helps maintain linkages between MMJSP and the women's group, tensions have emerged as men realized that the women's group is beginning to come into its own.

These meetings are held in a large hall in the offices of MMJSP in Ranpur, which is centrally located and easily accessible. The meetings are scheduled at 10:00 a.m., although women tend to arrive late due to transportation challenges, as women travel from 3 to 20 miles to get to the meeting venue. Some walk, others request a ride on a cycle or motorcycle from male relatives, and most take public buses, which can be erratic and unreliable. Due to the logistics, the effective meeting time is often less than three hours. Initially, predominantly middle-aged and older women attended these meetings, given their relative freedom to travel and lighter loads of household responsibilities, but increasingly younger women have started coming as the CWC has taken up forest-based livelihood activities that engage younger women. For the women, the informal interaction before and after the meetings is as important as the formal meeting and helps them to exchange news and seek advice. These meetings provide a sense of purpose and a social outing. One woman noted, "Men can gossip for hours in a tea-shop, while we cannot. We also need a place to go to."

Women's Action and Expansion of Spaces

As women gathered every month, they brought their forest-based livelihood challenges to the monthly meetings. In this section, I discuss how women engaged in gathering kendu leaves used the space within MMJSP to advocate for livelihood rights, and problems that were otherwise invisible have since become visible and a part of MMJSP's advocacy agenda.

Kendu leaves are an important source of livelihood for the poor in central India, especially during the lean summer months when few other sources of employment exist. In Orissa about 30 million person-days of work are created by leaf collection within a short span of three to four months. The trade in kendu is nationalized in Orissa, and hence the leaves can only be sold at government administered collection centers, or phadies. In the Ranpur area, there were no phadies, and thus women gathering kendu leaves were forced to sell them to private traders, who operated illicitly and offered only a fraction of the state-fixed prices. Women raised this problem at one of the women's meetings in 2000. At the athraha tarikh meeting in January 2001, women decided to take up this issue and organize a rally in Ranpur town. That April, about 2,000 women from ninety-five villages rallied to demand the phadies and sent a petition to the Chief Minister of Orissa. In response, the government established two phadies in 2002 and promised more later (but did not deliver).

Women continued demanding additional phadies through MMJSP. When these efforts failed, women staged another mass demonstration in Ranpur in November 2004. About 1,500 dalit and adivasi women gathered, and when this did not lead to any action by the state, the women decided to hold a sit-in demonstration (dharna) in front of the State Legislative Assembly. From 9 to 16 March 2005, nineteen women sat on a dharna in front of the assembly in Bhubaneswar.

The process of advocating for phadies has taken women into territories and spaces that they usually do not inhabit. Traveling to these places and spaces, both physically and metaphorically, has been liberating and empowering for women and has made them realize their power and potential as political actors. For women, their kendu leaf advocacy action was an important turning point. In my interviews, women recounted this struggle and saw their first rally at Ranpur in 2001 as an important marker in their becoming political actors. At a meeting in 2004 to discuss future courses of action, women were fast to suggest *"puni rally kariba* [let us do another rally]." The women who had gained from the first collective action felt obliged to continue with their advocacy efforts. They noted, "Because of everyone's efforts, we got a phadi. How can we now sit silent?"

Two women elected officials (*sarpanches*) were actively involved in the advocacy strategy meetings and brought with them their nascent experience in the formal political arena.[6] This advice, as well as counsel from other male leaders of MMJSP, helped women design multipronged strategies. For many of the women who went to Bhubaneswar for the dharna, it was their first visit to the capital city. Being in spaces and places alien to them and finding their feet in the new environment was in itself a novel experience. There was also the rare freedom from the drudgery of household chores and being in the company of other women. The streets of power in Bhubaneswar became their training grounds in the arena of political action and activism. There they met other people who had come with their demands, made friends, and shared stories and problems. They learned to deal with policemen who tried to drive them away, stray onlookers who stopped by, as well as the media and elected members of the Legislative Assembly (MLAs). MLAs from the opposition party especially expressed support and encouraged women to continue their fight. In the process, women also became very agitated at the lack of response from their own elected representative.

Their elected representative at that time was a woman who also held a ministerial charge. Women were particularly hurt by her apathy. During election campaigning, she had invoked sisterhood and claimed to understand women's problems. However, this *Apa* (elder sister) changed after getting elected, women said: "Now she does not recognize us. We are still the jungle-people, while she has become an urban dweller." Another woman added, "She is not a woman. She has become a man." After six days of dharna, Ranpur women went to meet this MLA. In the interaction that ensued, Kuntala Nahak, a dalit woman from Mardakoté village, took on the woman minister and reprimanded her for not doing anything about their problem (Singh 2007). In this exchange with the MLA, Kuntala, not bound by the awe of a minister and etiquettes of correct forms of behavior, was able to speak to power more directly by challenging authority and demanding accountability. Following this encounter, the MLA invited the representatives of MMJSP for another discussion and the government promised to open another phadi. While this was still short of their demands for several centers, the women saw it as partial success and felt that they were not going home empty handed.

Advocacy on the kendu leaf issue was not the only action by women in the newly emergent space within MMJSP. The women have also taken the initiative to organize around other forest-based livelihood issues. Biskia Jani, an adivasi woman leader, noted, "When we started meeting, we thought, only conserving forest is not enough, we need to get some income from these forests. So, we looked at our options. We looked at our existing activities [in the forest], for example, [collection of] *siali* leaves, and decided to improve our incomes from siali." (Siali leaves are used for leaf-plates to serve food.) Women decided to get machines to stitch siali leaf-plates and collectively market them. These nontimber forest-product-based livelihood activities have in turn helped strengthen nondestructive activities within forests, as well as helping women gain more economic independence and confidence.

Transformation in Spaces across Scales

Through their advocacy efforts and action in emergent spaces within MMJSP, women have displayed their power and determination to take control over their lives. MMJSP has also gained more visibility and popular support among women. Women's advocacy efforts and success has also helped the men to appreciate women's role and leadership potential. Over the years, there has been an increase in women's representation in the governance structure of MMJSP that consists of a general body, an executive committee, and a working body supported by an advisory committee, a task force for conflict resolution, and the women's subgroup. Initially, the general body consisted of the president and secretaries of all the village-level committees. Given the male domination at the village level, this meant that no women were part of the MMJSP's general body.

In 2000, however, this was changed to include the entire executive committee of village committees in MMJSP's general body. This has created more space for women and shows how institutional space can be used to favor their participation.

The general body of MMJSP usually elects its executive committee. Special provisions were made for including women in the executive committee even prior to 2000. Although the initial ad hoc executive committee of MMJSP formed in 1997 consisted of all men, a year later at the time of MMJSP's registration as a formal society, three women were included in the eleven-member executive committee, even though these women did not come through the same representational process (i.e., elected by the general body as men were). These three women included one dalit and two adivasi women. This inclusion of women initially remained notional but created space for subsequent more meaningful participation by women. The current executive committee of seventeen people has four women; however, until early 2006, none of the office bearers were women.

A working body was constituted to increase direct participation from villages in the functioning of the MMJSP. The initial working body in 1997 of thirty members had only one woman. The size of the working body and the proportion of women has increased steadily; by 2006 the working body had eighty-four members with thirty-one women. Thus, there has been a constant increase in the membership of women in the working body. The representation of adivasis and dalits has also been increasing. This is in stark contrast to the membership of women at the village level, which is quite low at 7 percent.

Even though the CWC started as a separate women's group, there has been synergy between men's and women's actions. As one woman leader said, "If we [women] are in the fore, they are behind [us]. And if they are in the fore, we are behind them [support them]. When we inform them about any problem, they cooperate with us to solve it." The women also feel that they now have more respect. As Kuntala noted, "Earlier, when we spoke the men did not listen. Now, it is different. Our opinion is heard now."

How does women's organizing at a higher spatial scale help to overcome patriarchal relations entrenched at the community scale? Identities and subject positions that are deeply entrenched at one scale become more fluid at another scale. For example, at the village level, a woman is more easily seen as someone's daughter-in-law, mother, or sister-in-law; it is more difficult for her to be just a woman, much less a person. Cultural taboos are also more relaxed outside of the immediate village boundaries.

As Kuntala's story shows, when a woman is able to take advantage of re-duced cultural obstacles to successfully engage in democratic spaces at a higher scale, her success gives her both the prestige and the confidence to expand her role at the community scale. After her participation in the demonstration at Bhubaneswar and exchange with the woman minister, Kuntala refused to sign a village resolution she disagreed with and de-manded certain changes in it. Previously this would have been unthink-able for her.

In several villages women have taken over broken-down forest protec-tion systems from men. After attending a CWC meeting, women from Dengajhari village decided to revive the forest protection system after sev-eral years of collapse. They decided to have two groups of women under-take forest patrolling on a rotation basis. Soon after they started protecting forests, women faced a serious confrontation with a timber-smuggling group. When a group of fifty to sixty men tried to steal timber from their forest, twenty-seven women confronted them and seized more than 1,500 logs. The village men who were too afraid to confront the timber smug-glers were amazed at women's courage, and this incident became a local legend. The leader of the women's group came to be known as "forester *mausi* [aunt]." She frequently narrated the incident dramatically, thus in-spiring women in neighboring villages to play a greater role in forest pro-tection. Men also became open to the possibility of a more pronounced role for women in forest protection. There are now several more instances in which women have started protecting forests on their own. As Kuntala said about the transformation in the space for women, "Due to participa-tion of women, the forest is well-protected. Now the question is whether men will participate in the process or resign from it. If they want to be involved, then they can join in at back, not in the front!"

While this transformation is taking place in certain villages, women members on the MMJSP committee are beginning to question the exclu-sion of women at the community level more generally. In the general body meeting of MMJSP held in 2007, Pramila Dash from Surkhabadi village of the Das Mauja cluster raised the contradiction between the rhetoric about women's participation at the block level and the reality at the village level, where they are simply expected to provide their signatures to en-dorse men's decisions. Thus, changes are occurring both because women who have achieved success at a higher level are beginning to stand up at the community level and because actors at the block level, where greater democratic space already exists for women, are lobbying for institutional-izing the same changes at the village level.

Continuing Challenges for Expanding the Spaces for Women

While there has been a transformation in women's participation in MMJSP, women's involvement in other community forestry federations remains a challenge. This is not unusual, considering that the community forest management groups are traditional institutions that derive strength from culture and traditional sources of authority. Their federations also draw on these strengths of culture and tradition, and often they do not know how to address power inequalities. In Orissa, only three of the twenty-five federations have taken steps to improve women's involvement. Most federations do not necessarily see marginalization of women or other social groups as a problem. While NGOs working with federations may want to tackle this, they do not necessarily prioritize their scarce resources to processes of long-term change.

In Orissa Jungle Manch, the state-level federation, women's involvement and participation still remain marginal. Other than their limited institutional presence, women also remain absent from different state-level policy forums, conferences, and workshops. Many factors contribute to this. Often it is leaders and those seen as experts who come to attend policy forums. Women find it difficult to get to such leadership and expert positions. When district federations nominate one or two representatives to represent the district at the state level, they tend to be men. For village women, travel to Bhubaneswar is also a constraint. It is difficult for women to get permission from family to travel unless they have a woman traveling partner. This constraint and the additional travel costs favor men's representation in state-level policy events.

Occasionally when some women do come to these meetings, they find it difficult to comprehend the discourse of policy and discussions about issues that seem far-removed from their immediate concerns. Men often do not take the time to fill in the details of past discussion, and there are also problems with the overly technical and managerial discourse.

Concluding Remarks

Women's marginalization in natural resource governance is a critical problem, especially in the Southern Hemisphere. In societies and contexts where hierarchy and unequal relations define the prevailing social order, addressing equity concerns is a formidable challenge, especially considering that top-down approaches to social reform often fail and bottom-up processes for social transformation are less likely to emerge in locales where these power relations are more strongly entrenched (Batliwala and Dhanraj 2006; Cornwall et al. 2006; Mukhopadhyay 2006).

But this case study of the MMJSP shows how change *can* come from certain locales and spaces: Everyday action and organizing by women to address their common problems may in the process allow them to gain voice and confidence to negotiate space at other scales. There are numerous such examples of women coming together in groups to save and invest or to fight against extractive industries that threaten their local environments, health, and economies (see Harcourt and Escobar 2005; Gibson-Graham 2006). In presenting this case, I draw attention to the extraordinary possibilities of leveraging space at certain scales to open and expand access in places where women have more difficult and often solitary struggles to wage. I suggest that closer attention to constraints and possibilities at different scales can help practitioners and development workers design strategies that are able to leverage space and foster processes that lead to participation and action at other scales. This requires being cognizant of interrelationships and enhancing communication and connections across scales.

For instance, constraints and possibilities for women's participation are clearly different across spatial scales. While cultural constraints restrict women's voices within their immediate community, they often have more knowledge about the workings at this scale. But at the macro-scale of region, nation, or globe, the techno-managerial discourse and language used can make it more difficult for village women (or men) to effectively participate, even though they may be encouraged to do so through affirmative action programs of NGO advocacy. At the same time, home is the site for women that is often the most resistant to change, and practitioners have pointed out that improved livelihoods and enhanced political space do not automatically translate into greater negotiating power within the closed doors of the family (Mendhapurkar 2004). In Orissa, the meso-scale of the region, where common issues of life and livelihood struggles could be clearly identified, provided an easier entry point to addressing issues of marginalization of women. Within the MMJSP, women were able to gain voice at the block level since they needed to take up advocacy at that scale to solve their common livelihood problem. This in turn helped nurture women's confidence and skills for becoming political actors.

Even though the concept of scale and cross-scale linkages has been drawing a lot of attention in social sciences in recent years, there has been inadequate appreciation of how democratic space across scales varies for different social categories and how social transformation can be facilitated by allowing the marginalized groups to jump scales. As I illustrate through my case, the constraints on and possibilities for democratic participation across scales are different. An appreciation of these differences can improve efforts to support transformation in power relations. I do not suggest a uniform prescription about the scale at which it is easiest to initiate the process of alteration of power relations, but only a need to pay close attention to the differences in the degree of entrenchment of power relations across locales. Even though the process of change is gradual, expansion of space at one scale has bearings on space and constraints at other scales.

Further, the environment as a topic has the potential to provide an apolitical entry point from which women can enter into more political domains and can help transform gender relations in families and communities. In the absence of formal rights over the forests that they protect, local communities rely on moral authority of "doing good" by protecting the environment (Singh 2009). Such a discourse and focus on altruistic dimensions of forest conservation turns sustainability into a common goal that can help overcome power struggles between genders to some degree. This partially explains why men have not responded in a hostile manner to women's increasing presence within the community forestry federations. The male members of MMJSP have welcomed women's conversion into environmental subjects through their increased involvement in community forestry (cf. Agrawal 2005) instead of resisting their increased involvement. This suggests that some sectors or arenas of participation in the public sphere might provide easier entry points than others. It would be worthwhile for practitioners working on equity issues to focus their energy on such spaces and arenas for expanding space in other more politically sensitive arenas.

Acknowledgments

This chapter is a revised version of a chapter in my dissertation, "Environmentality, Democratic Assertions and Re-imagination of Forest Governance in Orissa, India" (Michigan State University). I gratefully acknowledge the support from the Social Science Research Council and the American Institute of Indian Studies for my research. An earlier version of this chapter was published as a book chapter in *Women's Livelihood Rights: Recasting Citizenship for Development*, edited by Sumi Krishna and published by Sage New Delhi. My thanks to John Kerr, Anne Ferguson, Dianne Rocheleau, Jim Bingen, Kundan Kumar, and Sumi Krishna for their comments on earlier drafts and to Arundhati Jena and Aurobindo Rout for their able field assistance.

Notes

1. Kendu (*Diospyros melanoxylon*) leaves are used for wrapping beedis, local cigarettes. This forest product is nationalized and can only be sold at government-operated purchase centers. Women in the area have been demanding opening up of kendu leaf collection centers, known as phadies.

2. *Dalit* refers to a caste traditionally regarded as untouchables. *Adivasis* are also referred to as tribals, believed to be the aboriginal population of India. Both groups tend to be discriminated against in rural India.

3. Maa Maninag Jungle Surakhya Parishad means Mother Maninag Forests Protection Forum. It is named after a local deity and its namesake hill, Maa Maninag. *Parishad* means forum or solidarity group, and MMJSP is locally referred to as the Parishad.

4. For example, menstruating women's entry to temples is a traditional taboo, and in many villages dalits are still kept out of temples. While these barriers are breaking down, they are by no means gone.

5. *Athrah* means eighteenth and *tarikh* means date in Oriya and refers to the meetings held on the eighteenth every month.

6. Sarpanches are the elected representatives in the Indian local self-governance system called the Panchayati Raj. In 1993, through the 73rd amendment of the constitution, one-third of all panchayat seats were reserved for women.

References

Agarwal, B. 1997. Environmental action, gender equity and women's participation. *Development and Change* 28(1):1–44.

Agarwal, B. 2001. Participatory exclusions, community forestry, and gender: An analysis for South Asia and a conceptual framework. *World Development* 29(10):1623–1648.

Agrawal, A. 2005. *Environmentality: Technologies of government and the making of subjects.* Durham, N.C.: Duke University Press.

Agrawal, A., and C. C. Gibson. 1999. Enchantment and disenchantment: the role of community in natural resource conservation. *World Development* 27(4):629–649.

Agrawal, A., A. Chhatre, and R. Hardin. 2008. Changing governance of world's forests. *Science* 320:1460.

Batliwala, S., and D. Dhanraj. 2006. Gender myths that instrumentalize women: A view from the Indian front line. In *Feminisms in development: Contradictions, contestations, and challenges*, eds. A. Cornwall, E. Harrison, and A. Whitehead, 21–34. London: Zed Books.

Beetham, D. 1999. *Democracy and human rights.* Cambridge, U.K.: Polity Press.

Brenner, N. 2001. The limits to scale? Methodological reflections on scalar structuration. *Progress in Human Geography* 25(4):591–614.

Brosius, J. P., A. Tsing, and C. Zerner. 1998. Representing communities: Histories and politics of community-based natural resource management. *Society and Natural Resources* 11(2):157–168.

Brown, C. J., and M. Purcell. 2005. There's nothing inherent about scale: Political ecology, the local trap, and the politics of development in the Brazilian Amazon. *Geoforum* 36(5):607–624.

Colfer, C. J. P. 2004. *The equitable forest: Diversity, community, and resource management.* Washington, DC: Resources for the Future Press.

Conroy, C., A. Mishra, A. Rai, N. M. Singh, and M. K. Chan. 2001. Conflicts affecting participatory forest management: Their nature and implications. In *Analytical issues in participatory natural resources management,* eds. B. Vira and R. Jeffrey, 165–184. New York: Palgrave Macmillan.

Cooke, B., and U. Kothari. 2001. *Participation: The new tyranny?* London: Zed Books.

Cornwall, A. 2004. New democratic spaces? The politics and dynamics of institutionalized participation. *IDS Bulletin* 35(2):1–10.

Cornwall, A., E. Harrison, and A. Whitehead. 2006. *Feminisms in development: Contradictions, contestations, and challenges.* London: Zed Books.

Flint, C. G., A. E. Luloff, and J. C. Finley. 2008. Where is "community" in community-based forestry? *Society and Natural Resources* 21(6):526–537.

Gibson-Graham, J. K. 2006. *A postcapitalist politics.* Minneapolis: University of Minnesota Press.

Guijt, I., and M. K. Shah. 1998. *The myth of community: Gender issues in participatory development.* London: Intermediate Technology Publications.

Harcourt, W., and A. Escobar. 2005. *Women and the politics of place.* Bloomfield, Conn.: Kumarian Press.

Kant, S., N. M. Singh, and K. K. Singh. 1991. *Community-based forest management systems: Case studies from Orissa.* New Delhi: SIDA, ISO/Swedforest, and the IIFM.

Lefebvre, H. 1991. *The production of space.* Oxford: Blackwell.

Lister, R. 1997. Citizenship: Towards a feminist synthesis. *Feminist Review* 57(Autumn):28–48.

Marcus, G. E. 1998. *Ethnography through Thick and Thin.* Princeton, N.J.: Princeton University Press.

Marston, S. 2000. The social construction of scale. *Progress in Human Geography* 24(2):219–242.

Mendhapurkar, S. 2004. From subjects of change to agents of change: A travelogue in Himachal Pradesh. In *Livelihood and gender,* ed. S. Krishna, 397–411. New Delhi: Sage.

Mohan, G., and K. Stokke. 2000. Participatory development and empowerment: The dangers of localism. *Third World Quarterly* 21(2):247–268.

Mukhopadhyay, M. 2006. Mainstreaming gender or 'streaming' gender away: Feminists marooned in the development business. In *Feminisms in development: Contradictions, contestations, and challenge,* eds. A. Cornwall, E. Harrison, and A. Whitehead, 135–149. London: Zed Books.

Oldfield, A. 1990. *Citizenship and community: Civic republicanism and the modern world.* London: Routledge.

Sarin, M., L. Ray, M. R. Raju, M. Chatterjee, and S. Hiremath. 1998. *Who is gaining? Who is losing? Gender and equity concerns in joint forest management.* New Delhi: Society for Promotion of Wastelands Development.

Sarin, M., N. M. Singh, N. Sundar, and R. K. Bhogal. 2003. Devolution as a threat to democratic decision-making in forestry? Findings from three states in India. In *Local forest management: The impacts of devolution policies,* eds. D. Edmunds and E. Wollenberg, 55–126. Sterling, Va.: Earthscan.

Singh, N. M. 2001. Women and community forests in Orissa: Rights and management. *Indian Journal of Gender Studies* 8(2):257–270.

Singh, N. M. 2002. Federations of community forest management groups in Orissa: Crafting new institutions to assert local rights. *Forest, Trees and People Newsletter* 46:35–45.

Singh, N. M. 2007. Transgressing political spaces and claiming citizenship: The case of women kendu leaf-pluckers and the community forestry federation, Ranpur, Orissa. In *Women's livelihood rights: Recasting citizenship for development,* ed. S. Krishna, 62–81. New Delhi: Sage.

Singh, N. M. 2009. *Environmental subjectivity, democratic assertions and reimagination of forest governance in Orissa, India.* PhD diss., Michigan State University.

Smith, N. 1993. Homeless/global: Scaling places. In *Mapping the futures: Local cultures, global change,* ed. J. Bird, 87–121. New York: Routledge.

Young, I. 2000. *Inclusion and democracy.* Oxford: Oxford University Press.

Yuval-Davis, N. 1999. The 'multi-layered citizen': Citizenship in the age of 'globalization'. *International Feminist Journal of Politics* 1(1):119–136.

CHAPTER FOUR

The Gender Dimensions of the Illegal Trade in Wildlife

Local and Global Connections in Vietnam

Pamela McElwee

An important aspect to remember in the study of gender is that it is not just about women. That is, analyses of the role of gender in environmental problems and sustainability, as this book has focused on, should ideally outline the differential roles of *both* men and women and highlight areas in which there is strong stratification between genders in terms of beliefs or practices. The global wildlife trade is one area of sustainability in which actors and stakeholders are highly gender differentiated. However, in reviewing the literature in this field, I have been struck by the absence of discussion of the gender dimensions of the problem: Producers, traders, and consumers of wildlife products are almost never defined by their gender in the major works on the subject (cf. Oldfield 2003). Yet in my own research in Vietnam, I have found no other environmental problem that is so tied into very divided gender norms as the hunting and consumption of wild animals. Therefore, the lack of attention to gender in global analyses of the international wildlife trade and proposed solutions to it are especially striking, and I argue in this chapter that treating wildlife trade in a gender-blind manner may prevent us from seeing particular problems as well as potential sustainable solutions that have a basis in gender divisions.

Many of the key links between gender and sustainability are tied to production, social reproduction, and consumption patterns, which in turn are linked to access and control of resources. This is particularly clear in discussions of wildlife. The hunting of wild animals is often seen as a "man's profession," both because of its perceived dangerousness and laboriousness and because it involves extended periods away from home. There are cultural taboos against women handling or consuming certain types of wildlife among some ethnic groups around the world, as well as in the case study in Vietnam noted here. Although the trade of wildlife is conducted by both men and women, it is predominated by men. This trade often involves bribes to officials to turn a blind eye to the illegal nature of the problem, which is seen as a role for men to deal with other men, as men are more likely to be government rangers, officials, or inspectors. Finally, the consumption of wildlife is highly gendered. Much of the eating of wild meats and consumption of wildlife for medicinal purposes is tied to culturally perceived masculinity and sexual prowess, along with male sociality and prestige. Dealing with the wildlife trade as a social issue, whether through local or global enforcement and legal efforts, thus needs to be understood through a gender lens at all levels.

The Global Wildlife Trade and Gender

Little academic work has been conducted on the gender aspect of the global wildlife trade. Several studies examined the relationships between women and animals, mostly coming out of ecofeminist writings, but none of the research dealt specifically with wildlife trade. Ecofeminist theory has tried to draw parallels between women's subjugation and the treatment of animals (Gaard 1993; Kruse 1999), but this work is not particularly useful in understanding the modern dynamics of wildlife trade and the complicated systems of access, control, and consumption patterns involved. Other studies looked at attitudes toward wildlife by women, suggesting that there are significantly gendered differences in how wildlife/animals are perceived by the sexes. One study of North American respondents concluded that "the strength and consistency of male vs. female differences were so pronounced as to suggest gender is among the most important demographic influences on attributes toward animals in our society" (Kellert and Berry 1987). In that study, the women surveyed were more likely to have moralistic and anthropomorphic feelings toward animals, whereas men had a greater tendency to see animals as utilitarian and in need of dominion and mastery. The authors concluded that socialized gender roles, such as women being raised to be more nurturing and caregiving, may explain part of this difference (Kellert and Berry 1987). Yet this study was limited to attitudes in North America. It is important to examine opinions toward animals in other cultures with much more direct and sustained contact with wild animals, such as where animals might play a important role in food provision, as we might expect in more rural areas of the developing world.

For the developing world, the literature on gender and wildlife is primarily limited to studies of hunting. Although there is relatively little literature on women as hunters, as compared to men, it is clear that in some cultures women do play this role (Noss and Hewlett 2001, p. 1024). The few studies we do have of gender differences in hunting have tried to explain why women are hunters in some contexts but not in others. Much of this work is rooted in human behavioral ecology, which focuses on identifying activities that enhance reproductive fitness. This has produced theories that women only hunt when the caloric intake from wild animals is greater than that from plant food gathering or agriculture, or that women do not hunt because they are constrained by child bearing and childcare tasks that hunting would endanger (Bird and Bird 2008). Yet, as one author notes, "Such theories explain absolutely nothing about why categorical divisions of foraging labor exist at all, why they are predicated on gender, or why women's hunting is almost universally either marginalized or proscribed" (Brightman 1996, p. 687). More culturalist explanations suggest that "Female hunting is more likely to occur when women have access to the means/technology of efficient hunting, male ideological/political control of women is minimal, and cultural precedents exist that enable women to obtain knowledge of and experience in hunting" (Noss and Hewlett 2001, p 1026). In other words, resource access and control are likely as important as biology in explaining why women have been relatively insignificant in hunting effort in many parts of the world.

In this chapter I make a first attempt to look with a gender lens at the global wildlife trade, through a local case study based in Vietnam. I highlight how understanding the role of gendered practices can be used to reach a more sustainable level of world trade in wildlife and combat the enormous underground, illegal, and unsustainable trade currently going on.

Methods

This chapter is based on research conducted since 1996 on environmental change in Vietnam. As part of several research projects, I have had the opportunity to travel to nearly all sixty-three provinces in Vietnam and to conduct research in many of them, particularly along the mountainous spine of western Vietnam known as the Annamite Cordillera. Research in Ha Tinh province in 2001 and in Quang Tri, Thua Thien Hue, and Quang Nam provinces in 2005 forms the basis for most of the material collected in this chapter, particularly surveys with hunters who were ethnically Vietnamese in Ha Tinh and ethnically Katu in Quang Nam. These interviews took place in communities next to the Ke Go Nature Reserve in Ha Tinh and the Song Thanh Nature Reserve in Quang Nam (see figure 4.1). Over the past few years, this work with local communities has been supplemented by ethnographic interviews of conservation NGO workers and government officials in Hanoi and elsewhere regarding the challenges of conservation in Vietnam, particularly with NGOs such as TRAFFIC and the Wildlife Conservation Society, who have focused their efforts on the interdiction of illegal hunting. In 2008 and 2009, I also interviewed representatives of the Convention on International Trade in Endangered Species (CITES) authority office in Vietnam regarding the extent of the wildlife trade and their activities to combat it.

The Illegal International Wildlife Market

Due to its underground and illicit nature, it is difficult to know how widespread the illegal wildlife trade is worldwide. The illegal trade thrives despite the existence of CITES, a global treaty to regulate this commerce. Under CITES, more than 800 animal and plant species (known as "listed" species in Annex I of the convention) are banned from international trade among the more than 160 parties to the treaty, and another tens of thousands of species are subject to legal, but restricted, trade (Annex II species). The legal trade in wildlife under CITES is estimated at more than US$300 billion per year (TRAFFIC 2008b). Of the wildlife that flows through legal channels and is documented under CITES, most is timber (65 percent), followed by fish (25 percent), nontimber forest products (7 percent), and other commodities, such as pets, bushmeat, and skins (3 percent) (Blundell and Mascia 2005).

A parallel black market in endangered species exists beside the legal CITES-regulated trade. In the late 1990s, it was estimated that this illegal market is worth US$10–30 billion a year and is dominated by commodities such as bushmeat and animals for traditional medicine and curios, such as trade in elephant ivory or rhino horns (Stoett 2002). The largest consumption of these illegal goods occurs in the European Union, China, and the United States (Engler and Parry-Jones 2007; Wyler and Sheikh

Figure 4.1. Map of Vietnam. Base map from Perry-Castañeda Map Library,
University of Texas

2008). The illegal trade appears to be on the increase, aided by the use of the Internet and new technologies to evade capture, even while importing countries have attempted to crack down on the trade with increased funding and enforcement actions, such as through Interpol.

Many potential implications of the illegal wildlife trade are beginning to be recognized. In most cases, the levels of trade are likely in excess of what can be sustainably harvested, given species reproduction rates (Bennett et al. 2002). International NGOs have warned that "the current level of over-exploitation for both legal and illegal wildlife trade are widely considered to be the single greatest threat to many species, over and above habitat loss and degradation" (Swift et al. 2007). The loss of certain endangered species has moral implications that many find unacceptable, as some highly lucrative species, such as tigers, are being hunted nearly to the point of extinction. In other areas, the illegal trade in wild animals is diminishing the availability of wild subsistence protein to local populations, with local health impacts, as wildlife has become highly commercialized and commoditized. Exotic and invasive species are also being introduced into new ecosystems as wildlife is smuggled across borders by long-distance trade (Broad et al. 2003). Further, there is increasing concern that emerging infectious diseases, such as severe acute respiratory syndrome (SARS), may be linked to zoonotic pathogens that originate in the movement and consumption of wild animals (Swift et al. 2007).

Southeast Asia, and Vietnam in particular, has been identified as an important node in the global wildlife trade. In a search for "illegal wildlife trade" on Google, Vietnam is the first country that emerges in the search results, due to a large number of high-profile smuggling cases that have been broken in recent years. Vietnam plays many roles in the illegal network: serving as a site of capture and export of some illegally harvested plants and animals, particularly mammals and reptiles; as a site of consumption of many threatened animals; and as a transport link between countries (World Bank 2005; Swift et al. 2007). Vietnamese hunters have also been implicated in the depletion of wildlife in other neighboring countries, such as Laos (Singh 2008). Within Vietnam the illegal wildlife trade is predominantly of live animals that are used in traditional medicine, as bushmeat, and as pets. The World Bank (2005) estimated that the illegal trade of wildlife in the country generates more than US$60 million a year. The parameters of this current-day commerce in wild species—the international trade of live-caught animals sold for cash—is significantly different than the history of hunting in Vietnam and reflects social changes that have only begun in the past decade or so.

The History of Wildlife Hunting in Vietnam

Within Vietnam, hunting has always been highly gendered. Some accounts of hunters indicate that there are taboos that men should not meet with women on the way to a hunt (Vu Hong Thuat 2002) and women should not handle certain types of hunting equipment for fear of cursing it. I can find little evidence that women were ever strongly involved in hunting among any ethnic groups in Indochina. This is consistent with interviews of contemporary communities where I was simply told that women did not hunt because they had no tradition or experience of doing so. For men, hunting and forest product collecting have traditionally played an important role in the lives of all the ethnic minorities in the north-central area of Vietnam. Among the Katu people, for example, hunting played a very important role not only in supplying meat for protein, but also in providing a way to express one's prowess and masculinity (Hickey 1993, p. 133). American researchers writing during the Vietnam War noted of the gendered divisions in hunting: "Hunting provides the bulk of the meat diet, as the Katu are skilled hunters using the trap, the crossbow (sometimes with poisoned arrows), imitative calls to attract birds, and hunting dogs. Katu women roam over large areas collecting herbs, roots, shoots, and edible leaves, fruits, and tubers. They use a sharp stick or small hoe to dig the earth for the roots and tubers. With the help of dogs, the women catch lizards, rats, snakes, squirrels, and birds" (Schrock 1966, p. 367).

Hunting trophies collected by Katu men would be displayed prominently, particularly in the communal house of the village (known as a *guol*), a practice that continues to this day. Access to these communal halls was traditionally restricted to men of adult age and used as a site to induct young men into the masculine cultures of the village. While communal halls are still used among many minority groups, gender law in Vietnam now mandates that they be equally open to both men and women. Despite this transformation of the guol to a gender-neutral site, the role of animals in the guol remains strong, with skulls and visual markers for important animals decorating the outside of most modern community halls I have seen among the Katu.

When omens were not followed or bad luck befell a village, hunting was carried out to find animals to sacrifice to clear the bad luck, or domesticated animals such as buffalos were obtained. Nancy Costello, who has worked with Katu in Vietnam and in Laos, noted that "The whole fabric of Katu society is intermeshed with the environment. The Katu must live in harmony with the world around them, which includes other people, animals, birds, trees, stones, water, traditions, and the many spirits. When this harmony is disrupted, through the breaking of taboos and traditions, which displeases the many spirits, the correct relationship must be restored through ritual and sacrifice" (Costello 2003, p. 163). Such sacrifices were also made at times of plenty, such as after a good harvest to thank the spirits for their blessings.

However, despite the cultural importance of hunts and animal sacrifice among many ethnic groups in Vietnam, such ceremonies are increasingly rare, for several reasons. In many cases, these practices were considered superstitious and discouraged by the communist authorities. In addition, after the reunification of Vietnam, new wildlife policies were enacted. The new state established a decree in 1975 that all hunting needed to be authorized by permit, as the state was eager to claim authority over wildlife management, just as it claimed collective authority over production and agriculture in the new socialist system. Faced with evidence of declining game populations and threats to several major species, these hunting controls were later further enforced with bans on personal weapons in the 1990s, an expansion of the area of land in protected areas, and increased interdiction efforts by forest rangers, whose numbers were increased with money provided by Western NGOs who were concerned about overhunting (Nash 1997).

Current-Day Patterns and Sustainability of Hunting

Despite laws against it, hunting of wild endangered animals still goes on in Vietnam. Yet despite many news reports about high levels of poaching in the country, the average rural family does not engage in hunting as they might have in the past. In surveys I conducted from 2001 to 2005, only a few households per village were found to be hunting at all, and most of those did not go regularly. The main factor was that wildlife populations were severely depleted by the early 1990s. Animals were rarely encountered in the course of walking through the forest; many children had never seen a wild mammal in areas where they were previously common. This was attributed to unrestricted hunting, which was common during wartime and in the late 1970s and early 1980s during the postwar reconstruction era. This hunting was carried out by soldiers and others not familiar with the local environment, who were more prone to overhunting than locals. Informants noted that many animals were regularly seen during the war, and the common ones like deer and boar were often the only sources of meat in the deprivations of the postwar era. Older residents discussed having seen tigers (*ho*), leopards (*bao*), and even elephants (*voi*) regularly up until the late 1970s. However, the accessibility of weapons left over from the war meant that heavily armed men could hunt wildlife with a great deal of accuracy and more efficiently than in the past, when bows and arrows were the methods of choice. The few animals that remained in the forest were increasingly difficult to find, and local hunters were often in competition with professional hunters from hundreds of miles away who would come to the area with orders for the most lucrative species such as tiger and bears. When I once expressed interest in going into a nearby forest around Ke Go Nature Reserve, a village headman told me such a trip was very dangerous and difficult. "First," he said, "there are leeches. And then mosquitoes. And then forest animals." When I asked what animals in particular, he exclaimed, "Oh, tigers, and bears, and elephants, and leopards!" When I then asked if he had seen all of them recently himself, he laughed and shook his head. "How can I see them? They are caught and sold immediately! I've never seen them! Only the hunters see them." He said the largest numbers of hunters were outsiders from other provinces, who were known for their connections with wildlife dealers in the north and would ship any live animals caught immediately north to China.

Thus while hunting can be highly lucrative for those with connections, mainly professional or semiprofessional hunters, for the average farmer, hunting was simply too difficult and not profitable enough. Less than 10 percent of ethnic Vietnamese families and less than 30 percent of minority households interviewed in the course of my work over several years admitted to hunting, and even these claimed to be only "irregular" hunters; the contribution to household incomes from this activity was less than 5 percent of household income (McElwee 2008). While some animals could be highly profitable, they were so difficult to find that the average person did not bother to look for a tiger or a bear, leaving those species to the professional hunters, while locals focused on small mammals, birds, and reptiles that were more easily obtained.

The few local people who continued to hunt at the time of my surveys in 2001 and 2004 had a variety of techniques to try to find the few animals that remained in forest areas. All hunters I interviewed were aware of the diminished supply of wildlife now, as compared with twenty or more years ago. As wildlife has become scarcer, it is increasingly common for hunters to have to travel quite far from home for up to months at a time, and in groups, in order to track and obtain animals. This was one reason why men were seen as the only suitable people to be hunters; it was not feasible or safe for women to travel so far from home. Many times, hunting was only done in conjunction with another activity, such as cutting timber, as it was not profitable enough on its own.

Snaring (*day cap*) was the most common technique for local hunters; it was low investment and required just wires (often old bicycle cables) laid over a stick and pulled taut for an unsuspecting animal to trip it. Snares were most often used to catch large mammals, such as pigs and deer, and ground birds, such as pheasants. Some hunters used small wire traps (*bay doi*) for small mammals like squirrels and rats. None of the hunters I interviewed used dogs (*cho duoi*) for sniffing out animals, but more experienced professional hunters coming into the area were said to use them frequently to catch weasels, monitor lizards, and snakes in particular. For certain tree-dwelling reptiles and amphibians, lights or head lanterns (*di soi den*) were used; the animals were blinded by the light and then scooped up with nets. Large nets were also used to catch flying birds.

These hunting practices are quite different than those used in Vietnam in the past, as there have been major changes in the methods and targets of hunting in recent years. The national ban on guns and rifles has meant that most hunters, both local and professionals, have now shifted to the use of dogs and/or snare traps for hunting. This has had an unfortunate consequence of actually increasing the amount of wildlife at risk from hunting, as traps are indiscriminate about what they catch, whereas guns are much more selective because they depend on hunters' skill in using the gun and tracking the animals.

The second major change in hunting is that the demand for meat from urban middle-class consumers in Vietnam and elsewhere has meant that traders want the freshest meat—and thus pay premium prices for live animals. There has also been an impact from improved road expansion and affordability of air travel, meaning animals can now be transported much farther away from where they are collected in a much quicker time period (Nguyen Van Song 2008). This has meant that hunters need either connections to quickly move live animals to markets elsewhere or suffer lower prices if they do not have access to holding areas or refrigeration. This situation has reinforced a shift to professional hunters who do have trading connections and access to technology (such as tranquilizers and means of transport) to move live animals.

There has also been a shift from social sharing of meat in communities to individual profit. In the past, hunters often shared the meat from their hunting trips with relatives and even whole communities if a large animal was the prize. Yet I was told that since around 2000 in my study areas, local hunters no longer share meat or even eat it themselves, because they recognize the cash profit they can make from selling it. Older ethnic minority informants, though willingly participating in the trade as one of the sole sources of cash income in their villages, often decried the increasing commercialization of what used to be a shared resource. One Pa Cô headman said that before 2001, any hunter who caught a deer would share the meat with others in the village. After ethnic Vietnamese traders came to their village and proposed to buy animals, the practice of sharing meat ended. All animals were sold almost immediately, and there was very little local consumption of wild meat any more. The presence of new Vietnamese-owned shops in many previously remote locations has meant that wildlife can be killed and frozen for storage, and that especially valuable wildlife can be stored live while the trader phones to the coast for a pickup. These practices only became possible with the settlement of ethnic Vietnamese traders in the midst of ethnic villages, said local informants. Previously, locals simply did not have the ability to sell wildlife through these complicated trade networks.

Interviews with hunters in other areas of Vietnam confirm my findings that there is now a near-universal shift in wildlife hunting from local consumption to commercial selling (Newton et al. 2008). This shift from subsistence hunting to commercial trade has had another serious outcome: certain species are now more favored (civet, wild pig, deer, porcupine, pangolin, and snakes are most at risk) because these are the species demanded by urban consumers. In the past, when obtaining a subsistence meat supply was a main reason for hunting, a wider range of species were used. The new focus on a narrow range of species means these are more likely to face threatened or endangered status.

A final change in hunting practice has been the increasing restrictions on the legality of hunting, both by the state and by international conservation organizations. These organizations have been very interested in reducing threats to endangered species in Vietnam, and they have spent millions of dollars on conservation projects for animals such as elephants, tigers, and endangered primates (McElwee 2002). The international conservation organizations have conducted research on hunting among rural communities in attempts to find ways to reduce it, yet they have paid attention only to the economic importance in quantitative terms and made no attempt to put hunting in a larger cultural context (Le Trong Trai et al. 2003). No hunting studies have made any reference to the cultural importance of sacrifices or animal and ancestor spirits or to the role of hunting in local conceptions of masculinity, and no international organizations have proposed letting limited local hunting go on if communities made pledges to use meat for subsistence use only. In fact, hunting of all kinds has been actively discouraged by conservation organizations, even of common non-endangered animals like wild pigs, which often destroy crops if not kept in check. Local people had many complaints about the fact that the rarest of species were now overhunted by outsiders, while the most common and most nuisance animals, in local opinion, could not be legally hunted due to blanket restrictions banning all hunts.

All of these changes in hunting practice have had gender implications as well. None of the women I have interviewed take part in professional or long-distance hunting activities, but women are in fact intimately involved in other aspects of environmentally derived incomes, such as vegetable gardening, fuelwood collection, fishing, exploiting nontimber forest products, carrying goods to market, cassava cultivation, upland rice cultivation, cattle grazing and pasturing, and pig rearing, among other tasks. The fact that women have to do these activities and are also responsible for a larger share of housework and childcare means they have little chance to engage in hunting, which involves distant travel and is time consuming. In addition, because men have to travel farther for the scarcest game, this can increase household burdens on the women who are left behind. The only examples of women being involved in hunting wild animals nowadays are the collection of small reptiles, such as water monitors and turtles, which are collected by hand by both men and women in the course of working fields or looking for other forest goods. Another gendered aspect of the changes in hunting practices are that women stated they often have to spend more time acting as protectors of swidden fields, shooing away birds, rats, and pigs, often having to sleep in fields at night, now that households are not legally allowed to hunt animals in the periphery of important conservation protected areas.

Trading of Wildlife in Vietnam and the Expansion to Global Markets

As noted above, the markets for wild animals have changed radically in the past ten to fifteen years. Whereas once there was little commercial market for bushmeat, there is now widespread domestic and international demand for meat and other animal products, which has placed tremendous pressure on wildlife resources. While the trade involves relatively few people, it generates great sums of money. Just as hunters have changed from small-scale subsistence hunters to professionals with weapons and connections, traders too have been transformed. Wildlife traders are now usually well-connected middlemen who use cell phone technology and fax machines to track where wildlife has been caught and where it is being ordered (Nguyen Van Song 2008). Traders now are often responsible for long-distance transport of the most valuable wildlife; because big traders never accompany their products, an entire subsystem of runners and carriers is employed (Vu Hong Thuat 2002). These networks of illegal wildlife traders are shadowy and complicated, as the business involves neighboring countries, especially China and Laos. Wildlife smuggling now often occurs in concert with drug, gun, and human smuggling networks as well, and this has reinforced the gender divisions in this illegal trading world (World Bank 2005).

The lengths to which traders go to move wildlife around the country and into the global market can be astounding. As one report noted, "During the boom in prices of bear bile and bear parts in Vietnam in the early 2000s, smuggling of bears was accomplished by fake army vehicles, fake funerals, and even fake ambulances complete with the bear dressed as a patient and surrounded by concerned relatives" (World Bank 2005, p. 3). Early research into the animal trade in Vietnam in 1996 estimated that about 3.5 tons of wildlife was brought by air to Hanoi every week from the south of the country on the state-owned airline (Vu Ngoc Thanh 1997). There was even an incident in which an airplane en route to China via Hanoi returned to Saigon to avoid capture by Hanoi authorities. This indicates the existence of a significant coordination at high levels in the transport of live wild animals, and shows that while local people may be involved in the hunting, the real masterminds of this operation are people who have the power and resources to be able to commandeer aircraft for their trade.

Cross-border trade with China is a major factor in the pressure on Vietnamese wildlife (TRAFFIC 2008a). The increasing demand from China can be attributable to both a rising affluent middle class, as well as to Chinese state law from the late 1980s restricting the harvesting of numerous Chinese animals (the China Wild Animal Protection Law). This has resulted in large number of animals now being imported from outside China to meet internal demand (Yiming and Dianmo 1998). Trade in live animals is now the primary modus operandi in cross-border trade, and wildlife bound for China usually ends up as either bushmeat or in traditional medicine (Still 2003). Surveys on the Vietnam–China border indicate that an estimated 30 tons of wildlife passes through each day,

Figure 4.2. A slow loris is sold on the street, 2005. Lorises are banned from trade under Vietnamese law and are listed in Appendix II of CITES. Photo by the author

including many species on the CITES Appendix I lists and thus officially banned from international trade (see figure 4.2). During surveys of the cross-border trade, turtles were the species with the largest volume (nearly 60 percent of animals), whereas mammals made up a smaller 10 percent, of which pangolin and primates (macaques) were the most common (Yiming and Dianmo 1998).

How is this increasingly international trading sector gendered? There is no clear answer on this. In many reports on wildlife trade, the gender of the trader is not recorded, although in some reports there is evidence that women are indeed involved, particularly at the lower ends of the scale when wildlife is first purchased from the actual hunters (Hendrie 2000). This is in accord with my own research at the local end of the chain, where I interviewed several Vietnamese women who served as middlemen in moving illegally hunted wildlife away from remote rural areas and into larger cities, such as Ho Chi Minh City, Danang, and Hanoi. There have also been several high profile cases of women being caught with illegal wildlife goods in these cities, including a woman arrested for making tiger balm in her Hanoi apartment in 2007 and a woman arrested with two tons of wildlife skins and bones in a warehouse in central Hanoi in 2009 (Reuters 2007; Do Minh 2009). However, much of the higher end of the transportation chain involves men, particularly in the cross-border and international trade, due to the potential for danger and the need to use bribes and/or aggression with interdiction agents. As most government customs, police, and forest rangers are men, the traders who have to deal with them are men as well.

The Gendered Consumption of Wildlife Products

China is not the only destination for Vietnamese wildlife: A rising consumer demand from within Vietnam has been observed in recent years, attributed to a growing middle class. Vietnamese often joke that the only thing with four legs they won't consume is the table that dishes are served on. Primates, large and small carnivorous mammals, reptiles, and even endangered insects are on the menu at many wildlife specialty restaurants in urban areas. A recent survey of 2,000 Hanoi households revealed that 45 percent admitted to using wild animal products as meat, medicine, jewelry, and for other purposes (Venkataraman 2007).

One aspect of wildlife trade that should be highlighted is the strongly gendered dimension of consumption. The aforementioned Hanoi survey revealed that 60 percent of male respondents said they had used animal products, whereas only 34 percent of females did. In addition, the type of end product used was quite different between men and women. The women often bought ornamental animal products, for example, jewelry (such as pearl necklaces, tortoise shell combs, and coral bracelets), whereas men consumed wild meats and traditional medicines.

The consumption of wild meats in restaurants is a highly gendered practice and one that confers social status upon the purchaser. A recent report based on interviews with wildlife consumers in Hanoi noted the strong tendency that "Most interviewees consider wild meat rare and precious, and strongly associate it with wealthy, successful and high status individuals. These values are more important than the physical characteristics of the meat itself" (Drury 2009, p. 3). Ordering wild game is a way to show off in front of friends or, more often, in front of business clients one wants to impress. Men interviewed in wildlife consumption surveys often stated that going to eat wild meats as part of a group of male office friends or to cement a business deal is an important cultural practice. As a recent newspaper article put it, "The fact is that wildlife restaurants are most crowded after the work hours of offices and agencies. Eating wildlife dishes continues in every place where there are men. People go to wildlife restaurants when they have something to celebrate, to shed their bad luck, and to find good fortune" (Anonymous 2003). This was statistically confirmed in a recent survey on wild animal use, which revealed that almost no one ate wild meat alone, but rather it was a social activity. Businessmen and government officials had the highest wild animal consumption rates among all respondents, indicating that "Eating wild animals is strongly linked with occupational and social peer pressures" (Venkataraman 2007). If gender, affluence, and social status are the most important variables in explaining animal consumption, then these variables need to be considered in any discussion of enforcement or other policy efforts to try to curb wildlife use. Unfortunately, as I point out in the concluding section of this chapter, this is rarely the case.

Another important aspect of animal consumption is the large number of animals used in traditional medicine, both Chinese and Vietnamese (although there are important differences between the two systems), to treat male sexual dysfunction and to increase virility. A recent survey of the traditional medicine shops of Vietnam found around one hundred animals used in the traditional pharmacopeias, of which a large number were endangered or on CITES lists (Nguyen Dao Ngoc Van and Nguyen Tap 2008) (see figure 4.3). Tiger bone, tiger penis, and rhinoceros horn have been used in traditional treatments in the past. Given the highly endangered nature of both animals, there has been great concern that this aspect of traditional medicine needs to be controlled. The widespread availability of Viagra in Asia in the late 1990s led some conservationists to believe that this might lead to a decline in the demand for some medicinal goods, as Viagra costs much less per dose than tiger or rhino concoctions (Hippel and Hippel 1998). Studies have been suggestive, but inconclusive, that there has been a decline in trade in the main taxa associated with erectile dysfunction treatments since Viagra became widely available, but more needs to be done to understand this phenomenon (Hippel and Hippel 2002).

Part of the problem in reducing the use of animals in traditional medical treatments through substitutions, however, is that it is very difficult to sort out cultural beliefs from medical ones. In addition to the efficacy of medical treatments, the consumption of wild animals is also often associated with certain animal traits: "The fierceness of the tiger, the sexual

Figure 4.3. Medicinal pastes made of wild animals for sale in an airport gift shop in Vietnam, 2006. Animals used for these unguents include python, monkey, and gecko. Photo by the author

stamina of the rhinoceros, and the timidness of the deer are believe to be inherent in the products derived from these animals. People use preparations made from animal products both to restore health and vigor and to enhance their personal capacities according to the characteristics of the animal consumed" (Donovan 2004, p. 96). For example, bear bile is one of the most common wildlife products used in Vietnam. Bear bile is believed to cure fevers, liver ailments, and muscle injuries, and when brewed with rice wine and herbs and then consumed as a drink it is believed to improve strength and vitality and act as an aphrodisiac (Tran Dinh Thanh Lam 2003). Asiatic black bears, which are endangered in the wild and prohibited from trade under CITES restrictions, are captured in forest areas and put into cages or bred, and bile is extracted while the bear is still alive. The widespread use of bear bile is believed to have significantly reduced the populations of wild bears in Vietnam in the past ten years, and several NGOs have made strong campaigns for the prohibition of bear raising. Education for Nature, one of the few local NGOs in Vietnam to work on wildlife issues, enlisted a popular Vietnamese pop star, My Linh, for a television promo encouraging people not to consume bear parts or bile. Clearly targeted at men, the young, attractive female singer urges them to stop consuming bear products because they are cruel and further endanger the species. Paying attention to the gender of the consumers of wildlife and the social reasons for which they do their consuming can be an important driver toward reducing demand and the illegal trade that feeds it, leading to more sustainable outcomes.

Conclusions: How Attention to Gender Can Improve Policy Enforcement and Lead to Sustainability

How can the multiplicity of levels of the wildlife trade, from production to market to consumption, be better understood and potentially better regulated, and how can a gender analysis contribute to this effort? As this chapter has noted, all aspects of wildlife use, from forest to table, have gendered dimensions to them. This can inform how approaches to regulate hunting and wild animal trade should be formulated to reduce the illegal trade to more sustainable dimensions.

However, to date, the use of gender analysis has not informed potential options for regulating the animal trade, which has been focused mostly on policy and enforcement, not on social issues. NGOs and governments in Southeast Asia and elsewhere have advocated several possible interventions to try to reduce the unsustainable overharvest of wildlife, including regulating markets and pricing of products, legal restrictions and financial penalties, increasing community rights over lands and access to wildlife, consumer awareness campaigns, diversifying harvester incomes through alternative income projects, and closed hunting seasons and limits on hunting technology (TRAFFIC 2008b). Yet each of these approaches has both positive and negative social impacts, and there are other gender implications for different solutions as well.

For example, there may be immediate negative social impacts from hunting regulations aimed at the capture of wildlife, in terms of lost income and employment opportunities. In the case of Vietnam, the blanket hunting restrictions in place near most protected areas have significant downsides and are largely ineffective. Professional hunters ignore such bans, as they are able to elude or bribe rangers if caught, whereas local hunters are often the ones hurt by bans, both in lost income and the loss of crops to predatory wildlife. For example, in the globally important Vu

Quang Nature Reserve, two Vietnamese reporters found that one of the main reasons wildlife was still being hunted there extensively was that the head of the local government, a man who was named in the article, had been paid off after he requested a cut of all the wildlife proceeds. The poachers were interviewed: "'If you hunt endangered animals you could go to jail. Aren't you afraid of that?' 'Afraid of what? We always do it in the forest. People don't know where. If we have a tiger they also don't know. When they find out, by that time we have sold it already. Truthfully, in the three years past, we got three tigers. Did it in the forest. At the beginning of this year we already have caught one tiger'" (Nguyen Tuan 1999, p. 6). Hunting bans also do not discriminate among the kinds of species that are hunted. Members of several local communities stated that they would like permission to hunt species such as wild boar, deer, rats, and coucals, which were all predators of their crops and increased women's workloads if not kept in check. None of these are endangered or threatened species and not on CITES lists banned in international trade. Yet the practices of protecting fields from common pests were assumed to have as much impact on biodiversity as outsider poachers who came in and targeted highly endangered wild animals such as tigers, elephants, and primates, as the hunting restrictions make no distinction between the types of animals hunted and who collected them.

Thus, finding solutions to the problem by only focusing on the beginning of the wildlife chain, where animals are hunted, remains difficult to achieve and can often result in social inequity and uneven application. For example, many of the stakeholders now seeking solutions for the illicit wildlife trade in Vietnam are ironically culpable in its expansion. A recent report by the World Bank (2005) decrying the wildlife trade in Asia made little mention of the fact that the bank's portfolio of investments is heavily road- and infrastructure-centered in Vietnam, and that road expansion is a major culprit in opening up once-remote forest areas to professional hunters and migrants.

In another instance, newspaper reports have argued that government attention to local hunters through hunting and weapons bans is a smokescreen to hide the culpability of government officials who are easily bribed to turn a blind eye to trade or who are consumers of wild animals themselves. Recent articles in the Vietnamese press have noted that "Poachers holding pens are more dangerous than poachers holding saws, hammers or traps" (Nguyen Van Song 2008, p. 159). Another article noted, "Patrons of wildlife restaurants come by motorbikes and cars with blue registration plates (vehicles of state functional agencies). They include both junior and senior state employees. Maybe some of these senior officials have signed instructions or official documents prohibiting hunting wild animals or consuming wildlife meat. Some actual restaurant owners (some restaurants are managed by relatives) are state employees or local authorities, or even law practitioners" (Anonymous 2003, p. 4). Given that state employees in customs, police, and the forest ranger service are overwhelmingly men, attention should be paid to how changes in gender diversity in these forces might also have an impact on reducing their culpability in the illegal wildlife trade.

NGO campaigns to encourage Vietnamese to avoid consuming endangered species also need to pay attention to gender issues. The use of female celebrities in public service announcements aimed at men has been one relatively successful approach. A less useful one, however, has been a campaign to get young people to pledge to not consume wild animals and to resist efforts by colleagues and bosses to get them to do so in social settings. A recent video shown on Vietnamese television and the Internet shows a young man meeting an older gentleman for a drink at a bar; the older man orders bear bile wine and urges his young colleague to down it. The young man thinks hard, as visions of the torture bears go through to extract bile race across the screen, and he finally says dramatically, "No! I won't drink this!" and pushes the glass away. Unfortunately, appealing to young people to risk their social positions by refusing to drink with their bosses seems a quixotic approach, given how important social relations are and how common male socialization over wild animal meat or wine is in formal settings from business to government offices. If eating meat is about showing one's social status and treating distinguished guests, then refusing to eat or drink these products is a direct social affront to those of higher status.

More effective might be targeting the male bosses instead, through public service announcements featuring young women who state that men who use such products have little appeal for them. Other tougher public service announcements could be used to indicate the criminal penalties associated with violations of wildlife law and the loss of money and or prestige that would accompany being arrested on these charges. Clearly better enforcement of the existing laws prohibiting the sale and transport of CITES-listed species would also reduce the availability of wildlife products as well.

Some bright spots of hope do exist. In 2009, several members of Vietnam's National Assembly were given information by the NGO Education for Nature about bear bile farms and how they have become a popular stop on Korean tourist jaunts to Vietnam, whereby the (predominantly male) participants see the bile being extracted, consume some on the spot, and then buy more to take (illegally) home. The parliamentarians have contacted South Korea's Environment Ministry to ask their government to stop the transport of bear bile by their citizens returning from Vietnam. The parliamentarians stated they would work with Vietnamese NGOs to bring attention to the problem, such as by launching awareness campaigns on Korean Airlines to inform passengers of the illegality of the bear bile trade.

In the end, the enormous global illegal wildlife trade will only likely be solved by a variety of methods: some regulations, some enforcement, some market solutions like farmed wildlife, and campaigns to reduce demand by consumers. In each possible angle to the problem lies the need to understand the gender dimensions of the problem, including the effect of hunting bans on women's efforts to protect their fields, the lax enforcement of trade laws and domination by men in the bribery and fraud that characterizes much international trade, and the reasons why men and women consume various wildlife products in different ways. In each case, a gendered analysis of the problem is likely to lead to better, more sustainable solutions in the long run. But achieving this sustainability in wildlife trade is a long-term process and one that the world is nowhere near achieving, if current trade patterns are any indication. It will take a concerted effort along all points in the value chain to understand the effect of wildlife trade on species and populations and to identify solutions to bring wildlife consumption in line with reproduction and population growth rates so as to achieve long-term sustainability.

References

Anonymous. 2003. Wildlife meat and the Red Data Book. *The Pioneer Newspaper* 23 June.

Bennett, E. L., E. J. Milner-Gulland, M. Bakarr, H. E. Eves, J. G. Robinson and D. S. Wilkie. 2002. Forum: Hunting the world's wildlife to extinction. *Oryx* 36(4):328–329.

Bird, R., and D. Bird. 2008. Why women hunt: Risk and contemporary foraging in a western desert Aboriginal community. *Current Anthropology* 49(4):655–693.

Blundell, A. G., and M. B. Mascia. 2005. Discrepancies in reported levels of international wildlife trade. *Conservation Biology* 19(6):2020–2025.

Brightman, R. 1996. The sexual division of foraging labor: Biology, taboo, and gender politics. *Comparative Studies in Society and History* 38(4):687–729.

Broad, S., T. Mulliken, and D. Roe. 2003. The nature and extent of legal and illegal trade in wildlife. In *Trade in wildlife: Regulation for conservation*, ed. S. Oldfield, 3–22. London: Earthscan.

Costello, N. A. 2003. Katu society: A harmonious way of life. In *Laos and ethnic minority cultures: Promoting heritage*, ed. Y. Goudineau, 163–176. Paris: United Nations Educational, Scientific, and Cultural Organization.

Do Minh. 2009. Two warehouses of wildlife bones discovered in Hanoi. VietnamNet. http://english.vietnamnet.vn/social/2009/01/823491.

Donovan, D. 2004. Cultural underpinnings of the wildlife trade in Southeast Asia. In *Wildlife in Asia: Cultural perspectives*, ed. J. Knight, 88–111. London, Routledge.

Drury, R. 2009. Reducing urban demand for wild animals in Vietnam: Examining the potential of wildlife farming as a conservation tool. *Conservation Letters* 2(6):263–270.

Engler, M., and R. Parry-Jones. 2007. *Opportunity or threat: The role of the European Union in global wildlife trade*. Brussels, TRAFFIC Europe.

Gaard, G., ed. 1993. *Ecofeminism: Women, animals, nature*. Philadelphia, Pa.: Temple University Press.

Hendrie, D. 2000. *Complied notes on the wildlife trade in Vietnam*. Hanoi: Traffic Southeast Asia.

Hickey, G. 1993. *Shattered world: Adaptation and survival among Vietnam's highland peoples during the Vietnam War*. Philadelphia: University of Pennsylvania Press.

Hippel, F. A. V., and W. V. Hippel. 1998. Solution to a conservation problem? *Science* 281:1805.

Hippel, F. A. V., and W. V. Hippel. 2002. Sex, drugs and animal parts: Will Viagra save threatened species? *Environmental Conservation* 29(3):277–281.

Kellert, S., and J. Berry. 1987. Attitudes, knowledge and behaviors toward wildlife as affected by gender. *Wildlife Society Bulletin* 15(3):363–371.

Kruse, C. R. 1999. Gender, views of nature, and support for animal rights. *Society and Animals* 7(3):179–198.

Le Trong Trai, Dang Thang Long, Phan Thanh Ha, and Le Ngoc Tuan. 2003. *Hunting and collecting practices in the central Truong Son landscape*. Central Truong Son Initiative Report No. 3. Hanoi: World Wildlife Fund Indochina/World Wildlife Fund US.

McElwee, P. 2002. Lost worlds and local people: Protected areas development in Viet Nam. In *Conservation and mobile indigenous people: Displacement, forced settlement and sustainable development*, ed. D. Chatty and M. Colchester, 296–312. Oxford: Berghahn Press.

McElwee, P. 2008. Forest environmental income in Vietnam: Household socioeconomic factors influencing forest use. *Environmental Conservation* 35(2):147–159.

Nash, S. V. 1997. *Fin, feather, scale and skin: Observations on the wildlife trade in Lao PDR and Vietnam*. Petaling Jaya: TRAFFIC Southeast Asia.

Newton, P., N. Van Thai, S. Roberton, and D. Bell. 2008. Pangolins in peril: Using local hunters' knowledge to conserve elusive species in Vietnam. *Endangered Species Research* 6:41–53.

Nguyen Dao Ngoc Van and Nguyen Tap. 2008. *An overview of the use of animals in traditional medicine systems in Viet Nam*. Hanoi: Traffic Southeast Asia.

Nguyen Tuan. 1999. Vu Quang, khu bao ton khong yen tinh [Vu Quang, a nature reserve that is not peaceful]. *Lao Dong Newspaper* (Hanoi), 21 May, p. 6.

Nguyen Van Song. 2008. Wildlife trading in Vietnam: Situation, causes, and solutions. *Journal of Environment and Development* 17(2):145–165.

Noss, A., and B. Hewlett. 2001. The contexts of female hunting in central Africa. *American Anthropologist* 103(4):1024–1040.

Oldfield, S., ed. 2003. *The trade in wildlife: Regulation for conservation.* London: Earthscan.

Reuters. 2007. Endangered tigers killed for medicine. *Sydney Morning Herald Newspaper,* 9 May.

Schrock, J. L., ed. 1966. *Minority groups in the Republic of Vietnam.* Washington, DC: Headquarters, Department of the Army.

Singh, S. 2008. Contesting moralities: The politics of wildlife trade in Laos. *Journal of Political Ecology* 15:1–20.

Still, J. 2003. Use of animal products in traditional Chinese medicine: Environmental impact and health hazards. *Complementary Therapies in Medicine* 11(2):118–122.

Stoett, P. 2002. The international regulation of trade in wildlife: Institutional and normative considerations. *International Environmental Agreements: Politics, Law and Economics* 2:195–210.

Swift, L., P. R. Hunter, A. C. Lees, and D. J. Bell. 2007. Wildlife trade and the emergence of infectious diseases. *EcoHealth* 4(1):25–30.

TRAFFIC. 2008a. *The state of wildlife trade in China.* Beijing, TRAFFIC.

TRAFFIC. 2008b. *What's driving the wildlife trade? A review of expert opinion on economic and social drivers of the wildlife trade and trade control efforts in Cambodia, Indonesia, Lao PDR and Vietnam.* East Asia and Pacific Region Sustainable Development Discussion Papers. Washington, DC: East Asia and Pacific Region Sustainable Development Department, World Bank.

Tran Dinh Thanh Lam. 2003. Vietnam's elixir: bear bile. *Asia Times,* 20 August.

Venkataraman, B. 2007. *A matter of attitude: The consumption of wild animal products in Hanoi.* Hanoi: TRAFFIC Southeast Asia, Greater Mekong Programme.

Vu Hong Thuat. 2002. Follow the footprints of hunters. Paper presented at the American Museum of Natural History conference on Vietnam, April 2003.

Vu Ngoc Thanh. 1997. *Biodiversity and biodiversity loss.* Hanoi: Department of Vertebrate Zoology, Faculty of Biology, National University of Hanoi.

World Bank. 2005. *Going, going, gone: The illegal trade in wildlife in East and Southeast Asia.* Environment and Social Development East Asia and Pacific Region Discussion Paper. Washington, DC: World Bank.

Wyler, L. S., and P. Sheikh. 2008. *International illegal trade in wildlife: Threats and U.S. policy.* CRS Reports for Congress. Washington, DC: Congressional Research Service.

Yiming, L., and L. Dianmo. 1998. The dynamics of trade in live wildlife across the Guangxi border between China and Vietnam during 1993–1996 and its control strategies. *Biodiversity and Conservation* 7(7):895–914.

PART TWO

Gender and Water

Gender, Water Scarcity, and the Management of Sustainability Tradeoffs in Cochabamba, Bolivia

Amber Wutich

Sustainable governance requires humans to make decisions that strike a balance between environmental, economic, and social resource uses. While recent research has explored the costs and benefits of these sustainability tradeoffs, gender-oriented analyses are often absent from this literature. In particular, we know little about how gendered roles and responsibilities shape how communities make, enforce, and cope with decisions about sustainability tradeoffs. To address this gap, this chapter examines the gendered management of sustainability tradeoffs in a water-scarce community on the outskirts of Cochabamba, Bolivia.

Sustainability Tradeoffs

Sustainability can be defined as an approach to development that seeks to preserve the long-term well-being of social and ecological systems. A core challenge of sustainability is weighing the costs and benefits of different resource management choices (Brown et al. 1987). This challenge was recognized by early environmentalists, who struggled to resolve the conflict between environmental and human needs for resources (e.g., Ehrlich 1972). Later proponents of sustainable development sought ways to meet current resource demands without undermining future generations' capacity to do the same (Brundtland 1987). A new generation of sustainability scholars has begun to explore how tradeoffs among the three pillars of sustainability—environment, economics, and society—can be resolved to achieve sustainable development (de Vries and Petersen 2009). Recent studies have demonstrated how sustainability tradeoffs can yield different configurations of environmental, economic, or social costs and benefits. One common concern is the tension between ecological conservation and economic development (Spangenberg et al. 2002). These studies examine how economic development trades off against environmental conservation goals, or vice versa. In a recent example, Martinet and Blanchard (2009) demonstrated how reducing trawling in a shrimp fishery off French Guiana would enhance the long-term economic well-being of the fishery but could also negatively impact a protected frigatebird species that feeds off fishery discards. In this case, economic benefits would win out, causing ecological costs. Others have highlighted the conflicts among different resource conservation goals. For instance, in a study of global rice production, Mushtaq et al. (2009) suggested that water conservation may trade off against energy use because water-saving irrigation practices are more energy consumptive. Here, one kind of ecological benefit (water conservation) wins out, creating another type of ecological cost (energy consumption). Similarly, some have found that scarce resources prompt competition among different social groups. Woodward (2000), for example, examined how the current generation's pursuit of economic development may trade off against the economic welfare of future generations. Each of these studies highlights the ways in which locally specific conditions result in unique sustainability tradeoffs within and between the three pillars of sustainability.

In the new research on sustainability tradeoffs, there has been little, if any, discussion of gender. This is puzzling because gender has long been understood to play a crucial role in environmental management. Gendered roles and responsibilities shape the ways in which environmental resources are governed, extracted, allocated, and used (Rocheleau et al. 1996). Yet few have asked how gender affects the management of sustainability tradeoffs in determining who decides what tradeoffs will be made, who enforces these decisions, and who pays the costs. One exception is Palmer-Jones and Jackson's (1997) research on gender and tradeoffs between sustainable development and labor intensity. Drawing on an investigation of water provision projects in Bangladesh, the authors found that the adoption of treadle pumps championed by proponents of sustainable development burdened impoverished women with greater workloads, increased energy expenditure, and caused more physical injuries. In brief, an economic benefit (low-cost water extraction technology) traded off against a social cost (increased workloads for women). Based on these results, Palmer-Jones and Jackson called for more research into the ways in which sustainable development projects reshape gendered divisions of work and time allocation. Yet this call has been largely ignored. In this chapter, I take up the challenge to investigate the gendered management of water scarcity in Cochabamba, Bolivia. As Palmer-Jones and Jackson's research in Bangladesh demonstrated, water scarcity is a topic that provides unique insight into sustainability tradeoffs because gender plays such a prominent role in shaping water management.

Water Scarcity

Water scarcity is one of the world's most pressing environmental crises (UNDP 2006). More than 1 billion people currently live in regions where water is physically scarce, and another 1.6 billion are unable to obtain adequate water due to economic and political constraints even when it is abundant (UN-Water 2007). As a result, a fifth of the people living in developing countries have less than 20 liters of water per day (UNDP 2006), which is not enough water to meet even basic consumption and hygienic needs. The stresses on water supplies are only expected to increase in coming years, as water consumption is increasing twice as quickly as population growth (UN-Water 2006). By 2025, nearly 6 billion people are expected to live in countries that are water scarce or water stressed (Secretariat of the United Nations–Water 2005).

The health impacts of water scarcity are enormous. Inadequate water and sanitation is the world's leading cause of disease. Illnesses related to unclean and inadequate water include diseases caused by the ingestion of contaminated water such as cholera, typhoid, and dysentery; diseases caused by the use of contaminated water such as trachoma and scabies; and water-related insect-based diseases such as malaria and dengue (Gleick 2004). Each year, these diseases are directly responsible for between 2.2 and 5 million deaths, indirectly related to another 10 million deaths, and cause 4 billion diarrheal episodes (Hunter et al. 2000; Secretariat of United Nations–Water 2005; UN-Water 2007). Even if current water initiatives, such as the Millennium Development Goals, are successful, 32 million people are expected to die of water-related illnesses between 2000 and 2020 (Gleick 2004).

Beyond these health impacts, water scarcity has important implications for livelihoods. Water plays a crucial role in income generation activities for nearly all economic sectors, ranging from agriculture to manufacturing to services. When water is scarce, expensive, or contaminated, it has an inordinate impact on the poor's economic well-being (UN-Water 2007). In rural areas, increasing droughts, falling groundwater tables, and surface water scarcity and contamination have undermined the livelihoods of farming, pastoralist, and fishing communities (UN-Water 2006). In urban areas, the exclusion of shantytowns and squatter settlements from municipal water systems forces their residents to pay ten or twenty times the municipal fee for water (Garland and Herzer 2009). The high price of water prevents the urban poor from engaging in water-intensive home-based production, gardening, and informal labor, all of which could provide supplemental income and enhance economic well-being (UNDP 2006). As rural people, displaced in part by the agricultural water crisis, migrate to urban areas, the problem of urban water scarcity becomes ever more severe (Secretariat of the United Nations–Water 2005).

Gender and Water Management

Gender is widely recognized to play a crucial role in the management and consumption of water. There is now broad agreement that any solution to global water scarcity must include a gender dimension. For instance, major international water accords, such as Agenda 21 of the Rio Declaration (United Nations 1992), the Ministerial Declaration of the International Conference on Fresh Water (International Conference 2001), and the International Covenant on Economic, Social, and Cultural Rights General Comment on the Right to Water (United Nations 2002), all acknowledge the centrality of gender in water provision. While women and men both participate in water management in important ways, there is often a clear division of labor in gendered roles and responsibilities.

At the household level, women take primary responsibility for water acquisition, allocation, and use in many cultures. Women and girls are generally tasked with household water acquisition, including waiting for water distribution at the tapstand, walking to far-off water sources, locating water vendors and buying water, and carrying water back to the household (UNDP 2006). The responsibility for the allocation of scarce water supplies to different household members and water use tasks often belongs to women and girls (Ray 2007). In addition, women and girls perform the majority of water-related chores within the household, such as cooking, childcare, housecleaning, and laundry (Secretariat of the United

Nations–Water 2005). While the burden of household water management indisputably falls to women, Wallace and Coles (2005) and Ray (2007) recently argued for a reexamination of gendered water dynamics at the household level. As they noted, research on gender and water has been overly focused on women's roles, while the broader gendered division of labor at the household level—and men's contributions in particular—has been largely ignored.

At the community level, men are primarily responsible for water-related decision-making and management in many societies. Men's roles as community leaders, engineers, construction workers, mechanics, and heads of households all facilitate their disproportionate representation in water decision-making. In contrast, women's historic inability to own land and participate fully in governance excluded them from key roles in community water management (UNDP 2006). Since the 1990s, many initiatives have been designed to increase women's participation in water management (Ray 2007). Such programs have made real accomplishments in incorporating women in the development, administration, operation, and repair of community water systems (Fisher 2006). Even so, in many cases women's participation in water decision-making has been minimal, marginalized, or merely symbolic (Narayan 1995; Prokopy 2004; Singh 2008). Although women are at the table, their contributions are often stifled by gendered power dynamics, norms for women's deference, and men's greater experience with water management tasks (UNDP 2006). Research highlighting women's contributions may help improve the success of interventions designed to redress gender inequities in community water management.

Field Site

My fieldwork was conducted in the city of Cochabamba, located in central Bolivia. Driving from north to south across the Cochabamba Valley, disparities in water availability make a strong visual impact. The northern side of the city of Cochabamba is rich with greenery and abundant water, which overflows from surging artesian wells, spring zones, and alluvial fans (Antón 1993). Foliage-filled parks and tree-lined boulevards gradually give way to dusty streets and barren hillsides. The southern reaches of the city, crisscrossed with dry creeks and ditches, are undeniably water poor.

Political inequities overlay these patterns of physical water scarcity in Cochabamba. The city is often recognized as the site of the Water War of

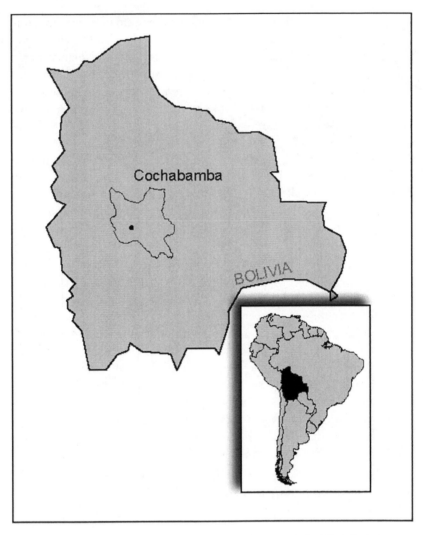

Figure 5.1. Map of Cochabamba, Bolivia. Map from Wutich (2011) by Jake Lulewicz

2000, a major conflict over the privatization of a municipal water system. After grassroots activists and protesters succeeded in halting the privatization scheme, the Water War was hailed as a success for the poor (Assies 2003). In reality, however, the municipality was not empowered to provide water to residents of squatter settlements in Cochabamba's south-side Districts 7, 8, 9, and 14 (Antequera Durán 2007). In 2004, the municipality's service area was officially enlarged to include the south side. However, due to water scarcity and budget shortfalls (Los Tiempos 2004), most south-side settlements have not yet received even a drop of municipal water. Currently, 30 percent of Cochabamba's population is dependent on water from unreliable informal sources including private water vendors, surface water sources, and loans from neighbors (CEDIB 2007). As a result, these south-side residents spend around 10 percent of their incomes to obtain less than 20 liters of water per day (Ledo García 2005).

This research was conducted in Villa Israel, a settlement located at the furthest tip of Cochabamba's water-scarce south side. Gentle hills roll above Villa Israel to the south, and the community enjoys a breathtaking night view of the city center below it to the north. For most of the year, the community's earthen streets are dry and dusty, but they spring briefly to green life during the wet season. Unlike the common stereotype of squatter settlements, residences in Villa Israel are often spacious. Settlers buy as much land as they can afford and gradually build houses out of brick or plaster-finished adobe, adding rooms as their incomes allow. Slowly, Villa Israel is transforming from a young settlement with small, unfinished houses to an established community with large, well-constructed homes. To support the population, the community hosts a Sunday market, fourteen small churches, bus and taxi lines, numerous corner stores, and a few modest restaurants and food stands.

Villa Israel's residents are mainly urban migrants of indigenous Quechua and Aymara descent. Nearly 90 percent of household heads work in the low-income informal sector as market vendors, taxi drivers, domestic servants, and construction workers. While the settlement now has formal legal and political status, it has not yet obtained access to municipal water supplies. Using its own groundwater, Villa Israel operates a common-pool water institution. Because the system's water output is very low, residents must supplement with water from other sources. All households buy water from private vendors, which provide notoriously high-priced and low-quality service. During the brief wet season, households capture rainwater; some also fetch water from a polluted creek. Taking into account water from all of these sources, the average Villa Israel resident is still unable to obtain 50 liters of water per day, the minimum amount of water recommended to safeguard health and hygiene internationally (Gleick 1996).

Gender relations in Villa Israel differ in some ways from national trends. In Bolivia, women clearly lag behind men for all economic indicators (UNICEF 2009). In Villa Israel, the vagaries of neoliberal economic restructuring have, to some extent, inverted this trend. As formal sector jobs disappeared, men with knowledge of mining, construction, and other forms of skilled labor were increasingly unable to find work. In many Villa Israel families, women became the primary breadwinners, working in Cochabamba's enormous open-air market as fruit vendors, snack sellers, and laundresses. Weismantel (2001) documented the ways in which market livelihoods have historically empowered Andean women economically and socially. In Villa Israel, female heads of household are common—both in households that lack an adult male and in those where women work while men stay at home. While there is a degree of tenuous economic equality between women and men in some Villa Israel households, the same cannot be said for the political realm. At the national level, women are typically excluded from powerful roles in Bolivian politics (Deere 2009). In Villa Israel, too, men hold nearly all of the primary leadership and decision-making roles, whereas women are only rarely selected to serve in the local government or lead major community initiatives. This research examines how gendered roles in community governance and household economics shape water management in Villa Israel.

Methods

This fieldwork was conducted in Villa Israel between 2003 and 2005, with a follow-up visit to verify the results in 2008. To begin, I conducted five months of participant observation at the height of the wet and dry seasons of 2003 and 2004. During the wet season (November–March), I investigated how people collected and stored rainwater, used the seasonal creek for washing, and attempted to cleanse contaminated water from these sources. During the dry season (May–September), I learned how people obtained scarce water by chasing down private water vendors; begging other community members to sell, lend, or give them water; waiting hours for their turn at the tapstand; and even carrying their laundry far into the foothills to find clean sources of water for washing. Throughout the wet and dry seasons, I attended meetings of the local government, participated in community construction and development projects, observed daily water distribution at the tapstands, and struggled to find sources of safe water for my own use.

Throughout the participant-observation phase, I was careful to note how gender affected people's knowledge of, participation in, and benefit from water provision. My access to participant-observation data was inarguably affected by my own gender position in Villa Israel. As a childless, college-educated foreign woman, I did not fit easily into female or male roles in the community. I could not master the water-saving cooking and sanitation techniques that Villa Israel women excelled in. I was more comfortable with the development and government tasks generally reserved for men. Initially, my inability to conform to local gender roles in a competent and culturally appropriate manner was somewhat distressing to me. In time, I realized that it facilitated my access to data by allowing me to interact more freely with both men and women than I might have otherwise.

After the intensive participant observation ended, I assembled and trained a Bolivian field team that was matched to Villa Israel's demography in terms of gender (male/female), ethnicity (Quechua/Aymara), and religion (Catholic/evangelical). Together, we developed an interview protocol over a two-month period of pretesting, revision, cognitive interviewing, and translation. Open- and closed-ended questions addressed migration history, household demography, livelihood strategies, social networks, community politics, and experiences with water scarcity. We then drew a simple random sample of 96 households from a map of 425 residences in Villa Israel. After obtaining consent from the community at a series of meetings and from individual households and participants, 73 households (76 percent response rate) participated in the study.

Alongside the field interviewers, I conducted a series of five interviews in each household over a ten-month wet-to-dry-to-wet season cycle. In 66 percent of households, we were able to interview both female and male household heads, defined as those responsible for the acquisition and distribution of household goods. Having data on men's and women's experiences in the same household allowed me to tease apart intrahousehold gender dynamics. In the remaining households, there was only one household head (usually female) or one of the household heads refused to participate (usually male). Interviewers were matched to participants by gender, unless a participant requested a specific interviewer. Interviews were conducted in Spanish, Quechua, or Aymara, depending on the participant's preference. Average interview times ranged from 1 hour 49 minutes in the first wave of the study to 21 minutes in the fifth wave.

The goal of the analysis was to determine how gender shapes the management of sustainability tradeoffs in Villa Israel's community water system. The analysis proceeded in two parts. First, to determine how the water system functioned and what sustainability tradeoffs were involved, I conducted an institutional analysis (Ostrom 2005). Using the data collected during participant observation, I identified the community water system's rules-in-use and norms. Because there were no policy documents I could use to cross-check my observations, I iteratively verified my findings with key informants. Once I understood the water institution, I reanalyzed the participant-observation data to identify sustainability tradeoffs, defined as institutional rules-in-use and norms designed to prioritize one need (e.g., environmental) over another (e.g., social).

Second, to determine how gender shapes the management of sustainability tradeoffs in the community water system, I conducted text analysis. Using data from interviews and participant observation, I searched for: (1) gendered norms; (2) the socially sanctioned suspension of gendered norms; and (3) idiosyncratic violations of gendered norms in my observations of the following activities: governmental meetings, water committee meetings, interactions with water development NGOs, preparation and solicitation of grant funding, maintenance of wells and pumps, monitoring of the wells and tapstands, water collection at the tapstands, alternative forms of water acquisition, and water use in the household. Regarding sustainability tradeoffs, I searched for gendered behavioral norms in rule making, rule enforcement, and the payment of costs.

The results are presented in two sections. In the first, I describe Villa Israel's community water system. In the second, I discuss sustainability tradeoffs. In each section, I explore how the gendered nature of economic and political work in Villa Israel shapes water governance and management.

Gender and the Governance of a Community Water System

Technical Operations and System Expansion

Villa Israel owned two small wells located in the hills above the settlement. Well water was piped down the hillside and delivered to community members through a series of public tapstands. Villa Israel residents owned, operated, and maintained the well infrastructure. In addition, the community received technical assistance and some funding from NGOs. In recent years, there have been technical challenges, such as siltification and water leakage in the community water distribution system. For the most part, however, the system was well monitored and well maintained.

Men took on primary responsibility for the technical operation of Villa Israel's hillside wells. Working with a foreign-born female engineer employed by a local NGO, they monitored and maintained the wells' output. While men dealt with most of the technical aspects of the water system, women assisted in the maintenance of the infrastructure. For example, in 2003 Villa Israel undertook major construction on the water system,

Figure 5.2. Men of Villa Israel lead at the head of a community project, while women provide the manual labor to build a footbridge over a local waterway. Photo by Ashley Yoder

which required dozens of laborers to work on the main hillside pipeline. For these tasks, women and men worked together to dig ditches, remove large rocks with pick-axes, and lay pipe. While they did not have a central leadership role, women did make important contributions to system maintenance.

Community Governance

Villa Israel's Junta Vecinal (Neighborhood Council) governed the operation of the water system. The Junta Vecinal was led by a Mesa Directiva

(Board of Directors) elected by the community. General meetings of the Junta Vecinal were a popular event in Villa Israel. On the first Sunday of each month, women, men, and children flooded the street in front of the Junta Vecinal office to attend the monthly meeting. The Junta Vecinal's Mesa Directiva used general meetings to plan for any needed maintenance of the water infrastructure, charge a monthly fee for water users, hand out yellow punch cards that conferred the right to obtain water for one month, and address any concerns or complaints regarding the system's function. In addition to official activities, the meetings drew local vendors, and *pasankalla* (puffed corn), ice cream, and other snacks were shared among friends and neighbors.

At general meetings of the Junta Vecinal, the vast majority of discussions—both by leaders of the Mesa Directiva and community members—were dominated by men. The Mesa Directiva was primarily male, with just a few women serving during the time I was in Villa Israel. The female Mesa Directiva members were involved in projects such as land titling, development of the local market, and the improvement of the community's daycare and preschool services, but they were not highly engaged in water governance. Women's involvement as community members was also less active than that of men. As several long-time female residents explained to me, women felt that their input was neither welcomed nor valued. As a result, women generally sat on street curbs during general meetings, a short distance from the action, knitting, chatting, and looking after children.

Occasionally, women did break into the male-dominated discussions. When they did so, it was often to raise a grievance or suggest a resolution to a conflict. A heated exchange, in which the male leader of the Mesa Directiva was impeached, provides a clear example of this dynamic. It began when an elderly woman accused the leader of corruption. She testified that the leader had charged her US$100 for a utility hook-up, failed to connect the services, and refused to return the money—and produced a receipt for US$100 with the leader's signature as proof. After this testimony, a melee broke out; the entire community seemed to demand the leader's resignation all at once. From the angry crowd, another woman's voice rang out. She argued that, as a Christian community, the people of Villa Israel should show forgiveness and give the leader an opportunity to make amends. The crowd was convinced and the community decided collectively to give the leader a chance to correct his errors and repay the elderly woman. As this event demonstrates, women's contributions in Junta

Vecinal meetings, while rare, often shifted or refocused the conversation in significant ways.

Tapstand Zones

Tapstands, which were located on street corners at regular intervals throughout the community, were constructed by local residents. The residents within tapstand zones were responsible for organizing themselves, raising the funds for tapstand materials, building the tapstand, and performing repairs. Tapstand construction, like any collaborative effort, could be a source of stress and tension for participants. Disagreements over the purchase of bricks, laying of pipes, responsibility for maintenance, and rights to long-term use were not uncommon among residents of tapstand zones. Due to the investment of time and funds required, not all zones in the community were able to construct a tapstand. At the time the research was conducted, there were approximately ten functional tapstands operating throughout the community. One tapstand was under construction, and another zone was in the planning stages for new construction. Only one tapstand, which was choked with silt, had fallen into disrepair and disuse.

The organization of new tapstand zones was normally initiated by the male leader of the Comité de Agua (Water Committee). Targeting zones with a large enough population to provide the necessary investment in funds and labor, he methodically encouraged residents—often women—to organize themselves. In my interviews with community members, women were generally more interested in the benefits of tapstand construction than men. Similarly, women were more concerned with the details and difficulties of organizing residents of the local tapstand zone. In one example, a family had committed to participate in the construction of a new tapstand. The family struggled economically and was unable to contribute all of the materials they had promised to provide. While both the man and woman were at fault, it was the woman who took on the burden of talking to neighbors, taking responsibility for the family's failing, and trying to make amends. This example illustrates how the onus of tapstand construction was, to a large degree, on women.

Water Distribution

Water was distributed each morning, Monday to Saturday, at the community's tapstands. A tapstand monitor was responsible for overseeing the distribution of water through the community water system. The tapstand monitor was a community employee, who was selected by the Comité de Agua and paid a stipend by the Mesa Directiva of the Junta Vecinal. Rising each day at 4:00 a.m., the tapstand monitor unlocked the padlocked tapstands one by one, and blew a whistle to alert local residents of their turn at the tap. Each dues-paying household was allotted one yellow punch card, which enabled them to retrieve their daily water allotment. The monitor checked the punch cards and supervised residents as they lined up to ensure that there was no jostling, line skipping, or water overuse.

According to a former leader of the Comité de Agua, the person chosen to serve as tapstand monitor was always a man. When I asked why, he said that only a man could keep the women who use the tapstand in check. He expressed doubt that a woman could command the authority needed to enforce community rules. The women who used tapstands were often long-time acquaintances and neighbors. Some had longstanding alliances or grievances—even dating back to their shared hometowns. Yet, these women often depended on each other for help at the tapstand. Neighbors helped each other by holding buckets in place under the tap, helping to lift water into a wheelbarrow, or filling another household's buckets when its representative was unable to wait in line. As in the case of tapstand construction, men were generally in change of decision-making and water distribution, whereas women provided much of the raw labor for menial tasks.

Water Acquisition

Each household normally sent a representative to retrieve its water. This representative was responsible, first, for listening for the monitor's whistle, which could sound at any time between 4:00 and 9:00 a.m. Early in the morning, some household representatives lined up the family's buckets in order to save their place in the line. Once the whistle trilled, household representatives usually went to the tapstand alone. While in line, representatives safeguarded their family's interests by ensuring that their right to water was respected and that they were able to retrieve the quantity of water that was rightfully theirs. At the head of the line, household representatives filled two jerry cans or large buckets with the household's daily water allotment and lugged the heavy water one or two blocks to their home. At home, tapstand water was generally stored in kitchens, where it was reserved for cooking and drinking because of its purity.

Figure 5.3. Tapstand users line up their jerry cans in front of a tapstand in Villa Israel. Water is distributed only once a day, and each family is allotted a maximum of two jerry cans (40 liters) of water. Photo by the author

The acquisition and use of water in Villa Israel was, for the most part, women's work. Most households sent either an adult woman or adolescent girl to retrieve their water from the tapstand. As a result, women reported much more often than men that they wasted time waiting for the tapstand monitor's whistle to be blown, standing in line to retrieve water, and transporting water home. A number of women reported that their incomes declined due to the time wasted retrieving tapstand water, while their husbands' incomes were less likely to suffer in this way. Even when men were in charge of the household while women went out to work, I found that female household members (usually adolescent girls) were often responsible for retrieving tapstand water. The exceptions that I found to this rule were households containing no able-bodied woman. In one household headed by an elderly woman, for instance, an adolescent boy was responsible for retrieving tapstand water. However, most households did contain women or girls who were capable and responsible for water retrieval.

Gender and the Management of Sustainability Tradeoffs

Prioritizing Environmental Sustainability over Social and Economic Sustainability

In Villa Israel, the environmental pillar of sustainable development (water resource sustainability) was consistently prioritized over the remaining two pillars (economic and social sustainability). The community instituted a number of rules designed to prevent groundwater overdraft, safeguard the wells' longevity, and ensure that groundwater was distributed fairly over tapstand zones and users. Wherever possible, these rules contained adaptive mechanisms that adjusted the system's functions based on water availability. For example, one such rule dealt with the amount of water households were allowed to collect from the tapstand each day. During periods of normal water output, the daily water allotment was set at 40 liters per household per day. During periods of low output, generally during the dry season, daily water allotments were lowered to 20 liters to ensure that as many households as possible received some water. As a result, water distribution ranged from 8 to 4 liters per capita for an average five-person household, less than 20 percent of the minimum international daily water use recommendation. Here, the sustainability of the water system was prioritized over social and economic sustainability.

Despite these low standard allotments and seasonal adjustments in water distribution, there were periods in which the community's water stores were exhausted before water could be delivered to every tapstand. When this occurred, water distribution halted before a complete cycle was finished, and some tapstand zones could be left without water. The next morning, water distribution was reinitiated from the same point where it had halted the previous day. That way, zones that were left out one day received the highest priority the following day. Even with this precautionary mechanism, there were occasionally extended periods of time in which the water system's output was low or nonexistent. During those periods, water distribution was suspended indefinitely. Whatever their level of need, all households were unable to use the community's tapstand system until an acceptable level of water flow returned. Here, too, long-term environmental sustainability won out over social and economic needs for water.

Villa Israel's Junta Vecinal, Mesa Directiva, and Comité de Agua made the rules that shaped water distribution under conditions of scarcity. As I explained previously, men were primarily responsible for decision-making in these governance bodies. While a minority of women served in the Mesa Directiva and women did attend meetings of the Junta Vecinal, their leadership was generally muted, particularly as relates to the governance of the water system. At the tapstand level, too, the male monitor was responsible for deciding when water output was low, when to decrease water allotments from 40 to 20 liters per capita, and when to cut off water distribution completely. In a number of governance realms, then, men were primarily responsible for adjudicating the environmental facet of sustainability tradeoffs.

Environmental Sustainability Trades Off Against Social Sustainability: The Case of Socially Excluded Groups

While tapstand users had to endure occasional exclusion from the tapstand system during dry spells, three social groups were prevented from accessing water from the tapstands as a matter of policy. The most visible example was the exclusion of renters and new landowners from the water system. The rationale was that these groups had not contributed money, materials, time, and labor to construct the water system and, therefore, should not be allowed to use it. While new landowners could theoretically buy in to the system by paying back fees, this rarely occurred. The back fees were prohibitively expensive, particularly given the low output of water from the system and the need to supplement with water purchased from private vendors. Unlike new landowners, renters were completely locked out of the system; they could neither vote in Junta Vecinal meetings nor buy their way into the tapstand system. In addition, even landowners who participated in constructing their zone's tapstand could be excluded if they did not have the time or money to purchase their punch card. The exclusion of renters, new landowners, and residents without punch cards helped safeguard scarce water resources by lowering overall demand. However, it also forced the costs of sustainability tradeoffs onto some of Villa Israel's most vulnerable social groups—those with least access to the political, social, and economic capital to attain water supplies. In this way, environmental needs were elevated above social and economic needs.

Given the stresses that these sustainability tradeoffs put on renters, new landowners, and residents without punch cards, people from these groups periodically approached their local tapstands with pleas to bend or break the water distribution rules. Formally, the responsibility for enforcing the rules belonged to the male tapstand monitor. In reality, however, tapstand monitoring was a cooperative activity; women at the tapstand played an active role as arbiters of community members' claims to water. One case, in which a female renter asked users of her local tapstand to give her two jerry cans of water, illustrates this clearly. Women at the tapstand were initially split over the request. While one woman argued vociferously that renters should not be allowed to take advantage of the water system because they had not contributed to its construction, another woman prevailed. She argued that this particular renter had always been a good parent to her three children, was a faithful parishioner at a nearby church, and was genuinely in need. The latter woman convinced the others at the tapstand, and all agreed to give the renter the water she had requested.

As in this case, the women at the tapstands normally worked together to evaluate the worthiness of unauthorized requests for water. Each woman contributed her knowledge of the supplicant and her family. Relevant information included questions such as: Is this a needy child or elder? If an adult, has this person contributed to the community in important ways? Does this person have a record of caring responsibly for her children or helping her neighbors? Does this person have a legitimate reason for being in need? If the women came to a consensus about the merit of a claim, the tapstand monitor normally enforced their will. If there was no consensus, however, the tapstand monitor would enforce the letter of the law. In this way, women took the primary responsibility for the decision-making and rule enforcement at the tapstands. Even when a man held the formal authority, he deferred to the knowledge and judgment of the women when the survival of the community's most vulnerable households was at stake. This illustrates the ways in which—within the constraints of a system in which men had prioritized environmental sustainability over social and economic sustainability—women found small ways to redistribute the costs more fairly across different social groups.

Environmental Sustainability Trades Off Against Social Sustainability: The Case of Household Well-Being

Water scarcity at the tapstand impacted all user households sooner or later, through low yields, seasonal shutdowns, or permanent exclusion. As a result, the heaviest costs of Villa Israel's sustainability tradeoffs were paid at the household level. To survive, households carefully economized their water use. In nearly all households, people lacked sufficient water to bathe comfortably. Residents bathed less frequently or thoroughly than they would like; this was especially stressful for young people who felt pressure to maintain strict hygienic standards at school. Most households also reported that their water provisions were insufficient for washing clothes and cleaning their homes. The inability to maintain sanitary conditions in kitchens and bathrooms, in particular, posed a health risk for residents. At times, water was so scarce that households had to forgo essential water use tasks, such as cleaning, bathing, and even cooking meals, for days at a time. In the worst cases, families were forced to subsist on bread rolls or leftover potatoes until they had enough water to cook again.

The burden of subsistence in water-scarce households was initially borne by women and girls. In most households, they were responsible for cooking, cleaning, and washing. They were the ones who had to scrimp on water, laboring longer and harder with insufficient water provisions to ensure that dishes were washed, clothes were cleaned, and children were bathed. Men, however, were also highly sensitive to water scarcity and its impacts on the household. This first came to my attention in my discussions with men about household conflicts; their responses were surprisingly similar to those of the women I interviewed. Like the women, men told me about household tensions that arose as a result of water insecurity. In many cases, the men reported scolding their children when they wasted water by spilling, playing, or purposely dumping clean water onto the floor. In addition, men reported bickering, often with their wives, over impending water shortages. While women were the first to notice when water stores were running low, men were keenly aware when water shortages affected household members' ability to complete sanitation tasks. After a close comparison of men's and women's accounts of water shortages, I found that men were just as likely as women to recognize when the household ran out of the water needed for bathing, washing laundry, or cleaning the house. Furthermore, men were as likely as women to take action to ensure that the household had enough water to survive.

That men and women reacted similarly to water shortages was clear in patterns of emergency water acquisition. Aside from the tapstands, the main way that people in Villa Israel acquired water was private water trucks. These vendors circulated the community, selling water in 200-liter increments. Because of the dearth of vendors and high demand for water in Villa Israel, it could take hours for residents to find an available water truck. Even when vendors were available, they were often very selective about their clientele—preferring to sell to clients with easy-to-reach houses and those with enough money and storage capacity to make large purchases. Thus, members of the impoverished families or those who lived on the community's edges often pleaded with several private water vendors before finding one who was willing to sell them water. My interviews and observations indicated that men and women were equally likely to engage in the time-demanding and difficult process of emergency water acquisition from water trucks. Both men and women could be seen running up and down Villa Israel's streets, trying to reach an elusive water truck. Women and men alike reported that they participated in the demeaning act of begging water vendors to sell them water. As the household's need for water become more urgent, gender roles became less influential in shaping household water monitoring and acquisition.

Do Stark Sustainability Tradeoffs Produce Flexible Gender Norms?

At first glance, water management in Villa Israel appeared to fall along familiar lines of gendered division of labor. Men were primarily responsible for governance and decision-making. They served as leaders of all major community governing bodies, including the Junta Vecinal, Mesa Directiva, and Comité de Agua. As community leaders and decision-makers, men were also primarily responsible for making decisions about sustainability tradeoffs in the management of the community water system. It was men who decided to prioritize water conservation over other social and economic needs in Villa Israel's community water system. Following recent trends in development thinking, women had been included in some aspects of decision-making. Women held a few seats on the Mesa Directiva and they contributed, to some extent, in the general meetings of the Junta Vecinal. Yet women's roles in governance did not extend deep into the water decision-making realm. Rather, women's chief water-related responsibilities were at the household level. They were charged with retrieving water from the tapstands; allocating water to different household uses; and doing the cooking, washing, and cleaning. These gendered roles and responsibilities closely follow the trends widely documented in Latin America, Asia, and Africa.

Yet when we look more closely at the role of gender in managing sustainability tradeoffs, we see a very different picture. Gendered roles and responsibilities shaped how community members enforced and coped with decisions about sustainability tradeoffs in unexpected ways. At the tapstand, a man held titular control as the community's appointed tapstand monitor. However, women played a crucial role in determining how the social costs of water conservation would be distributed across vulnerable community members. Using their unique knowledge, women assessed their neighbors' relative water needs, evaluated their value as community members, and decided the extent to which the community's water conservation rules would be bent to accommodate their water needs. Men's dominance of decision-making in the community water system was subverted, as women took primary responsibility for the enforcement of institutional rules and protection of scarce groundwater resources at the tapstands. In this way, women gained some control over the ways in which environmental sustainability traded off against social sustainability.

At the household level, women were primarily responsible for water acquisition and use. These responsibilities included monitoring water levels and acquiring water at the tapstand. However, when household water stores began to run dangerously low, men also became actively involved in water use and acquisition. Men carefully monitored dwindling water levels, scolding children who did not help to conserve remaining water stores. Men also joined women in the search for new water sources, particularly in the time-consuming and difficult pursuit of a private truck to buy water. During household water shortages, women's primacy in household reproduction was moderated, as men became actively engaged in the household's struggle to obtain subsistence-level water provision. In this way, men became involved in managing the ways in which environmental sustainability traded off against social sustainability in times of crisis. As in the case of women's monitoring at the tapstand, men's participation in household water acquisition and use transgressed gendered norms of water management in Villa Israel.

Why, then, did gendered norms become more fluid in the management of sustainability tradeoffs? While the data presented here do not provide clear answers, they do suggest some possibilities. Under normal conditions, conventional gendered divisions of labor went largely unchallenged in Villa Israel. However, the community's approach to sustainability tradeoffs, which prioritized environmental sustainability over social sustainability, forced men and women to engage in a broader range of water management activities. The burden of water scarcity was so heavy that it exceeded the abilities of those performing conventional gender roles to carry it alone. Under these emergency conditions, competence and ability mattered more than the power dynamics that ordinarily kept gender norms in place. As a result, women's expertise about emergency water management, household need, and social justice, which would normally be marginalized in water decision-making, was respected at the tapstands. Similarly, men's capability to acquire household water and shepherd its use—tasks that men would normally distain—become central to the household's survival. If the struggle to survive in subsistence-level conditions forces the blurring of gendered divisions of labor, it is possible that flexible gender norms can be found in a range of communities that are faced with stark sustainability tradeoffs.

This question provides an intriguing opportunity for future research and, perhaps, an opportunity to reengage the problem of women's exclusion from water-related decision-making. Highlighting women's contributions to water governance, such as those of women at Villa Israel's tapstands, may help improve the success of interventions designed to redress gender inequities in community water management. As communities around the world struggle with increasing water scarcity, many will have to make difficult decisions about sustainability tradeoffs. The findings presented here indicate that, in such situations, women's knowledge and expertise in water governance may be recognized, respected, and valued. If so, the management of sustainability tradeoffs may offer an opportunity for women to provide critical leadership in community water decision-making.

References

Antequera Durán, N. 2007. *Territorios Urbanos: Diversidad cultural, dinámica socio económica y procesos de crecimiento urbano en la zona sur de Cochabamba.* Cochabamba: CEDIB-Plural.

Antón, D. J. 1993. *Thirsty cities: Urban environments and water supply in Latin America.* Ottawa, Canada: International Development Research Centre.

Assies, W. 2003. David versus Goliath in Cochabamba: Water rights, neoliberalism, and the revival of social protest in Bolivia. *Latin American Perspectives* 130(30):14–36.

Brown, B., M. Hanson, D. Liverman, and R. Merideth. 1987. Global sustainability: Toward definition. *Environmental Management* 11(6):713–719.

Brundtland, G. H. 1987. *Our common future.* Oxford: Oxford University Press.

Centro de Documentación e Información Bolivia (CEDIB). 2007. *Datos de la Zona Sur de Cochabamba.* Cochabamba: Centro de Documentación e Información Bolivia.

Deere, C. 2009. Q & A: Bolivian women a force behind power, but still powerless. Inter Press Service New Agency. http://ipsnews.net/news.asp?idnews=49620

de Vries, B., and A. Petersen. 2009. Conceptualizing sustainable development: An assessment methodology connecting values, knowledge, worldviews and scenarios. *Ecological Economics* 68(4):1006–1019.

Ehrlich, P. 1972. *The population bomb.* London: Ballantine.

Fisher, J. 2006. *For her it's the big issue: Putting women at the centre of water supply, sanitation and hygiene.* Geneva: Water Supply and Sanitation Collaborative Council.

Garland, A., and L. Herzer. 2009. Water for the urban poor: Integrated solutions. *SAIS Review of International Affairs* 29(1):101–107.

Gleick, P. 1996. Basic water requirements for human activities: Basic needs. *Water International* 21(2):83–92.

Gleick, P. 2004. *The world's water, 2004–2005.* Washington, DC: Island Press.

Hunter, P., J. Colford, M. LeChevallier, S. Binder, and P. S. Berger. 2000. Panel on waterborne diseases: Panel summary from the 2000 Emerging Infectious Diseases Conference in Atlanta, Georgia. *Emerging Infectious Diseases Journal* 7(3):S544–545.

International Conference on Fresh Water in Bonn, Germany. 2001. *Ministerial Declaration.* New York: International Institute for Sustainable Development.

Ledo García, C. 2005. *Inequality and access to water in the cities of Cochabamba and La Paz–El Alto.* Geneva: United Nations Research Institute for Social Development.

Los Tiempos. 2004. Inauguraron proyecto para dotar de agua a 120 familias de la zona Barrios Unidos. *Los Tiempos,* 20 December.

Martinet, V., and F. Blanchard. 2009. Fishery externalities and biodiversity: Trade-offs between the viability of shrimp trawling and the conservation of frigatebirds in French Guiana. *Ecological Economics* 68(12):2960–2968.

Mushtaq, S., T. Maraseni, J. Maroulis, and M. Hafeez. 2009. Energy and water tradeoffs in enhancing food security: A selective international assessment. *Energy Policy* 37(9):3635–3644.

Narayan, D. 1995. *The contribution of people's participation: Evidence from 121 rural water supply projects.* ESD Occasional Paper Series No. 1. Washington, DC: World Bank.

Ostrom, E. 2005. *Understanding institutional diversity.* Princeton, N.J.: Princeton University Press.

Palmer-Jones, R., and C. Jackson. 1997. Work intensity, gender and sustainable development. *Food Policy* 22(1):39–62.

Prokopy, L. 2004. Women's participation in rural water supply projects in India: Is it moving beyond tokenism and does it matter? *Water Policy* 6:103–116.

Ray, I. 2007. Women, water, and development. *Annual Review of Environment and Resources* 32:421–449.

Rocheleau, D., B. Thomas-Slayter, and E. Wangari, eds. 1996. *Feminist political ecology: Global perspectives and local experiences.* London: Routledge.

Secretariat of the United Nations–Water. 2005. *Water for life, decade 2005–2015.* New York: United Nations Department of Public Information.

Singh, N. 2008. Equitable gender participation in local water governance: An insight into institutional paradoxes. *Water Resources Management* 22:925–942.

Spangenberg, J., I. Omann, and F. Hinterberger. 2002. Sustainable growth criteria: Minimum benchmarks and scenarios for employment and the environment. *Ecological Economics* 42(3):429–443.

United Nations. 1992. *Agenda 21 of the Rio Declaration on Environment and Development.* Rio de Janeiro: Earth Summit.

United Nations. 2002. *General Comment No. 15 on the right to water* (ICESCR, Articles 11–12). Geneva: United Nations.

United Nations Children's Fund (UNICEF). 2009. The situation of women in Bolivia. http://www.unicef.org/bolivia/children_1538.htm

United Nations Development Programme (UNDP). 2006. *Beyond scarcity: Power, poverty and the global water crisis.* New York: United Nations Development Programme.

UN-Water. 2006. *Coping with water scarcity*. Rome: United Nations Food and Agriculture Organization.

UN-Water. 2007. *Coping with water scarcity: Challenge of the twenty-first century*. Rome: United Nations Food and Agriculture Organization.

Wallace, T., and A. Coles, eds. 2005. *Gender, water and development*. Oxford: Berg.

Weismantel, M. 2001. *Cholas and pishtacos: Stories of race and sex in the Andes*. Chicago: University of Chicago Press.

Woodward, R. 2000. Sustainability as intergenerational fairness: Efficiency, uncertainty, and numerical methods. *American Journal of Agricultural Economics* 82(3):581–593.

Wutich, A. 2011. The moral economy of water reexamined: Reciprocity, water insecurity, and urban survival in Cochabamba, Bolivia. *Journal of Anthropological Research* 67(1):5–26.

CHAPTER SIX

Gendered Fruit and Vegetable Home Processing Near the US–Mexico Border

Climate Change, Water Scarcity, and Noncapitalist Visions of the Future

Stephanie J. Buechler

A more rapid pace of change has been evident in San Ignacio, a community in Sonora, Mexico, near the border with the United States, for many years and in many different forms, including through globalization, livelihood transformations, and environmental degradation. Perhaps most worrying, the area is experiencing water resource pressures as well as increasingly visible impacts of climate change and climate variability. These climate changes have had significant gender impacts, with ripple effects on socioeconomic relations in the community. Where once the community depended on agricultural production and processing, especially fruit and vegetable cultivation and canning, such livelihoods have been made more tenuous. Due to environmental changes, the future of agricultural production and processing in this area is at risk. As one resident, Maria, worried aloud, "All of my neighbors' wells are drying up or have already dried up. Like our trees, my neighbors' trees are being dug up and they are not planting new trees when they die from too little water. There is very little work with the economic crisis, and soon there won't even be orchards" (interview, March 2009).[1]

This chapter examines how sustainability issues are related to gender divisions in fruit and vegetable production and processing in San Ignacio. Currently, men are involved in agricultural production in more commercial fields on a daily basis, whereas women are more involved in

smaller-scale agriculture in the orchards located within the home compound (*solar*). In addition to gender divisions in production, agricultural
processing enterprises also see division: women are involved in the canning and candying of fruit and the pickling of vegetables and olives,
whereas other processing enterprises, such as the production of quince
jelly and jam on a more commercial basis, involves both men and women
at different stages. These divisions of labor activity are also reflected in
different visions of economic reproduction for the future and thus are
deeply entwined with long-term sustainability issues. Women's visions for
the present and future are geared toward family ties, social networks, and
noncapitalist relations, whereas men have different paths. Men's visions
do include family ties, but overall are more focused on agricultural production for the market, thus prioritizing capitalist relations.

In this chapter, I examine these alternative visions of Sonoran women
and men that stem from their engagement in home processing of agricultural goods and their exchange of these goods within social networks.
An important finding of this study is that women, to a greater extent than
men, are able to maintain noncapitalist visions of the present and future.
They do this by retaining a conviction that there are important linkages
between agricultural production and commerce on the one hand, and the
reciprocal aid and affection of family and friends on the other, which need
to be constantly nurtured. These alternative, noncapitalist visions ensure
a degree of social and economic sustainability for women and for men,
albeit in different ways.

However, the dynamic environmental conditions in the area are beginning to have detrimental effects on agricultural production and, by extension, agricultural processing enterprises. I argue that this could lead to a
fundamental restructuring of social organization that could adversely affect these future visions of the women and men producers and their entire
community. This community extends beyond the geographical boundaries of their village and fields to include family and friends in other cities
and towns in Mexico as well as across the border in the United States. This
research is an attempt to gain a deeper understanding of how women and
men in San Ignacio envision their future in the context of this environmental change, and how they have incorporated their long-term visions
into present-day practices, with concomitant effects on sustainability at
the local level.

Such a focus is much needed, as water resources and climate are critical
factors affecting the sustainability of agricultural production. The impacts
are clearly also going to be affected by gender, yet researchers have just
begun to study gender differences concerning the effects of water scarcity

for agriculture (Buechler and Zapata 2000; Zwarteveen and Meinzen-Dick 2001; Ahlers 2005; Buechler 2005; Buechler 2009a; Buechler 2009b). Research on gender, agriculture, and the long-term effects of climate change is an even newer area of inquiry (see Denton 2002; Nelson et al. 2002; Roy and Venema 2002; Ahmed and Fajber 2009; Buechler 2009a; Buechler 2009b; Khamis et al. 2009; Nelson and Stathers 2009; Lambrou and Nelson 2010). My study of agricultural production and processing in Sonora contributes to this emerging area of inquiry on climate change and livelihoods in developing countries that includes studies in geography and anthropology (e.g., Eakin 2000; Eakin and Bojórquez-Tapia 2008; Eakin and Webhe 2008; Osbahr et al. 2008). This study of Sonora adds a focus on gender and water to this literature, and it contributes to work on gender, environment, and sustainability in Mexico generally (e.g., see Vázquez-García 1999; Cruz-Torres 2001; Vázquez-García and Hernández 2002; Pablos 2003; Radel 2005; Soares 2006; Chambers and Momsen 2007).

Research Site and Methodology

This study was conducted in the village of San Ignacio, Sonora, Mexico (see figure 6.1). San Ignacio has a population of 1140 people (INEGI 2010b) and is located less than 10 kilometers from Magdalena, a city of 29,707 people, and 75 kilometers from the twin cities of Nogales, Sonora, and Nogales, Arizona, in the United States, with a combined population of approximately 241,000 people (INEGI 2010a; US Census Bureau 2010). Hermosillo, the capital city of the state of Sonora, is located about 200 kilometers to the south.

The study presented here is part of a larger, ongoing research project that was initiated in October 2007. For the part of the project presented here, seventy-five ethnographic interviews were conducted with women and men who reside in San Ignacio. Most interviews conducted lasted from thirty minutes to two hours, depending on the time the respondents had available, and were structured in the form of a conversation. Follow-up interviews were undertaken with about two-thirds of the interviewees to gain an understanding of daily and seasonal rhythms and the effect of location (such as home, field, other workplace in the community), social interactions (inside and outside the home), and the effects of particular national and local environmental, economic, and social events on livelihoods. Participant observation was conducted in different settings, including while living with a local family, in orchards, at community events, in village streets, and in the main plaza. Ethnographic research

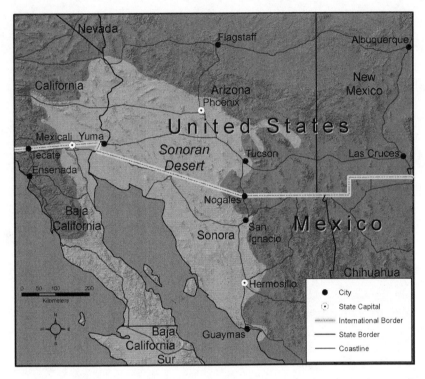

Figure 6.1. Map of San Ignacio, Sonora, Mexico. Cartographic design by Gary L. Christopherson, University of Arizona

facilitated deeper insight into gender and local perceptions surrounding the importance of agriculture-related activities for the sustenance both of livelihoods and social networks. It also helped shed light on local perceptions of the current and future impact of environmental change, such as the effects of climate change on water resources, on these economic and social relations. Some of the exact words of the interviewees were written down and used to help bring out the voices of the women and men of the community.

Gender and Work in San Ignacio

Both the globalization of the economy and the location of the community close to the US border have affected agriculture-based livelihoods in this area in many ways. Community, culture, and gender are all important units of analysis in a region such as the Mexico–US border where, as Álvarez (1995, p. 451) stated, "the massive exchange of commodities, both human and material, dramatically affects life and behavior." Most agriculture-dependent households at the study site have at least one immediate or extended family member residing in the United States, and thus remittances are an important source of income in the community. In 2007, Mexicans working in the United States sent back an estimated US$24 billion to their families (Malkin 2008). However, due to the global economic recession, dollar remittances fell by 4.9 percent in January 2009 over the same month in 2008 (El Economista 2009). Return migration from the United States to Mexico has increased as jobs are lost by migrants or heightened surveillance leads to their deportation. Due to stricter border controls, proposed legislation such as Arizona's infamous SB1070 law, and the economic crisis, it is now also less common for women and men to work in the United States during the week and return home to Mexico on the weekend (Buechler 2009c). This is placing added pressure on the local economy in San Ignacio and nearby city of Magdalena, as more people compete for the few available jobs.

The women and men of San Ignacio are employed in both nonagricultural and agricultural activities. However, no single activity is sufficient to support a household, and women and men normally must engage in multiple means to gain a living. Due to the lack of public transportation to the surrounding areas, including the cities, women's ability to obtain employment in the urban areas is limited. Women, unlike men, often do not own their own vehicle, do not know how to drive, or have limited access to a shared vehicle. Women frequently reported that the vehicle they share with other household members is not in good repair and that they did not know how long it would keep running. A few women with children find work in the community's small grocery stores. Some women also run snack stands or other small businesses from their homes, including meal preparation for tourist groups who come to see the community's historic mission church. Men also have small businesses, usually related to the construction industry and supported by migrant remittances. Most men are employed as workers in the nearby foreign-owned greenhouses and in the mines. Women and men also find work in other local businesses in Magdalena; men work in the construction industry and auto repair shops, whereas some young women and men work in multinational assembly plants (*maquiladoras*) in Magdalena. However, a week's salary in these plants is only slightly higher than weekly agricultural wages, and the number of hours of work obtained per week (therefore wages earned) fluctuates due to flexible production schedules tied to changing demand for the products with downturns in the global economy. Most of these nonagricultural forms of employment are therefore combined in some way with agriculture.

Water Resources and Climate Change in Sonora

Sonora is the most drought-affected state in Mexico, with unpredictable, heavy rainfalls that makes the area vulnerable to erosion (Vásquez-León and Bracamonte 2005). San Ignacio is located at the edge of the Sonoran Desert and is therefore quite dry. The annual rains the study area receives in July and August are termed the North American Monsoon (Ray et al. 2007, p. 3). Long-term temperature data from the Sonoran Desert show winter and spring warming trends, with fewer occurrences of freezing temperatures, longer periods without freezes, and increased minimum temperatures in the winter. The pace of these trends is expected to increase, causing changes to vegetation and the projected expanding boundaries of the Sonoran Desert (Weiss and Overpeck 2005, p. 2075). Studies on soil and air temperatures and on rainfall reveal a more rapid rate of localized warming in Sonora than across the border in Arizona, mainly because of desertification caused by land clearing, deforestation, buffelgrass invasion, and overgrazing, all of which cause a loss of biodiversity and declining economic potential of the land.

Due to climate change, Mexico may experience a reduction in summer precipitation as well as an increase in winter precipitation of as much as 10 to 20 percent (Magaña and Conde 2000). One study on climate change in the southwestern United States predicted temperature increases of 2–3°C by 2030 and 4–7°C by 2090; the authors warned that this would put even more pressure on already scarce water resources in part because of resulting higher evaporation rates and increased demand for water (Sprigg and Hinckley 2000). Water resource scarcity will adversely impact water availability for irrigation, and a combination of less water and warmer temperatures harms plant health, such as reduced resistance to pest attacks and drought, and decreases agricultural productivity (Appendini and Liverman 1994; Ingram et al. 2008; Adams et al. 2009).[2]

Water Resources in San Ignacio

Water resources used for agriculture in San Ignacio include water from springs, wells, and the Magdalena River. The Magdalena River originates in the Cocóspera water channel and the Concepción River, which originates near Cananea. A Mexican National Water Commission report in 2002 revealed that the Magdalena River basin is in deficit, meaning that more surface and groundwater is extracted from this river basin than is recharged through rainfall. The Magdalena aquifer, from which groundwater is pumped, is one of nineteen aquifers in the Magdalena River basin. The Magdalena aquifer has been under the protection of the government since 1978, when it was included as a groundwater protected area where no new drilling of wells could occur. New wells are only legally allowed to be drilled when they replace old wells (Martínez Peralta 2007). However, increasing volumes of water are being transferred from rural areas near San Ignacio to supply the growing urban area of Nogales, in seeming contradiction of the groundwater policies.[3] The population of Nogales grew from 159,103 inhabitants in 2000 to 212,533 inhabitants by 2010 (INEGI 2000; INEGI 2010a). Certain institutions as well as some wealthy users, such as the foreign owners of greenhouses located close to San Ignacio, have been able to circumvent restrictions in the drilling of new wells, which in turn affects the amount of groundwater available for other water users locally.

Gendered Agricultural Processing and Exchange

Agriculture remains an important source of income in San Ignacio for the landless and land-poor as well as those with larger landholdings. Fruit, vegetable, and dairy production predominates, and this production has created on- and off-farm employment. Quince, peaches, persimmons, pears, figs, and citrus fruits are produced in orchards located either near other fields or within the house compound. The types of vegetables produced include mainly chilies, spring onions, cabbage, carrots, cilantro, and broad beans. Women usually tend the orchards within the home compound, whereas men tend the further afield orchards and vegetable plots, with the participation of women during the harvest season (see figure 6.2). Women and men in San Ignacio also work in the production of canned fruits and vegetables, quince jelly and jam, and dried fruit flowers (for teas) either as laborers or as part of their own family enterprises. Those with land sell part of their produce and often retain part of their produce for canned and candied processing. They then sell the processed products and retain a portion for home food consumption and gift exchanges.

The production of canned fruits and vegetables is directed mainly by women in San Ignacio. The fruit is obtained from family orchards, or it is purchased from farmers in San Ignacio or in the surrounding communities. Often, the fruit is obtained from both family land and the market. Men have easier access to greater amounts of fruit because they are more deeply involved in agricultural production on a larger scale, whereas women have access to smaller amounts of fruit from their orchards in their home compounds. Women and men go together (often with children) to harvest fruit from other farmers' fields, paying the farmer for the quantity they harvest, which is usually just enough for canning or to make jam. Vegetables are also purchased in or outside the community and can sometimes be obtained free of charge from large producers in the community, particularly by those men and women who work as day laborers for the landowners.

For the canning, women draw in family members who reside within the community, nearby, or sometimes even distant urban areas, including urban areas in the United States. They use this family labor to help them wash and peel the fruit or wash the vegetables in preparation for canning. For example, a local woman, Maribel, revealed that before canning fruit, she enlists the aid of her aging parents who live in Magdalena to prepare it. Some women canners explained that they obtain new or used glass jars for canning from relatives living in the United States, as the jars are less expensive than those available in Mexico. A few women sell these jars to other women in San Ignacio. One of these women is Julieta; her grandson works in a store in Nogales, Arizona. He purchases the jars there at a worker's discount and transports them to his grandmother on a regular basis. The canning process is in many ways a path by which family ties that might otherwise be weakened through absence are strengthened. In this manner, women gain access to important sources of labor, which is crucial because of the labor-intensive nature of their work and the fact that most lack capital to hire labor (Buechler 2009a). They also secure critical commercial networks for the purchase and sale of inputs like jars.

These products are used by women to help secure social networks in other ways as well. Fruit and vegetable preserves are given as gifts to maintain reciprocal relationships, particularly in kin and fictive kin networks, or to important figures in the community such as the priest. Cora produces lemon preserves in the winter to sell from her home and at gatherings where there are visitors to the community. She produces about eighty jars of the lemon preserves to sell, twenty to give away, and a few for herself, her husband, and guests. When she visits her children and other relatives, "I go to each one handing them [the preserves] out." Another informant,

Figure 6.2. Woman irrigating an orchard in San Ignacio in June 2009. Photo by the author

Selena, revealed her method of product retention for gift giving and home consumption: "I keep two boxes of canned peach jars and four boxes of quince jelly bars to give as gifts. I also keep one box of canned peaches and a few pieces of quince jelly but these are for my household. I keep some fruit to make fruit juice for my family and also to eat as snacks." Jars or bars of quince jelly are also often given to other family members in need. For example, one woman gave her college student daughter cut fresh fruit with chile sprinkled on it and canned fruit to sell in front of the main entrance to the university as a way of helping her earn money to support her education. Another woman gives her relatives who live in Arizona fresh and canned fruit when they come to visit her, and they in turn give her canned food and flour from the United States, goods that are less expensive than in Mexico.

These exchanges are important to women, because they depend on mutual aid arrangements in the form of reciprocal gifts, as well as reciprocal labor arrangements in which women help each other by providing labor for agriculture and small-scale enterprises. They can also fulfill their responsibilities as mothers by giving their children goods that help them secure needed income. June Nash helped to elucidate why these roles are so necessary: "Women's mediating positions linking families to communities and communities to larger political, economic, and social circuits become crucial to survival where global development processes have undermined social reproduction" (2005, p. 145). The production of canned goods helps women in San Ignacio fortify these critical linkages.

Because quince is more commercial, the production cycle varies from that of traditional canning. In quince jelly and jam production, women and men are involved in different stages of the process as either unpaid or paid labor, and those who hold the means of production utilize the finished product in different ways. Both men and women wash the quince and cut it. Children and the elderly often also share in these tasks. Some who help are adult children who are living in other villages, towns, or cities in Mexico or the United States. Some elderly parents who lend a hand are from Magdalena or other nearby areas. Men mainly perform the tasks of stirring the hot quince jelly in the very large copper pots over the fire, which is considered to be heavy work, and the cutting of the cooled jelly into blocks that are later individually wrapped. Men sometimes have the capital gained from other activities and from the sale of the jelly to hire male workers to help with the heavy work of stirring and cutting, unlike women canners, who have less capital and therefore perform all of the work themselves with the aid of family members. Women and men wrap the blocks of quince jelly in plastic and place them in boxes for sale. Mostly women workers are hired for this stage. However, similar to canned produce production, family members are drawn in to contribute free labor to this work. Men mainly sell the quince jelly and jam, whereas women mainly retain it for household food consumption throughout the year and for gifts.

Fresh fruits and vegetables as well as canned fruit, jams, and jelly are sold to a wide variety of buyers. For canned fruits and vegetables, the main marketing outlets used by women are local vendors with stands along the highway who come to the producers' homes to purchase the products for resale; customers from the community or surrounding areas who come to the producers' home; and stands set up near fields to sell to religious pilgrims walking to area mission churches in October. Quince jelly is sold mainly by men to small community grocery stores, urban grocery chain stores, and urban municipal markets in Hermosillo and Nogales, as well as to bakeries in Hermosillo for pastries.

Visions of the Future and Gendered Implications for Livelihoods

The modes of both family and commercial fruit and vegetable production and the diverse set of purposes attached to this production (social, political, monetary, and household sustenance) generate an alternative vision among the producers in San Ignacio that includes both capitalist and noncapitalist visions of family and community, including cross-border networks. But the future of such social relationships and the economic support systems these foster in this community are imperiled by environmental change. Questions pertaining to the socioeconomic and environmental sustainability of this canned and candied fruit and vegetable production raise questions about the past, present, and future. Although the word *sustainability* is not an emic word in the community studied, in-depth interviews helped to illuminate some of the ways in which women and men combined traditions of the past with present-day social and economic practices, which were in turn also shaped to a large extent by their views of the future. This study responds to the call by Persoon and Perez (2008) and Persoon and van Est (2000) to better address local visions of the future in ethnographic research focused on environmental sustainability. These visions of the future are not homogeneous in a study population; instead, this study of Sonora points to the importance of including gender as a framework to better understand differences related to predictions about the future in the context of locally palpable environmental change.

Farmers interviewed in San Ignacio contend that ever since government water agencies started pumping water to Nogales, they have noticed lower water levels in their wells, necessitating the deepening of wells. They also often noted, "It doesn't rain like it used to, things are bad." Farmers also notice lower water levels in their irrigation channels that flow with spring water. In response to these growing water resource challenges, the water judge who organizes one of the spring water user associations in the community has stated that he plans to obtain help from the state to line the earthen irrigation channels with cement. In order to secure state aid to undertake this project, however, he must obtain official land titles for every plot of land owned by the spring water users in his water user association. This will require considerable work and multiple trips to the state capital, Hermosillo, to examine records of land deeds in his community. At the national level, increased attention is being placed on improving irrigation efficiency to save water, as evinced by pronouncements made by Mexico's National Water Commission director, José Luis Luege Tamargo, at the

World Water Forum in March 2009. Tamargo's statements surrounding the projected increase in funding for programs designed to save water in agriculture were made in the context of a session on strategies for adapting to climate change (El Financiero 2009).

In addition to coping with environmental changes through formal institutions, farmers have also altered the varieties of fruits they produce. Plum and apricot production once predominated in San Ignacio, but these fruits have almost completely disappeared. Fig and olive trees have also become much rarer in the area. The producers in the area stated that they changed their cropping patterns due to water scarcity (which has been particularly evident, they claimed, in the last eight years), warmer average temperatures, and pest infestations. Community members with tree nurseries noted that an increasing number of saplings die due to higher temperatures. In early 2009 Lidia, a woman in her nineties who has produced and processed fig and quince fruit since she was a child, exclaimed, "Now you cannot be sure of anything. The trees flower early and then the cold and wind kills them so there is less fruit." Quince fruit ripened much earlier than normal in 2008 due to warmer temperatures; the harvest ended in October rather than the normal time at the end of November. Diana, an olive producer, explained with a worried expression, "The climate has changed a lot. In 2008 the cold did not come in November or December." Celia, a woman in her sixties who cans peaches and helps other family members with quince jelly production, relayed that in terms of quince and peach production and processing, "There has never been a worse year for me than 2008." Her son told me separately that he had to buy much of the quince that they candied from other sources, and because of the higher cost this entailed they only produced 386 boxes (with 52 bars in each box) of quince jelly in 2008 compared to 800 boxes the year before. He said in 2009 that he would fertilize his quince trees well "and take care of them and hope to have a better year. The demand for quince jelly is always very good." He has also branched out into the purchase and resale of vegetables from San Ignacio and surrounding communities to make up for his local shortfall.

If climate change predictions hold true, the array of crops that can be produced in a future with less water and higher temperatures is likely to be further reduced, thus further restricting livelihood options. By 2050, it is predicted that climate change could cause species extinctions of 15 to 35 percent (Thomas et al. 2004). This will reduce agro-biodiversity that communities, and especially women, depend on to be able to hedge their risks against climate change. In addition to warmer temperatures, precipitation variability associated with climate change is likely to intensify in the future, further impacting farmers' livelihoods. Flooding along the river banks could occur with greater frequency, ruining fields and crops. Past experiences in San Ignacio are sobering: due to large-scale deposits of sediment on farmers' fields, land near the river had to be abandoned in the late 1990s after a flood.

Extreme events are also on the rise. Unseasonable frost and hail in April 2008 was followed by very heavy wind and rain the following month, first freezing and then blowing away many of the flowers that would have formed fruit on trees. When asked whether the government would compensate farmers for their resulting losses, José, a fruit farmer in San Ignacio, replied, "My friends and I were sitting yesterday in the plaza talking about our crop losses and had a good laugh. One friend said with a smile, 'I have insurance.' Another friend replied, 'I have insurance, too,' and then I joined in and said 'I have insurance, too. I have the assurance that when I die I will be carried down this street right here, on the way to the cemetery over there.'"

These farmers' words reveal that those involved in agriculture envision an insecure future due in part to the lack of a supportive policy environment. The dismantling of several forms of state support to farmers such as subsidized seed, fertilizer, machinery, and credit accompanied the suspension of crop insurance in the late 1980s and the early 1990s (Buechler 2005). Credit in the form of a government-supported revolving loan fund was also cut off recently to farmers in San Ignacio who are members of a water user association due to the lack of repayment by some owners of larger farms with larger loans.

Gendered Responses to Climate Change

The heightened climate variability and growing water scarcity are affecting gendered livelihoods in San Ignacio. Women's responses to questions about the future of agricultural production in San Ignacio have centered on the provision of food for themselves and their household members. Cecilia, a woman who cans fruits and vegetables, explained that if agricultural production declines in San Ignacio and canned products are not produced, there will be increased seasonal food insecurity. She asked, "What will people eat in the winter?" Maria, another woman who cans fruits and works with her husband to produce quince jelly, relayed how important fruit production was to her family because it offered a degree of food security in the form of fruit, fruit juice, and canned products as well as income through sales. The importance of this source of food was increasing, she emphasized, due to the rising cost of food.[4] She explained that the future of this production was in jeopardy, however, because of growing groundwater depletion.

Women canners often depend on proximate orchards for part of the fruit that they preserve. These orchards are irrigated with groundwater, often by the women themselves. However, with declining groundwater levels and the need for greater volumes of water for irrigation due to the changing climate, there is now often insufficient water to irrigate the orchards. Maria said that she and her husband had one open well and one drilled well in their *solar*. However, two years ago these wells dried up and, in order to irrigate the persimmons, peaches, oranges, and grapefruit trees in their *solar*, she had to begin drawing water from her neighbor's well. She predicted that the orchards would soon disappear, compounding community members' problems created by the economic crisis. Cecilia, similar to other women fruit and vegetable processors interviewed, also saw the value of the processed goods for food security, particularly during lean times of the year. Women commonly associated water scarcity and climate change with growing challenges related to producing the crops that they use in their businesses and on social and household reproduction. Women's concerns primarily centered on whether they would be able to continue providing food for their families in the face of these environment challenges, which were compounded by the current employment and food and fuel price crises.

In contrast, men's concerns about the future tended to center on water availability for irrigation of their fields and climate variability that leads to crop loss, particularly of their commercial crops. In response, male community figures such as the president of the spring water irrigation user association were taking steps to reduce inefficient water use in agricultural production. José, a quince orchard farmer, noted, "With little rain, and less water in the canal [spring water], there were few quince . . . not even a third of what there was the year before. I have been making quince jelly for nine years, and this was the worst year. To make the quince jelly, I had to buy quince from [other communities] but the quince from there were expensive." He added, "I sell most of my jelly to supermarket chains, which is better paid but often with delayed payments, and to small stores that pay less but [can] pay right away".

Aware of these constraints, women and men have attempted to diversify their income sources across household members, but with only limited success due to low remuneration attached to alternative income sources and to a lack of employment sources aggravated by the economic crisis.

Remittance income was also declining, and some migrants were returning to San Ignacio, thus intensifying dependence on agricultural production and processing as sources of food security and income.

Given the double exposure of climate change and these global economic crises, the worries that both men and women have expressed about the future are not insignificant. Flooding, frosts, hail, heavy winds, and higher temperatures, all associated with climate change, are natural disasters for populations such as those studied in Sonora, and the effects of these are often gendered. As noted in this case study, however, climate change is often combined with other pressures, creating local dynamics that are exacerbated by economic crises and price hikes that have increased under globalization. For example, Quisumbing et al. (2008) shed light on the gendered implications of the current food price crisis by showing that in the 1980s under structural adjustment "rising prices . . . tighten[ed] women's time constraints by forcing them to travel longer distances to obtain lower prices and to prepare cheaper, but more time-intensive foods." Such changes in food availability, and the concomitant effect on the use of food in social networks and household reproduction, is likely to happen again, given pathways of environmental change that now seem all but inevitable in San Ignacio.

Concluding Remarks

Climate change and resulting water resource variability have gendered impacts that in turn affect socioeconomic relations in communities. In this study of a community in Sonora, the effects of these physical processes related to climate and water on the socioeconomic sustainability of gendered livelihoods can be examined through women's and men's economic practices and gendered visions of the future. Because agricultural production and processing enterprises in San Ignacio are used to maintain social networks, women in particular depend on these pathways being available to them. Maintaining strong networks with relatives who live across the US border is important for women in order to retain access to less expensive jars and labor for their enterprises. Social networks are also used to cement ties between community members and with those who have moved out of the community, such as sons or daughters in nearby towns and cities; nonmonetary exchanges between these actors sustain a web of economic and social support that crosses spatial boundaries of village, city, and even nation. This web is increasingly important in an environment in which the state has dismantled many programs that supported agricultural producers, food prices are rising, and employment is difficult to obtain and retain.

Noncapitalist relations have endured in San Ignacio, and these still exert an important influence even as the community has physically changed, such as in cross-border migration. However, climate change and water scarcity, which impact the viability of fruit and vegetable production, is likely to have a significant negative effect on these family enterprises. If agricultural production fails due to environmental change, and takes with it the family enterprises based on it, these noncapitalist visions of San Ignacio's women and men may disappear, harming future social sustainability if webs of social support can no longer be nurtured. Women are likely to be more vulnerable in the absence of these noncapitalist relations, due to their weaker position in the labor market. They are also likely to be more vulnerable because of their gendered responsibilities related to the provision of food and other household needs at the same time that they are experiencing diminished access to less expensive or free nutritious food. Another factor contributing to women's greater vulnerability during environmental crises is that women's access to and control over natural resources and technology declines even more than men's (Lambrou and Piana 2006; Dankelman and Jansen 2010).

By focusing on these women's and men's perspectives about the future, it is clear that men have centered their actions around their concern that the future of agricultural production will be less certain under conditions of heightened environmental variability. They have begun taking action by attempting to raise their water use efficiency and by emphasizing one set of agricultural activities over others (for example, resale of purchased vegetables to compensate for poor fruit harvests). Women are also concerned about their future ability to retain food for household consumption and for the redistribution of food among community members, part of their noncapitalist vision of a healthy family and community. Women centered their responses to this concern on diversifying their own and their children's income sources. However, as remittance income falls and some migrants return home, increasing pressure is placed on these existing employment options.

What can be done to help the people of San Ignacio cope with the changes, both environmental and economic, that threaten to overwhelm them? Sustainable development programs for agricultural communities such as the one studied here could include collaborations with local and extra-local producers to focus on a few globally profitable yet hardier crops. For example, global demand for pomegranate fruit has risen as it has been linked to an anti-cancer diet, and producers could be aided in capturing a share of this global market. (Pomegranate trees resist temperature extremes better than, for example, citrus fruits.) Of course, any recommendations would need to examine the different products that could be made from each particular crop by gender-differentiated actors in or near their homes. Research focused on contexts of rapid change need to incorporate views of the past, present, and future into data gathering and analysis. This would serve to reject static models that do not take into account how dynamic environmental, social, and economic processes shape local responses to livelihood impacts. Ethnographic research such as the present study can reveal differences between women's and men's views concerning the sustainability of livelihoods increasingly influenced by climate change, water resource pressures, and economic uncertainty. The future of their production hangs in the balance, as does their ability to mold a noncapitalist vision of community and family that extends beyond local and national geographic boundaries.

Acknowledgments

The author gratefully acknowledges the funding sources for this study, which include a Fulbright–García Robles border grant from August 2008 to May 2009 and a grant from the Resource Center for Urban Agriculture and Food Security from October 2007 to April 2008.

Notes

1. All names used are pseudonyms to protect the identity of the author's informants.

2. A recent study on piñon trees showed that if the climate is warmer, then it takes a shorter drought to kill the trees. Shorter droughts are much more common historically than longer droughts (Adams et al. 2009).

3. The water supply system is organized by Organismo Operador de Agua Potable y Saneamiento de Nogales, with permission from the national-level water agency, Conagua.

4. By March 2008, the unit price of the imported food basket had risen by 62 percent with respect to its level in 2005. Mexican consumers have been most affected by price increases in corn, wheat, soy, and powdered milk (Villareal et al. 2008).

References

Adams, Henry D., Maite Guardiola-Claramonte, Greg A. Barron-Gifford, Juan Camilo Villegas, David D. Breshears, Chris B. Zou, Peter A. Troch, and Travis E. Huxman. 2009. Temperature sensitivity of drought-induced tree mortality portends increased regional die-off under global-change-type drought. *Proceedings of the National Academy of Sciences* 106(17):7063–7066.

Ahlers, Rhodante. 2005. Gender dimensions of neoliberal water policy in Mexico and Bolivia: Empowering or disempowering? In *Opposing currents: The politics of water and gender in Latin America*, eds. Vivienne Bennett, Sonia Dávila Poblete, and Maria Nieves Rico, 53–71. Pittsburgh, Pa.: University of Pittsburgh Press.

Ahmed, Sara, and Elizabeth Fajber. 2009. Engendering adaptation to climate variability, Gujarat, India. *Gender and Development* 17(1):33–50.

Álvarez, Robert R. 1995. The Mexican–U.S. border: The making of an anthropology of borderlands. *Annual Review of Anthropology* 24:447–470.

Appendini, Kirsten, and Diana Liverman. 1994. Agricultural policy, climate change and food security in Mexico. *Food Policy* 19(2):149–164.

Buechler, Stephanie. 2005. Women at the helm of irrigated agriculture in Mexico: The other side of male migration. In *Opposing currents: The politics of water and gender in Latin America*, eds. Vivienne Bennett, Sonia Dávila Poblete, and Maria Nieves Rico, 170–189. Pittsburgh, Pa.: University of Pittsburgh Press.

Buechler, Stephanie. 2009a. Gender, water and climate change in Sonora, Mexico: Policy and program implications for agricultural development. *Gender and Development* 17(1):51–66.

Buechler, Stephanie. 2009b. Gender, water and climate change dynamics of fruit and vegetable production and processing in peri-urban Magdalena, Sonora, Mexico. In *Women feeding cities*, eds. Alice Hovorka, Henk de Zeeuw, and Gordon Prain. Leusden, Netherlands: Resource Center for Urban Agriculture and Food Security Foundation, and Ottawa, Canada: International Development Research Centre.

Buechler, Stephanie. 2009c. Migration in the context of the current economic crisis: Household-level responses in central and northern Mexico. Paper presented at the conference "Reconceptualizing migration: Economies, societies, biopolitics," sponsored by the Committee on Global Thought, Columbia University, April 2009.

Buechler, Stephanie, and Emma Zapata, eds. 2000. *Género y manejo del agua y tierra en comunidades rurales de México*. México, D.F.: International Water Management Institute and Colegio de Postgraduados, Montecillo.

Chambers, Kimberlee J., and Janet Henshall Momsen. 2007. From the kitchen and the field: Gender and maize diversity in the Bajío Region of Mexico. *Singapore Journal of Tropical Geography* (28):39–56.

Cruz-Torres, Maria L. 2001. Local-level responses to environmental degradation in northwestern Mexico. *Journal of Anthropological Research* 57(2):111–136.

Dankelman, Irene, and Willy Jansen. 2010. Gender, environment and climate change: Understanding the linkages. In *Gender and climate change: An introduction*, ed. Irene Dankelman, 21–54. London: Earthscan.

Denton, Fatma. 2002. Climate change vulnerability, impacts and adaptation: Why does gender matter? *Gender and Development* 10(2):10–20.

Eakin, Hallie. 2000. Smallholder maize production and climatic risk: A case study from central Mexico. *Climatic Change* 45:19–36.

Eakin, Hallie, and Luis Bojórquez-Tapia. 2008. Insights into the composition of household vulnerability from multicriteria decision analysis. *Global Environmental Change* 18(1):112–127.

Eakin, Hallie, and Monica B. Webhe. 2008. Linking local vulnerability to system sustainability in a resilience framework: Two cases from Latin America. *Climate Change* 93(3–4):355–377.

El Economista. 2009. Caen 11.88 percent los envíos de remesas a México. *El Economista*, 27 February, 19–24.

El Financiero. 2009. Dominan cambio climático y financiamiento jornada de Foro del Agua Nacional. *El Financiero*, 17 March.

Ingram, Helen, John M. Whiteley, and R. W. Perry. 2008. The importance of equity and the limits of efficiency in water resources. In *Water, place, and equity*, eds. John M. Whiteley, H. M. Ingram, and R. W. Perry,1–32. Cambridge, Mass.: The MIT Press.

Instituto Nacional de Estadísticas, Geografía e Informática (INEGI). 2000. Censo de población y vivienda, tabulados básicos.

Instituto Nacional de Estadísticas, Geografía e Informática (INEGI). 2010a. Censo de población y vivienda por localidad. Sonora. http://www2.inegi.org.mx/sistemas/mapatematicomexicocifras3d/default.aspx?e=26&mun=36&sec=M&ind=100200 0001&ani=2010&src=0&i=.

Instituto Nacional de Estadísticas, Geografía e Informática (INEGI). 2010b. *Principales Resultados por Localidad 2010*. San Ignacio, Magdalena, Sonora. http://www3.inegi.org.mx/sistemas/iter/entidad_indicador.aspx?ev=5

Khamis, Marion, Tamara Plush, and Carmen Sepúlveda Zelaya. 2009. Women's rights in climate change: Using video as a tool for empowerment in Nepal. *Gender and Development* 17(1):125–136.

Lambrou, Yianna, and Sibyl Nelson. 2010. *Farmers in a changing climate: Does gender matter? Food security in Andhra Pradesh, India*. Rome: Food and Agriculture Organization.

Lambrou, Yianna, and Grazia Piana. 2006. *Gender: The missing component of the response to climate change*. Rome: Food and Agriculture Organization of the United Nations.

Magaña, Víctor O., and Cecilia Conde. 2000. Climate variability and freshwater resources in northern Mexico, Sonora: A case study. *Environmental Monitoring and Assessment* 61(1):167–185.

Malkin, Elizabeth. 2008. Mexicans barely increased remittances in 2007. *New York Times*, 26 February.

Martínez Peralta, Claudia Maria. 2007. *El flujo de agua virtual en la producción agrícola: El caso del Río Magdalena*. Thesis. Specialty Diploma in Integrated Water Basin Management, Colegio of Sonora, Hermosillo.

Nash, June. 2005. Women in between: Globalization and the new enlightenment. *Signs: Journal of Women in Culture and Society* 31(1):145–167.

Nelson, Valerie, and Tanya Stathers. 2009. Resilience, power, culture, and climate: A case study from semi-arid Tanzania, and new research directions. *Gender and Development* 17(1):81–94.

Nelson, Valerie, Kate Meadows, Terry Cannon, John Morton, and Adrienne Martin. 2002. Uncertain predictions, invisible impacts and the need to mainstream gender in climate change adaptations. *Gender and Development* 10(2):51–59.

Osbahr, Henny, Chasca Twyman, W. Neil Adger, and David S. G. Thomas. 2008. Effective livelihood adaptation to climate change disturbance: Scale dimensions of practice in Mozambique. *Geoforum* 39(6):1951–1964.

Pablos, Esperanza Tuñón, ed. 2003. *Género y medioambiente*. Plaza y Valdés, México: Ecosur, Semarnat.

Persoon, Gerard A., and Padmapani L. Perez. 2008. The relevant context: Environmental consequences of images of the future. In *Against the grain: The Vadya tradition in human ecology and ecological anthropology*, eds. Bradley B. Walters, Bonnie J. McCay, Paige West, and Susan Lees, 287–306. Malden, Mass.: Rowman & Littlefield.

Persoon, Gerard A., and Diny M. E. van Est. 2000. The study of the future in anthropology in relation to the sustainability debate. *Focaal* 35:7–28.

Quisumbing, Agnes, Ruth Meinzen-Dick, and Lucy Bassett. 2008. *Helping women respond to the global food price crisis.* International Food Policy Research Institute Policy Brief 7 (October). Washington, DC: International Food Policy Research Institute.

Radel, Claudia. 2005. Women's community-based organizations, conservation projects and effective land control in southern Mexico. *Journal of Latin American Geography* 4(2):8–34.

Ray, Andrea, Gregg Garfin, Margaret Wilder, Marcela Vásquez-León, Melanie Lenart, and Andrew C. Comrie. 2007. Applications of monsoon research: Opportunities to inform decisionmaking and reduce regional variability. *Journal of Climate* 20(9):1608–1627.

Roy, Marlene, and Henry David Venema. 2002. Reducing risk and vulnerability to climate change in India: The capabilities approach. In *Gender, Development and Climate Change*, ed. Rachel Masika. Oxford: Oxfam Press.

Soares, Denise Moraes. 2006. Mujeres, leña y desarrollo: Estudio de caso sobre género, y recursos naturales en los altos de Chiapas. In *Gestión y Cultura del Agua*, Vol. II, eds. Verónica Vázquez-García, Denise Soares Moraes, Aurelia de la Rosa Regalado, and Ángel Serrano Sánchez, 293–312. México, D.F.: Secretaría de Medio Ambiente y Recursos Naturales, Instituto Mexicano de Tecnología del Agua and Colegio de Postgraduados.

Sprigg, W. A., and T. Hinckley. 2000. *Preparing for a changing climate: The potential consequences of climate variability and change.* Report of the Southwest Regional Assessment Group for the US Global Change Research Program. Tucson: Institute for the Study of Planet Earth, University of Arizona.

Thomas, Chris D., Alison Cameron, Rhys E. Green, Michel Bakkenes, Linda J. Beaumont, Yvonne C. Collingham, et al. 2004. Extinction risk for climate change. *Nature* 427:145–148.

US Census Bureau. 2011. Arizona's census by cities, counties. http://www.azcentral.com/community/pinal/articles/2011/03/10/20110310census-arizona-new-2010-numbers-brk10-ONbox.html.

Vásquez-León, Marcela, and Álvaro Bracamonte. 2005. *Indicadores ambientales para la agricultura sustentable: Un estudio del noreste de Sonora.* Sonora, Mexico: El Colegio de Sonora, and Tucson: University of Arizona, Bureau of Applied Research in Anthropology.

Vázquez-García, Verónica, ed. 1999. *Género, sustentabilidad y cambio social en el México rural.* México, D.F.: Colegio de Postgraduados en Ciencias Agrícolas, Estudios de Desarrollo Rural.

Vázquez-García, Verónica, and Aurelia Flores Hernández. 2002. *Quién cosecha lo sembrado? Relaciones de género en un área natural protegida mexicana.* Plaza y Valdes: Colegio de Postgraduados.

Villareal, Héctor J., Juan Carlos Chávez, Ricardo Cantú, and Horacio González. 2008. *Impacto del Incremento en los Precios de los Alimentos en la Pobreza en México.* Working Papers 20081. Centro de Estudios de las Finanzas Públicas, H. Cámara de Diputados.

Weiss, Jeremy L., and Jonathan T. Overpeck. 2005. Is the Sonoran Desert losing its cool? *Global Change Biology* 11(12):2065–2077.

Zwarteveen, Margreet, and Ruth Meinzen-Dick. 2001. Gender and property rights in the commons: Examples of water rights in South Asia. *Agriculture and Human Values* 18:11–25.

CHAPTER SEVEN

Meaningful Waters

Women, Development, and Sustainability along the Bhagirathi Ganges

Georgina Drew

The need for gender inclusion in debates over resource management and sustainability has long been recognized. Academics, environmentalists, and development practitioners, among others, are working to increase awareness of and attention to the gender dimensions of resource concerns around the world. This work has become more critical as development activities and climate change jeopardize access to life-giving sources such as water. While the physical hardships that scarcity exerts on women must be addressed, the nonmaterial implications should not be overlooked. This chapter argues for a broadening of the notion of sustainability to include the continuity of resources and livelihoods as well as the diverse relationships between humans and the environment. Although scholars and activists have made similar calls, I contextualize this argument in debates over the management of the Bhagirathi River, commonly recognized as the primary tributary of the holy Ganges, in the Indian Himalayas. As I show here, a holistic concept of sustainability opens up a range of possibilities for the engagement of gender perspectives on development and ecological change. This can lead to a more nuanced approach to gender inclusive collaboration in environmental praxis.

Culture, Ecology, and Sustainability on the Bhagirathi Ganges

Flowing some 1,560 miles and supporting more than 400 million people, the Ganges River is recognized as one of India's most important freshwater sources (Chapman and Thompson 1995). Direct and indirect users rely on waters from the Ganges for a range of domestic, agricultural, commercial, and industrial uses. In addition to the river's physical significance, the Ganges has many cultural and religious facets. For millennia, people seeking purification and spiritual guidance have worshiped the river. This reverence is established in Hindu epics such as the Ramayana and the Mahabharata (Darian 1978). It is also embodied in daily practice. Devotees consider the river to be the Goddess Ganga, and they confer upon her the status of a mother. As a sign of respect and a literal identification, the river is called Ma Ganga (Mother Ganges).

Unfortunately, the health of this multifaceted water resource is in jeopardy. According to scientific reports, the Himalayan glaciers that contribute to surface flows are receding significantly (IPCC 2007), and rivers such as the Ganges have already become seasonal (Immerzeel et al. 2010). While controversy persists over the short-term implications of climate change, it is likely that environmental shifts such as glacial melt will contribute to long-term water stress. This will amplify problems in a nation that, in 2003, ranked 133 of 182 countries for water availability per capita (UNESCO 2003). Within India's borders, great inequities persist between those that have access to adequate, potable water supplies and those that do not, and these disparities are highly gendered (Lahiri-Dutt 2006). For this reason, it is important to attend to the concerns of Himalayan women, many of them part of India's rural and semi-urban poor, living along the Bhagirathi Valley where the primary tributary of the Ganges flows.[1] In this region, gender vulnerabilities to shifting water availability are exacerbated by current approaches to water resource management that include the proliferation of hydroelectric dams.

Within the context of shifting water resource availability and development along the revered and symbolic Ganges River, the concept of sustainability is inadequately summarized by the most commonly used definition, from the Brundtland Commission's 1987 report. Their widely quoted notion entails enacting development practices that meet present needs without compromising the ability of future generations to meet their own (Brundtland et al. 1987). While this is one aspect of sustainability, it does not encapsulate the full range of human needs and desires that vary according to cultural belief and religious systems. In its intent to stress the continuity of the human race, it also makes the anthropogenic error of understating the human-nature relationships around which civilizations are organized and that support life while informing worldviews, cosmologies, and behaviors.

This chapter seeks to engage a holistic approach to sustainability that encapsulates diverse cultural beliefs and practices. It is grounded in the conviction that human relationships and concern for natural resources are important for policy formation because modalities of action in relation to the environment are intimately linked to perception (Ingold 2000). In this effort, I employ insights gained during ethnographic research along the river's Himalayan reaches. My work documenting human reactions to changes along the primary tributary of the Ganges indicates that, beyond material concerns for water availability to support human livelihoods, a real need for residents, and women in particular, is access to the river for the maintenance of sociocultural traditions that are tied to livelihoods, life cycles, and identities. This is because the Ganges is not just a "resource," it is part of a cultural model of nature in which the river's nonmaterial dimensions are highly valued.[2] Although I recognize that cultures are dynamic and ever-changing and that humans create novel cultural practices over time and especially when faced with the need to adapt to new circumstances, the emphasis on culture in this text aims to honor the concerns that people express on their own terms. I explain the theoretical importance for this later in the chapter.

Damming the Ganges: Issues and Implications

Because of the multiple uses and meanings associated with the Ganges River, conflict erupts when attempts are made to harness its waters for the production of hydroelectric power. This was the case along the upper reaches of the river, which I henceforth refer to as the Bhagirathi Ganges, in the Himalayan district of Uttarkashi in Uttarakhand State (see figure 7.1). In that region, a series of three hydroelectric projects were the subject of intense regional and national conflict. Despite protests by activists in the Himalayas and New Delhi, two of the dams (of 480 to 600 megawatt potential) were in the early to middle stages of construction by 2010. Although these dams offered some employment for laborers, they posed numerous concerns for the people living in the dam-affected regions and beyond.

Ecologically, the dams were to be set in a seismic zone and in a fragile mountain ecosystem where landslides are frequent. Proposed in an area that has little infrastructure, the dams would be less than 40 miles below the Ganges' glacial source. In a region where ice loss is expected to

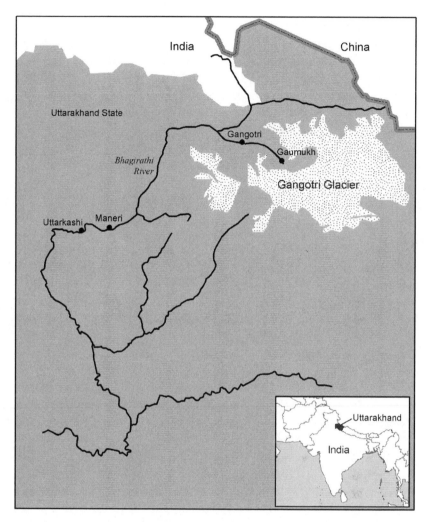

Figure 7.1. Map of the Bhagirathi River in Uttarkashi District, Uttarakhand. Map created by Amanda C. Henley, GIS Librarian, University of North Carolina, Chapel Hill. Data sources: ESRI Data and Maps 9.3., Environmental Systems Research Institute; National Geospatial-Intelligence Agency; and OpenStreetMap shapefiles India

continue or even accelerate, the power generation capacity of such dams was uncertain. It was probable, for instance, that as the melting glaciers deposited more sediment into runoff, the high silt content would have hindered energy production. This silt might also have increased the rate of corrosion of turbines and other machinery needed to generate electricity (Dharmadhikary 2008). Factoring the reduced lifespan of the proposed dams due to decreased water availability and increased quantities of silt, an independent economic analysis asserted that the money spent on the dams' construction could have exceeded the potential gains from energy production (Jhunjhunwala 2008).

In light of these and other concerns, numerous social movements and NGOs worked from 2006 to 2010 to raise public awareness and activism in response to the proliferation of development projects along the Bhagirathi Ganges.[3] Several of these groups, for instance, supported three *bhukh hartal* (fast unto death) programs undertaken by a retired professor of the reputed Indian Institute of Technology, Kanpur, in 2008, 2009, and 2010. The fasts—lasting from fifteen to thirty-eight days—were grounded in ecological, cultural, and religious concerns for the well-being of the river. Such actions prompted decisions by the central government to declare the Ganges a "national river" and to establish a regulatory body, the National Ganga River Basin Authority, to monitor projects on the river and promote its sustainable use. After extended pressure, the Indian government suspended and later canceled the construction of new hydroelectric projects along the Bhagirathi Ganges.

Despite these developments, it is unclear how the river's national status will translate to proactive measures to protect its flow or how long the dams will remain suspended/canceled. In the case of dam building, decisions can be reversed until binding legislation is passed to protect the river. This was the history of the Tehri dam, which was halted and resumed over decades before it was finished in 2006.[4] As long as dams are considered to be key vehicles to support India's accelerated growth, there will be continued pressure to expand hydroelectric production in the Himalayas. It is important, therefore, to examine the impact of past projects in order to understand the potential they pose to disrupt livelihoods as well as the cultural practices that add meaning to human existence. In this effort, I focus on the comments and knowledge of women residing along a stretch of the river's flow.

Within the larger debate over development, Himalayan women living near the Bhagirathi Ganges have a particular vantage point from which they interrogate the presence and proliferation of dams in the context of glacial melt and climatic change. The inclusion of their perspectives, I argue, can expand the regional and global understanding of what is at stake in a time when the river's longevity is in question. This is not to say that men are not concerned about the river's fate; the leaders of several social movements and NGOs addressing the Ganges' condition were, in fact, male. With the exception of a few extraordinary women who joined them, these men frequently traveled back and forth from the plains to the mountains raising awareness about their concerns for the river. While men and women shared numerous preoccupations for the river's health and sociocultural significance, many rural and semi-urban Himalayan women expressed an especially strong sense of urgency. This is, in part, due to their reduced capacity for mobility and migration (relative to men) in the face of water resource decline. Their socially delegated and highly demanding responsibilities in domestic and agricultural spheres also help to foster distinct perspectives on ecological change along the Bhagirathi Ganges.

Methods

To understand the gender dimensions of concern with and connection to the river's flow, I worked along the Ganges' upper reaches over twelve months from 2008 to 2009. My Himalayan field site spanned from the river's glacial source to the city of Uttarkashi some 80 miles below. The focus on this region built upon previous studies of Himalayan resource conflict as well as efforts to address the sociocultural implications to the Ganges' (mis)management, including work that explored responses to the river's polluted stretches in the Indian plains (Alley 2002). In my ethnographic research, I focused on livelihood struggles, daily practices, and human-nature relationships. I was especially interested in Garhwali women's engagements with the river and their preoccupations with its continuity. During the course of fieldwork and in four additional months of organizational research in places such as New Delhi, I conducted nearly a hundred semistructured interviews, ten life-history interviews, and ten focus group sessions. I also participated in twenty-five movement events and fifteen cultural ceremonies in which devotion to the river was central. These research activities exposed me to a range of concerns about the river's condition.

Integrating Women's Resource Knowledge: Insights from Nagpuri Village

My work on the gender dimensions of development and climatic change along the Bhagirathi Ganges reveals two key points relevant to the topic of gender and sustainability. First, approaches to natural resource management should be holistic in order to include the continuity of ecological integrity *and* the human relationships with the natural world that engender cultural diversity. Beyond environmental degradation, as I show below, some women who live and work along the Bhagirathi Ganges contend that development projects increase physical hardships while rupturing their honored connections with the river, their personal sense of belonging, and their cultural sense of place. The projects, in short, threatened to impact daily practice and everyday life in the region. Second, and in light of these observations, there is room to expand the range of women's development and environmental concerns in the work of social movements and NGOs.

Insight for the first point comes from conversations with various women living along the Bhagirathi Ganges in the Indian Himalayas. To illustrate, I focus on the words and concerns of women in Nagpuri village (a pseudonym) below the already-established Maneri Bhali Hydroelectric Project. Over the period of fieldwork, I visited Nagpuri an average of once every three months and spent several nights there at the home of a female village leader, Usha Devi (also a pseudonym), who is the head of a women's committee known as a *mahila mangaldal* (see figure 7.2). In extended conversations with Usha, women's committee members, and other villagers (both men and women), I came to understand the harsh environmental and economic realities of Nagpuri, made even more difficult due to the upstream Maneri dam. Over time, the villagers' problems came to epitomize the hardships that could befall many if hydroelectric development and climatic change accelerate across the Himalayas. The postdam challenges of Nagpuri also illustrate the need for more collaboration with women in decisions related to development in the Himalayas.

Nagpuri is a few miles upriver from the district capital of Uttarkashi and close to the India–Tibet border. Situated at the base of a hillside along the Bhagirathi Ganges, the village of about 150 families is accessible from a main road by two swing bridges that straddle the riverbed. Despite the presence of an adjacent ashram complex that mainly caters to foreigners, many of the villagers in Nagpuri have few economic opportunities. Although several women in the village have working knowledge of Hindi

Figure 7.2. Usha Devi, the leader of the women's committee, at her home with a view of the Bhagirathi Ganges. Photo by the author

(one of India's national languages), many are most comfortable when speaking a regional dialect of Garhwali. The emphasis on Garhwali is an indication of low levels of formal education combined with infrequent travel beyond Garhwali-speaking communities. The lack of education and mobility also reflects highly gendered workloads in a region where women are responsible for most of the domestic and agricultural labor (Manjari 1996). Whereas men travel in and out of their villages in search of work, economically underprivileged women often remain behind to tend to the daily needs of *ghar* (home), *gai* (cow/livestock), and *khet* (agricultural field) (see figure 7.3). Rural life for women in places such as Nagpuri, therefore, develops deep familiarity with the dynamic localities in which they live (cf. Agarwal 1994). As the comments of women in Nagpuri demonstrate, daily practice along the Bhagirathi Ganges also fosters insights into the effects of development projects such as the Maneri dam located some 5 miles upstream.

Construction for the Maneri Bhali Hydroelectric Project began in the 1970s. Due to the high level of silt in the glacier-fed Bhagirathi Ganges and the erratic nature of the river's seasonal flow, however, the dam produces less than half of the 90 megawatts it was supposed to generate,

Figure 7.3. A woman in Nagpuri village tends to the summer rice crop before the coming of the monsoon. Photo by the author

according to a faith-based activist group who retrieved data on the dam through India's Right to Information Act. Built in an era of accelerated hydroelectric proliferation, the dam's construction spiked hopes for employment and development in a region that is sometimes referred to as "backward" (Rangan 2000). With some exceptions, however, most of the skilled and unskilled jobs went to workers from other areas. Although the lack of employment was disappointing, a greater source of concern for the residents of Nagpuri was the paucity of fresh water they suffered after the dam's construction. Although villagers were not opposed to hydroelectric development on principle, they now question the benefits of such projects while complaining that the scant river flows and the destructive impacts of tunnel construction have left them vulnerable to water stress.

In a low-lying Himalayan village like Nagpuri, a lack of potable water is an anomaly. Many villages in Uttarkashi district are fed by freshwater springs and/or have access to groundwater supplies. Prior to the construction of the Maneri dam, Nagpuri village had ample water sources. According to residents, the creation of the dam's underground tunnels for river water diversion tapped into and drained Nagpuri's water supplies.[5] Although agitations were able to secure a pipeline for the villagers, the new water source is located nearly 15 miles away. Women in Nagpuri complain that the water flowing in the pipeline, if it reaches the village at all, is frequently polluted. Improper maintenance means that villagers, especially children, often get sick from consuming the piped water. Due to failures in their water service, women are now only able to plant rice in years when the July rains are abundant. If the rains are insufficient, the fields go uncultivated and no rice is produced.

Although some might argue that such localized disturbances are a necessary cost of development in the region, members of the women's committee in Nagpuri disagree. Their extensive conversations, fostered through regular meetings on topics of mutual concern, sensitized them to the many problems they and others experienced in the dam's aftermath. In sharing these insights with me, a frequent refrain was that development had in fact not taken place in or near their village. Several reasons were given to substantiate this argument.

The complaints often began with the observation that the river had thinned significantly over the years. As one woman commented during a focus group session that took place on a porch overlooking the river, "Today Gangaji [a term of respect for the river and the goddess] is flowing, but in winter you can't even see her. So where is this development?" Shaking a fist in the direction of the dam upstream she quickly answered, "This is not development, this is detriment!" The denunciation was followed by the observation that periods of low flow witness an increase in intervillage conflict due to disintegrating riverine boundaries downstream from the dam. Where once outsiders had to enter Nagpuri on swing bridges, now people can indiscriminately cross the riverbed in search of cattle fodder and other goods when the water level is scant. The rise in resource plunder upsets social relationships, increases commodity scarcity, and augments vulnerability.

The seasonal variation in water availability in Nagpuri village, I was told, also makes access to the river a matter of survival. While dam proponents sometimes argue that people do not depend on river water for livelihoods because the district is not a water-deficit area, members of the women's committee such as Usha Devi stressed that the river sustains them in times of scarcity. Although the flow may be nominal in difficult winter months, the little that trickles down is used for drinking, cooking, washing clothes, and other household uses. When asked what they would do without these waters, Usha retorted that a total lack of flow would be like a death sentence. This, she reasoned, would not only be due to the loss of water but also because of the reduced incentive for pilgrims to travel to the region for a sight of the river's revered water. As Usha and the other women's committee members readily pointed out, these tourism activities are a lifeline for many people living along the river, as the earnings trickle into and help sustain village economies.

Despite the high material stakes, the physical changes along the river are only part of the preoccupations. Members of the women's committee worry that their location vis-à-vis the Bhagirathi Ganges is in jeopardy. "Gangaji is sacred, and she is flowing right before us," one woman pointed out. "People come from far and wide to see her. This is how we give importance to where we live. It is part of our *pehchaan* [identity]." Nodding agreement, another woman stressed her deep connection to the river as a companion through life. "This is the land in which we were born," she said pointing to the mountains and the thin line of water below. "We watch the river day and night. It is like [the beating of] our heart. Even though we sometimes take it for granted, we are proud that the Ganges is ours." Such comments illustrate the "fluvial intimacies" (Raffles 2002) that some women express for the river. They also suggest that it acts as a cultural artifact that mediates self-understandings (Holland and Lave 2001). If the river's flow is further hampered by development projects and the predicted effects of climate change, respondents in Nagpuri expressed a fear that their lives would become "zero" or meaningless.[6] Instead of being motivated by the notion of becoming developed (Shrestha 1995), women worry over the river's loss and the ways that this will impact their sense of identity and belonging in the sacred geography of the Himalayas (cf. Holland and Lave 2001).[7] This echoes the findings of Orlove et al. (2008), who described how cultural identities are challenged by retreating glaciers and shifting water resource availability.

Linked with identity concerns, women in Nagpuri worry that a further reduction in the flow of the Bhagirathi Ganges will significantly alter their ability to fulfill cultural prescriptions for conduct. As dutiful wives, for instance, many women fast regularly for the welfare of their husbands. The fast includes prayer and worship at the river's banks. Access to the river is therefore tied to intimate notions of womanhood and domesticity.

In addition to jeopardizing gender codes of conduct, the inability to access the river also impacts the observance of cultural rites of passage in the Hindu life cycle, known as *sanskar* (or *samskara*). Water from the Ganges is meant to sustain a person from the moment of birth by washing away physical and spiritual impurities. Immersion in the Ganges is especially critical for the performance of death rituals because the river is believed to be a direct bridge to heaven for the deceased who are placed in its waters. The thought of omitting such culturally and cosmologically significant rites in the event of nominal flow is deeply disturbing for many who live along the river. To continue their traditions despite low water levels in the winter season, residents of places like Nagpuri state that they already have to beg for water to be released from the Maneri dam during traumatic times of death. Shaking her head at the state of affairs, Usha Devi lamented that they have lost their rights to the river and, by extension, the Goddess Ganga. "If we have to ask permission to see and touch her," she explained, "then she no more belongs to us." In such a perspective, the diverted and depleted water supply amounts to the appropriation of a physical, cultural, and spiritual commons.

While the above example is linked with the significance of cultural and religious rites, arguments were also made about maintaining intimate relationships with a river that, for many, is also an actor. As one woman shared in a pause between tending to her fields, "We want Ganga's flow to be constant. Gangaji is our mother. If [one day] She is no more, then what will we do without our mother?" As mentioned, the concept of the Ganges as a mother goes beyond a term of endearment; women, men, and children across South Asia honor the river as a physical guardian who protects and cares for her children's well-being (Haberman 2006).

The river's agency is also evident in some interpretations of glacial retreat. As another women's committee member explained to me, "Gangaji has become angry. That is why she is disappearing." The reason given for her anger was too much human sin. To substantiate the increase in moral decay, the woman pointed to the high levels of pollution in the environment and a growing disrespect for the places that demarcate the sacred geography of the Himalayas.

Honoring Place(s) and the Gods Who Inhabit Them

The importance given to the river and to the Himalayas in which it flows involves a reverence for place that bears exploration. Known as *dev bhoomi*, the region is a famed land of gods and goddesses (Gulia 2007).[8] The region's prominence in Hindu epics gives it added heritage value. The cultural sense of place and sacrality in the Himalayas has a strong lure for tourists and pilgrims, who come in droves every year to enjoy the scenery and visit the many holy sites that dot the landscape. Although it has a long history of human struggle and resource management conflicts, the Himalayas occupy a special position in the global imagination as a land of purity and spirituality (cf. Rangan 2000). Such imaginings will be tested as the place and places of the Himalayas transform along with the rapid social, cultural, and ecological changes underway.

In speaking of place, I draw from Massey (1994), who described place as a nexus of relations, a patterned logic and ethos of contingent connections rooted in a particular way, anchored in a given space and time. This notion of place is dynamic. Socially, place continues to be important to human meaning-making wherever people engage with and experience a particular location in connection with their everyday lives (Escobar 2008). As important sites of knowledge and wisdom (Basso 1996), places are articulated within local-global networks of action and interaction (Dirlik 1998). In the Himalayas, as in other locations, place is a domain where worldviews are formed and informed through interactions with the environment.

Because much human action is grounded in the localities in which we live, place is an important site of agency. Given the gendered dimensions of social life, places are also critical sites of power contestation and resistance for women (Harcourt and Escobar 2005). The concerns of women in Nagpuri show how place-based knowledge of the Bhagirathi Ganges informs understandings of ecological change and shapes critiques of development. Cultural notions of place along the Bhagirathi Ganges also demonstrate the many facets of risk involved in the river's potential loss.

Among the many concerns is the potential loss of access to the Goddess Ganga, an entity that gives added cosmological value to the region. The river's social and cultural construction as a living goddess, I argue, must be taken seriously because it informs human behaviors. Engaging belief in the Goddess Ganga has implications for the pursuit of sustainability. My conversations with people living along the river, in Nagpuri and elsewhere, show that many are worried about protecting not only the flow of water but also their ability to interact with the divine being who resides within. This means that the material as well as the nonmaterial implications of resource management must be considered in decision-making processes.

Along the Bhagirathi Ganges, holistic practices and policies could work to ensure flows sufficient enough to nourish biodiversity while simultaneously supporting the conditions of cultural and religious diversity from which human existence draws its rich heritage. There are promising signs that such an approach might be underway: When the Indian government canceled the proposed and under-construction dams along the Bhagirathi Ganges in 2010, they noted that their decision was informed by religious and environmental reasons that kept in mind, "the very special features and unique status of the sacred Ganga in our culture and in our daily lives" (Mukherjee 2010).

Such decisions honor our complex relationships with natural entities. They also offer an opportunity and a challenge to engage multiple views on the coexistence of humans and the divine. This requires interrogating the assumption running through modern political thought that gods and spirits are "social facts." Critiquing the limitations of this approach and the impositions on subaltern worldviews that it entails, Chakrabarty (2000) flipped the normative social science perspective to argue that the question of being human involves the question of being with gods and spirits. Working with indigenous populations, Marisol de la Cadena (2010) also urged us to honor multiple approaches to the natural and the supernatural world. Speaking of indigenous beliefs of a sentient being embodied by an Andean mountain in Peru, she imagined the possibilities for a politics that incorporates the sentiments of indigenous intellectuals without negating them as superstitions or "respecting" them as mere cultural beliefs. How can we form plural politics, she asked, and what would it entail? Of particular importance for her is the issue of taking beliefs associated with sentient beings *literally* (my emphasis) instead of metaphorically or symbolically, as anthropologists and other social scientists were once accustomed to doing. This is a challenge that is as relevant in the Indian Himalayas as it is in the South American Andes.

In the case of the Bhagirathi Ganges, a holistic approach would mean taking the river on the terms presented by people living along her banks. Julie Cruikshank (2005) provided a strong model for this in her collaborative sharing of Alaska Native relationships with glaciers. By "listening for different stories," Cruikshank presented an unjudged world of belief where glaciers can hear, smell, and respond to human action. Approaching human-nature interactions in such a way involves a continual chipping away at the idea that nature is a scientifically knowable domain separate from the social and cultural (Latour 1991). These arguments make poignant links between theory and practice that are important to keep in mind with attempts to include, and collaborate with, women along the Ganges.

Collaborating for Sustainable Livelihoods: Cautions and Suggestions

To promote sustainability along the river, people-centered and ecologically sound approaches to development are needed to support the economy of the region for the benefit of its residents without jeopardizing people's personal, material, and cultural needs to be in contact with the Bhagirathi Ganges. To find such solutions, more engagement and dialogue is needed. Many development agencies recognize the value of such efforts. Some even call for the incorporation of "local knowledge" in resource management and development decisions. As the United Nations said in their 2006 *World Water Development Report*, "Local knowledge must be the starting point for all development projects. Local or indigenous knowledge is internationally recognized as vital to sustainable development and environmental management. Many of the activities affecting, and affected by, water management and use are performed by local people who may have little formal education but maintain a strong understanding of the water systems on which they rely" (UNESCO 2006, p. 38).

Such calls to include multiple knowledge(s) are significant, as they signal an intention to avoid top-down management approaches. The challenge for development practitioners promoting "local" knowledge, however, will be to accept propositions that run contrary to their training. The United Nations' water report, for instance, encouraged an expansion of hydroelectric projects (UNESCO 2006). The organization is particularly optimistic about the potential for economic development through the proliferation of small dams. The experiences of women in Nagpuri, however, attest to the damage that modest-sized dams can do. Their call to "let the Ganges flow" is a demand that, dams or no dams, the focus should be on providing a constant supply of the river's life-giving and culturally meaningful waters. The stance of such women is not just reactionary. They understand, as does the United Nations, that climatic change and glacial decline will impact the health of ecosystems downstream, and they want to ensure the continuation of livelihoods along the Bhagirathi Ganges. They also worry that a further reduction in the river's flow due to the development of run-of-river dams could impair river-related tourism and income. When crops are failing and rainfall is increasingly erratic, the thought of losing this regional source of revenue is disheartening. The reverberations of such income loss would likely increase pressures on already limited and highly exploited forest areas for fuel, food, and fodder. As for the employment created by dams, women in villages like Nagpuri are quick to point out that the temporary income men earn for construction labor is nominal compared with the needs of current and coming generations. Stressing women's roles and responsibilities as caretakers, they argue for long-term solutions that will keep food on the table for their children.

As for the practices of inclusion of women's resource concerns, there is scope to increase the involvement of women living along the Bhagirathi Ganges in discussion, activism, and decision-making forums. Although many initiatives and organizations encourage women's participation, these sometimes consist of one-time events with limited impact. The lack of repeated institutional engagement reflects the difficulty of accessing and coordinating people in dispersed mountain villages, communication challenges, and the constraints on rural women's time. Even when there is involvement in environmental campaigns and awareness-raising events, women, such as Usha Devi in Nagpuri, cite a lack of postevent updates on the result of their actions. The dearth of information is discouraging; it leaves women wondering about the efficacy of their efforts and fosters skepticism about the value of expending precious energy on such activities when the return is uncertain.

When women do participate in defense of the river, there is little consensus on why they choose to take action. In February 2008, for instance, 5,000 people—most of them women—walked from the river's source to the capital city of New Delhi to protest dam construction in the Himalayas. When asked to explain the reason for the substantial involvement of rural Himalayan women (many of whom exhausted limited savings and sacrificed two weeks of work), the demonstration's leader attributed their participation to a "natural" connection with the river. Such essentialism does little to improve our understanding of the range of women's concerns, motivations, and relationships with the environment. It also misses an opportunity to explore linkages between culture, religion, and environmental action. Although not all reverence for nature translates into ecologically sound behavior because of our resource demands and complex relationships with the environment (Nagarajan 1998), women's willingness to expend limited time, money, and energy in defense of the Bhagirathi Ganges demonstrates the extent to which diverse connections to its flow and faith in its goddess can inspire human action. To improve the efficacy and gender sensitivity of environmental campaigns, therefore, more effort is needed to comprehend the varied motivations that can inspire women's participation.

Concluding Remarks

Although there is potential for the inclusion and collaboration of women in addressing the future of the Bhagirathi Ganges, there is also reason for caution. For instance, critics question the value of work done by groups whose stated aim is to improve the physical and social situation of women in the Himalayas. Noting the difficulty with which organizations translate donor dollars into programs that support women's health and social mobility, some warn of the "fallacy of women's empowerment" in the Himalayas.[9] Concerns like these are a reminder to be wary of the "NGOization" of women's issues (Mohanty 2006) and to increase critical analyses of gender imbalances in groups and organizations that operationalize women's inclusion into their work (O'Reilly 2007).

This is not to say that efforts to include women in water management and development decisions must always require that women play a central part. As Ray (2007) noted, participation can take many forms. Because women of various ages as well as caste and class backgrounds will have different desires or capacities to contribute, they should be allowed to select their level of involvement. For some, this might mean giving time to attend and listen silently at meetings. For others, it could mean donating labor for projects. Those that wish to be directly involved in discussion and decision-making, however, must be actively supported in their efforts to do so. In the case of rural Garhwali women's participation, this would mean helping women to navigate the language and literacy obstacles that some face in Hindi or English. It would also entail valuing their time enough to organize meetings and programs that fit within pauses in the agricultural work cycle and overlap with periods in which women can travel freely without fear or social stigma (such as daytime hours).

Another option for increasing collaboration with Garhwali women would be to enhance work with existing groups such as the women's committees (*mahila mangaldal*) that are found in Nagpuri and many other villages along the Bhagirathi Ganges. In such committees, many women are already engaged in the regular discussion of their site-specific and regional problems. Some have concrete ideas for promoting the ecological health of the localities in which they live. Social and economic obstacles, however, often prevent the implementation of their solutions. To overcome this, work with women's committees could encourage the discussion of water management and development issues at set meeting times while providing the means for committees to send village representatives to local and regional forums where input and suggestions can be shared.

No matter what the level and duration of engagement, it is important to refrain from dictating the terms of gender inclusion. This means that the goals of collaboration should be discussed with the women whom programs seek to involve. While such an approach has organizational challenges and it requires more time for dialogue, it can enhance the long-term benefits and beneficiaries of such endeavors. For those efforts that aim to increase women's ability to deploy, access, and subvert power, a last caution is to remember that the "empowerment" of women can be a moving target. The meaning and practice of empowerment is continually redefined because the subjects involved engage in their own efforts to challenge, circumvent, and exceed the original designs of women's empowerment programs (Sharma 2008). This power play, as Singh explains in this volume, can involve jumping scales between bottom-up and top-down processes. Efforts to include women along the Bhagirathi Ganges in debates over environmental resource management and sustainability must, therefore, remain flexible and reflexive in their attempts at inclusion, collaboration, and empowerment. They should also be mindful of diverse feminisms and feminist subjectivities in different regional and socioeconomic contexts (Chaudhuri 2004).

The above points and cautions, however, must be combined with timely action. Given the dire predictions of accelerated water scarcity relative to demand and the increasingly fragile state of Himalayan ecologies, turning to the resource concerns and knowledge of women intertwined in the management of their mountain environments can expand our understanding of the risks we face and potential solutions. Doing so, I argue, would be a step toward a more holistic approach to sustainability because it would take into consideration the myriad perceptions of the natural world that motivate human action. For, as a project on water and cultural diversity asserted, we are far more likely to treat natural resources with respect and use them sustainably when we recognize the multiple ways of understanding and valuing nature (UNESCO-IHP 2008). This chapter is an effort toward creating more dialogue around the significances of a vital body of water, the Bhagirathi Ganges, that highlights gendered issues and concerns over its use. It is also a call, echoing that of Cruikshank (2005), to listen for "different stories" that may ultimately advance our appreciation of human entanglements with the natural world and their relevance for the pursuit of sustainable livelihoods.

Acknowledgments

The research for this chapter was made possible by organizations such as the Fulbright Hays; the National Science Foundation (grant no. BCS-0851193); and the Center for Global Initiatives at the University of North Carolina, Chapel Hill. I am grateful for their assistance as well as for the feedback on this chapter that I received from several people. Julie Cruikshank provided helpful comments on an early draft. Maria L. Cruz-Torres and Pamela McElwee also gave useful suggestions for improvement, as did Brenda Baletti and an anonymous peer reviewer.

Notes

1. In speaking of the "poor," I am identifying a low socioeconomic group and a category of people that self-identifies as *gareeb*, or impoverished.

2. Cultural models of nature involve the ways in which societies produce "use-meanings" for the material world that reflect diverse cultural values (Escobar 1999).

3. Social movements involved in efforts to improve the river's condition include the Ganga Bachao Abhiyan (Movement to Save the Ganges), Ganga Ahvaan (Call of the Ganges), and the Ganga Raksha Manch (Ganges Defense Forum).

4. Due to the opposition of social movements, the Tehri dam took nearly three decades to complete. When the dam, which was built to produce a maximum capacity of 2,400 megawatts, was completed in 2006, it displaced some 100,000 people, created a 28-mile reservoir up the Bhagirathi Valley that inundated large tracts of fertile land, and submerged the historic capital of Tehri district.

5. As opposed to reservoir dams, Maneri dam and the dams set for construction upstream are "run of the river" schemes that produce electricity after diverting water out of the riverbed and into underground tunnels.

6. The words *vayarth* (useless) and *zero* (nothing) were used to describe what life would be like without the river.

7. The significance of their proximity to the river travels as well. As one woman pointed out on 8 August 2008, when the village men journey to the plains in search of work, they win respect from others when they say they live along the Ganges. This helps explicate how proximity to the river fosters a sense of self-importance.

8. *Dev* refers to gods and *bhoomi* denotes a land, region, or even the Earth.

9. Semistructured interview with Dr. Bharat Jhunjhunwala on 15 August 2008.

References

Agarwal, Bina. 1994. The gender and environment debate: Lessons from India. In *Population and environment: Rethinking the debate*, eds. Lourdes Arizpe, M. Priscilla Stone, and David C. Major, 87–124. Boulder, Colo.: Westview Press.

Alley, Kelly. 2002. *On the banks of the Ganga: When wastewater meets a sacred river*. Ann Arbor: University of Michigan Press.

Basso, K. 1996. Wisdom sits in places. In *Senses of place*, eds. S. Feld and K. Basso, 53–90. Santa Fe, N.M.: School of American Research.

Brundtland, G. H. et al. 1987. *Our common future: Report of the World Commission on Environment and Development (The Brundtland Commission)*. Oxford: Oxford University Press.

Chakrabarty, Dipesh. 2000. *Provincializing Europe: Postcolonial thought and historical difference*. Princeton, N.J.: Princeton University Press.

Chapman, G. P., and M. Thompson. 1995. *Water and the quest for sustainable development in the Ganges Valley*. New York: Mansell.

Chaudhuri, Maitrayee. 2004. The Indian women's movement. In *Feminism in India*, ed. M. Chaudhuri, 117–133. New Delhi: Kali for Women and Women Unlimited.

Cruikshank, Julie. 2005. *Do glaciers listen? Local knowledge, colonial encounters, and social imagination*. Vancouver: University of British Columbia Press.

Darian, Steven G. 1978. *The Ganges in myth and history*. Honolulu: The University Press of Hawaii.

de la Cadena, Marisol. 2010. Indigenous cosmopolitics in the Andes: Conceptual reflections beyond 'politics'. *Cultural Anthropology* 25(2):334–370.

Dharmadhikary, Shripad. 2008. *Mountains of concrete: Dam building in the Himalayas*. Berkeley, Calif.: International Rivers.

Dirlik, Arif. 1998. Globalism and the politics of place. *Development* 41(2):7–14.

Escobar, Arturo. 1999. After nature: Steps to an anti-essentialist political ecology. *Current Anthropology* 40(1):1–30.

Escobar, Arturo. 2008. *Territories of difference: Place, movements, life, redes*. Durham, N.C.: Duke University Press.

Gulia, K. S. 2007. *Art and culture of Himalaya*. New Delhi: Isha Books.

Haberman, David L. 2006. *River of love in an age of pollution: The Yamuna River of northern India*. Berkeley: University of California Press.

Harcourt, Wendy, and Arturo Escobar, eds. 2005. *Women and the politics of place*. Bloomfield, Conn.: Kumarian Press.

Holland, Dorothy C., and Jean Lave, eds. 2001. *History in person: Enduring struggles, contentious practices, intimate identities*. Santa Fe, N.M.: School of American Research.

Immerzeel, Walter W., Ludovicus P. H. van Beek, and Marc F. P. Bierkens. 2010. Climate change will affect the Asian towers. *Science* 328:1382–1384.

Ingold, Tim. 2000. *The perception of the environment: Essays on livelihood, dwelling, and skill*. New York: Routledge.

Intergovernmental Panel on Climate Change (IPCC). 2007. *Climate change 2007: Impacts, adaptation, and vulnerability. Contribution of Working Group II to the Fourth Assessment Report of the Intergovernmental Panel on Climate Change*. Cambridge: Cambridge University Press.

Jhunjhunwala, Bharat. 2008. *Jal Vidyut ka Sach*. Lakeshmoli, India: Independent Publication.

Lahiri-Dutt, Kuntala. 2006. Reflections on gender and water. In *Fluid bonds: Views on gender and water*, ed. Kuntala Lahiri-Dutt, 22–50. Kolkatta: Stree.

Latour, Bruno. 1991. *We have never been modern*. Catherine Porter, trans. Cambridge, Mass.: Harvard University Press.

Manjari, Mehta. 1996. Our lives are no different from that of our buffaloes: Agricultural change and gendered spaces in a central Himalayan valley. In *Feminist political ecology: Global issues and local experiences*, eds. Dianne Rocheleau, Barbara Thomas-Slayter, and Esther Wangari, 180–208. New York: Routledge.

Massey, Doreen. 1994. *Space, place, and gender*. Minneapolis: University of Minnesota Press.

Mohanty, Chandra Talpade. 2006. Foreword. In *Playing with fire: Feminist thought and activism through seven lives in India*. Sangtin Writers: Anupamlata, Ramsheela, Reshma Ansari, Richa Singh, Shashi Vaish, Shashibala, Surbala, Vibha Bajpayee, and Richa Nagar, ix–xv. Minneapolis: University of Minnesota Press.

Mukherjee, Pranab. 2010. Letter to Dr. G. D. Agarwal from the Finance Minister. Government of India.

Nagarajan, Vijaya Rettakudi. 1998. The earth as Goddess Bhu Devi: Towards a theory of embedded ecologies in folk Hinduism. In *Purifying the earthly body of God: Religions and ecology in Hindu India*, ed. Lance E. Nelson, 269–292. Albany: State University of New York.

O'Reilly, Kathleen. 2007. 'Where the knots of narrative are tied and untied': The dialogic production of gendered development spaces in north India. *Annals of the Association of American Geographers* 97(3):613–634.

Orlove, Ben, Ellen Wiegandt, and Brian H. Luckman. 2008. The place of glaciers in natural and cultural landscapes. In *Darkening peaks: Glacial retreat, science, and society*, eds. Ben Orlove, Ellen Wiegandt, and Brian H. Luckman, 3–19. Berkeley: University of California Press.

Raffles, Hugh. 2002. *In Amazonia: A natural history*. Princeton, N.J.: Princeton University Press.

Rangan, Haripriya. 2000. *Of myths and movements: Rewriting Chipko into Himalayan history*. New York: Verso.

Ray, Isha. 2007. Women, water, and development. *Annual Review of Environment and Resources* 32:421–449.

Sharma, Aradhana. 2008. *Logics of empowerment: Development, gender, and governance in neoliberal India*. Minneapolis: University of Minnesota Press.

Shrestha, Nanda. 1995. Becoming a development category. In *Power of development*, ed. Jonathan Crush, 259–270. New York: Routledge.

United Nations Educational, Scientific, and Cultural Organization (UNESCO). 2003. *Water for people, water for life*. United Nations World Water Development Report. Barcelona, Spain: United Nations Educational, Scientific, and Cultural Organization.

United Nations Educational, Scientific, and Cultural Organization (UNESCO). 2006. *Water, a shared responsibility: United Nations world water development report 2*. Paris, France: United Nations Educational, Scientific, and Cultural Organization.

United Nations Educational, Scientific, and Cultural Organization, International Hydrological Programme (UNESCO-IHP). 2008. Policy brief on mainstreaming cultural diversity in water resources management. http://typo38.unesco.org/es/themes/ihp-water-society/water-and-cultural-diversity.html

PART THREE

Gender and Fisheries

CHAPTER EIGHT

Gender, Sustainability, and Shrimp Farming

Negotiating Risky Business in Vietnam's Mekong Delta

Hong Anh Vu

It was around 9:00 a.m. one January morning in 2008. The sun was up high and glaring, warning of a hot day to come. Sau, a local woman, and I joined a group of villagers at a local tea shop. Sipping from her little cup of green tea, Sau spoke of a recent spat with her husband: "My husband and I recently had a fight over how to pursue the coming [shrimp] season. While he wanted to invest in intensive shrimp farming, I prefer to do the first crop extensively. Once I have harvested that, he can do whatever he wants [with the farm]. But he would not listen to me and wanted to plunge into industrial shrimp farming immediately. We almost wrecked the hut arguing over this decision."

The incident between Sau and her husband reflects the contentions at many levels among coastal households in Tra Vinh province in the Mekong Delta of Vietnam. These changes have followed the promotion of commercial shrimp aquaculture in tandem with a new "farm economy" policy introduced in 2000, which sought to promote the production of high-value crops for export on a large scale by allowing greater land accumulation through removal of earlier land-holding regulations. Rapid expansion of shrimp farming areas, especially of an industrial shrimp farming model, is environmentally destructive. Relying heavily on chemical inputs, industrial feedstocks, and mass-hatched shrimp fries, industrial shrimp aquaculture has resulted in frequent disease outbreaks, rising indebtedness, and land loss among households. The conflict between Sau and her husband can be viewed within the context of these rapid changes in resource use and weakening of household buffers.

Adoption of commercial shrimp farming also means accepting the financial, environmental, and social risks it entails. Industrial shrimp farming models often require significantly higher capital, labor, and time investment compared to more extensive practices.[1] The former also promises larger returns. In fact, most of the new houses in the area have been built thanks to profitable industrial shrimp harvests. However, industrial shrimp farming has also resulted in the loss of whole or part of a household's productive assets. Like many households in coastal areas of the Mekong Delta that have lost, Sau's family must still settle a loan of more than 100 million VND (US$5,500) taken out for industrial shrimp farming back in 2003. The shrimp boom has also resulted in massive loss of mangroves, pollution of land and water resources, and loss of common property resources, which used to form a critical buffer for coastal households. Sau's preference for the extensive model, which yields a lower but more secure return, versus her husband's desire to persist with the intensive system, which promises higher returns, reflects not only differences in gender risk perceptions, but also coping strategies.

This chapter explores the dynamics of intrahousehold negotiations on resource use and livelihood decisions. In the Mekong Delta, women's interaction with the environment varies according to household livelihood strategies, predicated on available assets and economic circumstances. Comparing changes in the division of labor among three typical household categories with different livelihood trajectories following the shrimp boom, I show how women can support both environmentally destructive and environmentally friendly activities, depending on the livelihood strategies their households can afford. I argue that the distinction between men and women's strategies seems to be defined by their risk perceptions, which are shaped by their social roles and spaces. Through the discussion of changing gender division of labor in shrimp farming and women's contribution to household production activities, this chapter highlights some of the reasons why women may or may not support sustainability. Specifically, the chapter addresses the following questions: What changes have occurred in the gender division of labor and intrahousehold dynamics across household groups following the shrimp boom? What are the factors that resulted in these changes? And how do experiences of women and men across household groups compare in the face of transformations in the production system and broader socioeconomic changes?

Women, the Environment, and Sustainability

The women-environment relationship engaged a diverse group of scholars and activists during the late 1980s and early 1990s. I focus on two main strands of ecological feminism, namely ecofeminism and feminist political ecology.

Ecofeminism points out how oppression against women and nature is based on race, class, gender, sexuality, and physical abilities (Gaard 1994, p. 1). Ecofeminists such as Shiva (1989), Mies and Shiva (1993), and Davidson (1989) contended that due to domestic responsibilities such as collecting firewood, fetching water, and growing vegetables, women have developed a closer relationship with nature. It is through their interaction with nature that women have developed knowledge about and care for the environment. As a result, women and nature share the same fate as victims of patriarchal capitalist projects. Ecofeminism and its call for attention to women both as victims of patriarchal projects and environment managers became a subject of intense debate among supporters and opponents. As ecofeminism became the ideology that centered the WED discourse among NGOs and international organizations, it also came under heavy criticism.

Feminist political ecologists, including Agarwal (1991), Biehl (1991), and Jackson (1993), challenged the proposition of women as ideal environmental managers and noted the absence of historical contexts, as well as issues of class, caste, and ethnicity. Women across societies do not form a homogeneous group. Women's experience with the environment varies depending on their socioeconomic backgrounds (Agarwal 1991). In particular, Jackson (1993, pp. 1949–1950) proposed that an understanding of women-environment relationships should focus on the specificity of the historical, social, and economic contexts and the dynamics of political economies and agroecosystems. Women's interaction with the environment is affected by their multiple identities, sources of income, class, intra- and extragender relations, and social gender norms. While division of labor along gender lines, resource rights, and responsibilities are criteria that should be included in examining the women-environment question, studies should recognize how women's interaction with the environment is dependent upon their households' experience of environmental degradation, which is shaped by both outside factors and the act of one's own family, kin, and neighbors. Most importantly, women's relationship with the environment is mediated by livelihoods. This means that the most direct human-environment interaction can find expression in their daily involvement with strategies for survival.

Methods

My fieldwork was conducted between January 2006 and July 2007, and data were collected from multiple visits to the villages of My Quy and Cay Da and the Long Thanh Industrial Zone in the districts of Duyen Hai and Cau Ngang in Tra Vinh province. This province occupies the stretch of land between the Bassac and Hau Giang Rivers that the Mekong branches into before it meets the South China Sea (see figure 8.1). My first exercise in the field was to hold a meeting in each village with a group of approximately ten men and women from different social backgrounds. The exercise was designed to gain some understanding of the history of changes in the landscape and demography and to identify key informants and research assistants. I also took the time to test a questionnaire.

The second phase of intensive fieldwork started a month after my first visit. Initially, the idea was to spend as much time as possible on shrimp farms. However, it soon became evident to me that women were not welcome there because of a belief that they could bring bad luck and harm the shrimp. Thus, the difficulties I as a woman encountered in accessing the shrimp ponds and farms alerted me to the gender implications of household livelihood strategies as well as in shaping social interactions among households engaged in different livelihoods. To maneuver my way around this challenging situation, I recruited and trained two male assistants whose identity as local men could ease my access to shrimp farms. The research assistants also helped collect questionnaire data, covering a wide range of issues, including household income and expenditure, investments in shrimp aquaculture versus other crops, land ownership, and gender roles in production and access to resources such as land and bank loans. It was also during the process of conducting the questionnaire survey that I identified men and women knowledgeable about the social, economic, and environmental history and transformations since Vietnam opened its economy to market forces in the late 1980s, known as Doi Moi (new changes), and the adoption of commercial shrimp farming in particular.

Constrained by limited access to the shrimp farms and male farmers, I had to turn to women for help. The women who shared with me their experiences, knowledge, and advice come from different socioeconomic

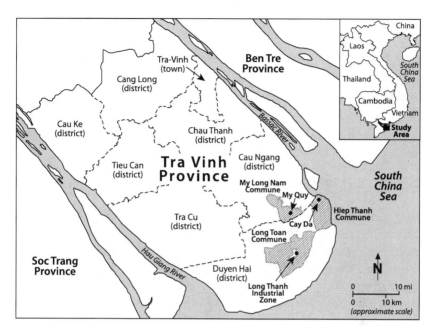

Figure 8.1. Map of Tra Vinh province, Vietnam. Map by the author

backgrounds: some were shrimp farmers themselves, others were house-wives, and a few of them held government jobs. They welcomed me into their homes and invited me to their meetings and social gatherings; some even set time to talk with me even when I showed up at their offices without prior notice. Intensive participant observation enabled me to see the complexity of gender divisions of labor along with changing livelihoods. But most importantly, women enabled me to see a different reality about the shrimp boom that is never included in the public discourse on shrimp aquaculture.

Instead of being passive observers, women showed me the importance of their labor not only in fulfilling domestic tasks, but in ensuring food security for their households while assisting the men with many tasks in the shrimp ponds/farms, an area that has often been strictly treated as a male domain. Contrary to the stereotypes I often heard about women as "knowing nothing" about and "doing nothing" with shrimp farming, women demonstrated their creativity in the strategies they adopted for assisting the men. Although shrimp aquaculture had altered gender roles and the ways household resources were used, women gained a measure of control over these resources by protecting household resources from risky undertakings. My interactions with women illuminated the struggles that they go through when household production activities are scattered and labor is split up. I also realized that a gendered approach to ethnographic research provides insights into women's role in maintaining the sustainability of the household and its members, in protecting the land and the environment, and thus contributing to social, livelihood, and environmental sustainability.

Changing Gender Divisions of Labor

In Vietnam's Mekong Delta, the shrimp boom since the early 1990s, backed by agricultural restructuring policies to pursue export-led growth, has resulted in fundamental transformations in the property regime, resource use, and social relations. The privatization of land and resources for the promotion of commercial crops has caused massive mangrove loss and loss of access to common waterways and resources that once formed the subsistence needs of coastal households, especially the landless and land-poor, poor women, and women-headed households.[2] At the same time, the shrimp boom has also seen a rise in social crimes that never existed before and general social disintegration as macroeconomic policies benefit some at the expense of others.

The shrimp boom has also highlighted the men equals commercial and women equals subsistence production dichotomy, a pattern common to other chapters in this book, as well as elsewhere, such as in many subsistence-turned-commercial farming communities in Africa (Burton and White 1984, p. 569). Changes in the gendered division of labor were most evident following the penetration of the industrial farming model as part of the promotion of the farm economy policy in the province since 2000. Male labor shifted to shrimp farming, whereas women had to take over agricultural and subsistence farming activities. Subsistence is strongly associated with female reproductive roles, minimum investment, and mundane tasks bound by female spaces within the home. Cash crops, on the other hand, are usually associated with high value, so male labor devoted to cultivating them is also valued higher than female labor.

This comparison follows the logic of the public/private, production/reproduction dichotomy, in which production activities are associated with the public sphere versus reproduction ones with the private sphere, that has long been a feminist critique of widespread asymmetric gender structure across the world (Rosaldo 1974). Despite recognition of women's economic contributions (Boserup 1970), the adoption of commercial cash crops as a growth strategy in many transitional economies tends to consolidate a patriarchal social structure. The transformations in production and gendered division of labor in the Mekong Delta have clearly caused women's physical exclusion from family land because shrimp aquaculture is seen as a masculine crop and a male domain.

The farming of shrimp can be divided into two stages. The first stage involves pond and farm preparation and the second nurturing activities. Digging soil for farm construction is considered the most physically challenging task, one that is exclusively done by men. Due to the hard work involved, prior to the introduction of the Kobe excavator,[3] households used to hire labor and spread the work out for a few years before a farm was completed (see figure 8.2). Once the pond is dug, water and lime powder are used to wash out the acidity in the soil. The second phase begins when the pond is filled with water and ready to welcome the shrimp fries. At this stage, the intensity of fries per square meter of water surface will set the stage for the production activities that follow. Extensive ponds often cast five fries per square meter of water surface, whereas intensive ponds have twenty to twenty-five fries per square meter. From this point, activities to nurture the shrimp become particularly labor intensive. Like newborn babies, shrimp fries require around-the-clock supervision during the ten days while acclimating to the new water environment. Because the likelihood of disease outbreaks is very high and can be overwhelming, farmers have to be alert to transitional phases in the growth process and sensitive to the changing needs of the shrimp as they grow older.[4]

Adoption of shrimp farming is not just an addition to household livelihood activities; it introduced a dramatic change in the production system. The rearrangement of responsibilities between men and women to adapt to the requirements of a new production system is based on traditional gender roles. The male/female dichotomy found in shrimp aquaculture reflects the gendered spaces embedded in Confucianism under which men represent the public sphere and women the inner sanctum of the household (Ho Tai 2001). Men are seen as more capable of handling risks, such as high investments and disease outbreak. They are entitled to greater mobility, develop larger social networks, and enjoy better access to information and services. Despite rhetoric about modernization and gender equality, many sexist prejudices against women continue to reign strong in Vietnamese society. In the past, women were considered "symbols of risks" and "causes of failures" and were blamed for losses in trading or exam failures (Nguyen 2006, p. 135). In the studied villages, the

Figure 8.2. A Sumitomo excavator reaches Ap Cho village in Hiep Thanh commune by boat. Photo by the author

notion of women as carriers of "bad luck," particularly among industrial farmers, creates a boundary that excludes women from shrimp ponds and farms. A less discussed issue is the fear of people having sexual intercourse near the shrimp ponds. Such beliefs—of women's menstrual and bodily subsistence as impure—were explained by Mary Douglas (1975). Fear inscribed in beliefs about menstrual pollution reflects structural dimensions of social order and serves the function of separating male and female social spheres. As a result, women in my research restrict their own mobility so as not to inflict themselves on sacred spaces and to protect themselves from blame. This also explains the small number of women engaging directly in industrial shrimp farming compared to men. For example, in the Long Thanh Industrial Zone, women managed only two of eighty farms. In the village of My Quy, men controlled all the twelve shrimp farms operating in 2007.

Greater priority given to shrimp aquaculture for its potentially higher economic value has also resulted in the shift of resources away from women's subsistence activities. Beyond the household, the spread of technology in shrimp farming has generated more employment opportunities for men while causing employment in the agricultural sector to dwindle. Men take up new employment opportunities such as the handling and repairing of motor engines used to pump water and Kobe machines used to dig ponds, remove earth, and clear groves. Fewer opportunities are available to women in shrimp farming. Typically, women are hired by households to sort shrimp at harvest time. Sorting shrimp pays reasonably well because this is a time when farm owners have good reasons to be generous. Sorting shrimp pays 50,000 VND (US$2.85) a day compared to 30,000 VND (US$1.71) for other agricultural work. In addition, farm owners often give workers a bonus of a kilogram of shrimp to take home. However, this rare opportunity only comes a few times in a whole year. While successful harvests are few and far between, those who are lucky with their shrimp investment usually reserve such jobs for their relatives, neighbors, and acquaintances. Women are also hired to sort and clean shrimp in processing factories. However, this job pays a modest wage. Depending on the worker's experience, she can earn a monthly wage of between 1 and 2 million VND (about US$60–100). Worse still, working in processing factories infested with toxic chemicals is known to have caused chronic illnesses among workers. As a result, few factory workers could survive such a working environment for more than five years. Those who have left the job have reported a decline in health due to long hours of working standing in the cold, with no health coverage provided.

While it may seem the adoption of shrimp aquaculture, a male-dominated production system, has reduced workload for women, ironically, it has not. In reality, women continue to help shrimp production in many ways. They provide logistical support such as cooking, cleaning, and preparing feed and herbal medicine for the shrimp. Here, the structural changes in the division of labor can find a connection with broader trends in the process of deagrarianization and the "housewifization" of the global economy. For example, Tinker and Summerfield (1999) and Bryceson (1999) observed that agriculture is increasingly feminized and undervalued as a result of the market economy and industrialized farming. Capitalism has also taken advantage of this housewifization process that treats women's reproductive labor as the cheapest production work, the exploitation of which is seen as necessary for the process of extended capital accumulation (Bennholdt-Thomsen and Mies 1999, pp. 33–34). In Tra Vinh, subsistence crops and rice cultivation that were once indispensable for households' food security suddenly became undervalued and undesirable, and they are being gradually eliminated. Farmers and policy-makers alike often cite the low value of rice and subsistence crops as a justification for persisting with risky shrimp farming. While women are taking on more work, the value of their reproductive labor, which has never been adequately recognized, has also been further reduced. The following analysis of allocation of work and responsibilities among households succeeding with different livelihood patterns since the shrimp boom demonstrates the dynamics in gender relations.

Gendered Division of Labor and Livelihoods

With commercial crops rapidly replacing subsistence farming over the past twenty years, livelihoods in coastal villages of Tra Vinh have undergone major transformations. Livelihoods in coastal areas of the province were traditionally diverse. Apart from rice cultivation, growing vegetables and keeping a few cows, goats, or pigs made up a household's livelihood. Wild fish were particularly important both for food and extra cash. This diversification has been rapidly displaced by the promotion of industrial shrimp farming and agricultural restructuring in formal policies since 2000. Most households now focus on at least one cash crop while subsistence sources shrink, as mangroves, waterways, and land have become private properties. I look at three livelihood trajectories, which represent contemporary patterns among households from different social strata: (1) households with their main income from shrimp aquaculture; (2) households that combine shrimp farming with agricultural production, with the latter being the main source of income; and (3) households that do not engage in shrimp farming.

Shrimp Households

By 2006, only a handful of households could maintain industrial shrimp farming as their main source of income.[5] Their successful shift to shrimp aquaculture indicates their ability to withstand the risks in this livelihood strategy. However, a large gap existed between those engaging in industrial shrimp farming in My Quy and the Long Thanh Industrial Zone and those doing extensive and semi-intensive shrimp farming in the village of Cay Da. In the village of My Quy, only 3 of the 164 households have successfully shifted to shrimp aquaculture. By and large, shrimp households in all the villages used to live on agriculture, but they also had a stable income from other sources. For example, a few households have family members holding government jobs, and others own a shop at the district market. These stable sources of income mean less worry about how to meet daily needs in between shrimp seasons.

Figure 8.3. A section of Sau's shrimp farm, located where the Bassac River meets the South China Sea. Photo by the author

In the village of Cay Da, however, where fishing has long been the main livelihood strategy and agricultural production is secondary, most households with land now engage in extensive shrimp farming. Only about 50 of the 500 households share the agricultural area of 34.19 hectares. Under the shrimp boom, this small area of agricultural land has come under attack. By 2006, landowners had turned 20 percent of the area to shrimp farming (see figure 8.3). Unlike other villages where industrial shrimp farming is the main model, few households in Cay Da have become rich because of shrimp aquaculture, but the extensive model provides them with a regular income throughout the year. Most of the households here continue to rely on wild catch or the harvest of fish in their ponds twice every month, according to the tides. This source of income has become the main buffer, supplying households with food and cash. Land continues to form the distinction between the rich and the poor. A couple of farmers in Cay Da have holdings of over 100 *công*, whereas the majority own about 2 *công* each.[6]

Although raising pigs, cows, or goats is more common among households as a buffer for shrimp farming, households with stable income sources such as shrimp traders can also invest in large-scale production and diversify into clam farming. Recently, clam farming in mudflat areas has emerged as a more desirable livelihood activity due to low investment and high returns. In 2006, with clam fetching 18,000 VND (US$1) per kilogram, it was estimated that profits from clam could be as high as 100 percent, a profit margin far greater compared with income from any other sources, including shrimp farming. Because clams require no feeding, investors only pay for the baby clams and hire guards to watch the mudflat area.

A third group of households that have been relatively successful in shrimp farming are a small number of owners of the industrial shrimp farms in the Long Thanh Industrial Zone. The zone was built in 2003 when canals were dug to supply water to eighty farms of approximately 20 công of land each. Of these eighty farms, forty-two belong to government employees, who rent the farm from the district and treat shrimp farming as an extra investment rather than the main source of livelihood. Because most of these investors are busy with their government jobs, they often hire labor to look after the farms. Actual owners pay frequent visits to monitor production. Nevertheless, these investors enjoy greater advantage over the remaining thirty-eight farms that belong to local farmers. Not only do they have a salary as a stable buffer, they also benefit substantially from an extended social network in the public sector that provides them with favorable information and credit access.

In both My Quy and Cay Da villages, women in shrimp farming households typically shift back to the domestic sphere while the men spend time on the farm. In some households, women leave men to look after the whole production process. However, in most households, women help out with some of the tasks. In Cay Da, women from households without agricultural land enjoy more free time during the shrimp season. In households with some agricultural land, women keep themselves busy with subsistence activities such as planting vegetables and keeping a few pigs, cows, and goats. Women's participation in extensive shrimp farming is quite common compared with the intensive model. This also means their work burden has increased due to the demand for their labor both at home and on the land.

Combined Shrimp and Agriculture Households

Most households that combine agriculture with shrimp aquaculture reside in the village of My Quy. These households were traditional farmers who had only adopted shrimp aquaculture since early 2000s, when the incentives to promote the farm economy model started to take effect. For these households, continuing to maintain both shrimp aquaculture and crops is an indication of failure rather than success because shrimp farming has created debts while continuing to burden household assets. Many households started out by shifting a portion of their agricultural land to shrimp farming. However, repeated crop failures forced them to shift back to agriculture. Some grow rice for domestic consumption, and most households grow watermelon for sale. Others grow vegetables and fruit on small plots for domestic consumption. By 2006, some households in this situation had sold their shrimp ponds, while a few were trying to hold on to the land that cannot be reverted to rice farming. Their reluctance to sell land is due to a decline in its value due to the failure in shrimp farming. The same land that sold for 15 million VND (US$850) per công in the immediate wake of the shrimp boom can barely fetch 6 million VND (US$333) now. Women in these households have experienced great pressure from agricultural production and domestic responsibilities because men's time is devoted to the shrimp ponds. They complain of heavier workloads while bearing the mental stress of losing household money on the plot of land that promises no certain return even though they only do it the "poor way."[7]

In the village of Cay Da, because most households have larger land-holdings, more households can rely on income from extensive shrimp farming. The lack of agricultural land has also prompted households to diversify in aquatic species such as fish, crab, and mussel. Income from wild catch remains an important source for sustenance for many households. In fact, collection of wild catch along with tidal waters twice a month provides households with income sufficient to cover daily basic needs. In addition, households also diversify into animal husbandry, and some grow vegetables for domestic use.

Households That Do Not Engage in Shrimp Farming

Households in the third group are those who have either given up shrimp farming or who are landless or land-poor. Some of these households have attempted to farm shrimp but failed and had to withdraw. For a few households, it was their engagement in shrimp aquaculture that led them to lose land and become indebted. The only choice that seems to be left for these households is to combine farming crops on small plots with working as day laborers, with the latter becoming the most important source of income. With meager and irregular incomes, these households are in constant search of on- and off-farm opportunities. This also means that households with members suffering chronic illnesses are most hard hit. In My Quy, landless households are not only poor because they have no assets or income to fall back on, but are constantly stressed by medical expenses for family members with chronic illnesses. The loss of land as the main productive asset makes life more difficult for both women and men. Women in these households have to gather small incomes from every source they can find, including growing vegetables, working as laborers in neighboring villages, and working in processing factories and other irregular jobs. Some women even have to take on hard-labor jobs on construction sites.

As demonstrated above, men's and women's relationships to productive resources are diverse and vary among households adopting different livelihood trajectories. While women in the first group tend to be driven away from household resources, women in households that can no longer persist with shrimp aquaculture actually spend more time on the land due to the increase in their presence in agricultural and subsistence production. This discussion also demonstrates how allocation of work and responsibilities by gender and livelihood strategies are interdependent; they fluctuate according to changing circumstances.

Risk-Aversion as a Coping Strategy

Intrahousehold decisions regarding resource use can be further understood by exploring how men and women react differently when household resources are at risk. In other words, gendered risk perceptions, shaped by their traditional social roles, influence resource use. Men's domination of the public sphere is often attributed to their ability to encounter and handle risks outside the household, whereas women's domestic sphere is viewed as more secure. Such perception of gendered risks is also translated into the economic domain, where male activities are more highly valued. That men's labor is considered more valuable than women's is not just because men are physically stronger, but their male identity provides them with the advantages in the public sphere that women are not entitled to.

Men's tendency to see risk as an opportunity versus women's instinct to safeguard household resources can find explanation in gendered social roles and spaces for husband and wife. Coastal communities of Tra Vinh often use *đăng* and *đó*, two essential components of a traditional fishing gear, as a symbol for the relation between husband and wife. The *đăng* comprises the main fish net that is long and wide, opening in a circle to let water flow through. The fish that pass through the net will reach the đó, which is attached to the bottom of the net. Once the fish are in the đó, there is no escape. Đăng performs the function of the man. It has to be wide open and broad to make way for wealth to flow in. The đó, on the other hand, has to be small, tight, and closed to hold the wealth and not let it escape. Đăng is related to đó just like a husband to his wife: They are close but not identical; they bear contrasting attributes but are not contradictory. Like đăng and đó, husband and wife perform complementary functions. The husband is expected to be generous, maintain extended social networks, and create opportunities for wealth generation. A wife is expected to preserve the fruits of the husband's labor. Her role is to guard the income wisely, to be thrifty and cautious. Thus, women and men represent two ends of the risk–safety spectrum. Men are usually the ones to initiate risky ventures that promise greater returns, whereas women usually demonstrate a conservative attitude toward risk-taking. A forty-seven-year-old woman farmer from Cay Da articulated the contrasting attributes of men and women as follows: "Women are petty-minded, thrifty, and careful. They collect small incomes. They are afraid of risk, and they are tending. Men, on the other hand, are proud, self-confident, sharp, fast, daring, and bold. However, when it is time to return bank loans, women often take money by themselves to the bank for fear that men would spend it on the way."

Even though the đăng and đó metaphor continues to be used to remind men and women of their appropriate places, intrahousehold gender relations in the Mekong Delta are not always restricted by these rules. In fact, there has been increasing acceptance of the swapping of gender roles along with greater market integration. Today, many women are said to carry the function of the đăng. For example, women are increasingly involved in the public sphere that once belonged to men through trading. Women dominate the banking sector as well. Many young women have also joined the labor force in processing factories, while others migrate to the city for work. But women who play the role of the đăng usually also assume the task of the đó, because men are easy spenders. They can be lavish when it comes to drinking and socializing with their friends. Therefore, leaving money with men is risky. It is probably the view of financial management as a feminine task that puts men who seize control of household money to shame through gossip among friends and acquaintances.

Nevertheless, like đăng and đó, the relationship between husband and wife is not an equal one in a patriarchal setting. One woman from Cay

Da said, "The đó is located within the đăng. If the man does all the hard work to make money, the woman has to safeguard it. A woman who does not know how to keep money is useless." However, even though women manage household income, this does not mean that they enjoy absolute freedom in decisions regarding the use of the money. Women can make decisions on small expenditures such as food and other essential items like detergent, household utensils, and clothing. Large investments such as purchasing a motorbike, buying production equipment, and building a house cannot be decided without men's approval. Although women increasingly have a greater share in household production decisions, in most cases, men have the final say. As one forty-seven-year-old woman put it, "Two types of agreement can be identified: consensual or forced. Most of the time, women are forced to agree [with men's decisions]. Men usually have the final word."

Unlike Africa, where women and men tend to manage their own land, farming activities, and income separately (Francis 2000), such division is not true of the Mekong Delta. Women's anxiety about the possibility of a decline in household resources has little to do with personal gain. They believe that a family's happiness depends on its economic security, which can only be achieved by cooperation between husband and wife. Households in which the husband and wife make plans and carry them out together and share decisions regarding use of household resources always fare better than those in which the husband and the wife disagree, quarrel, or fight frequently. Excessive drinking, gambling, and socializing by men can hurt the household's well-being. In my interviews, women expressed deep frustration over their husbands' drinking habit, because they know that without the man's support, a household can never be well-off, however hard a woman tries. Mekong Delta women's desire for a harmonious relationship with their husbands is not necessarily because they submit to the yin/yang model of unity and harmony, which has its roots in the Confucian doctrine that places collective well-being over individual desire (Tran Dinh Huou 1991). Rather, women consider "peace" between husband and wife to be *the* condition necessary to ensure a household's economic well-being.

Female Strategies

Some feminine qualities such as caring and nurturing have demonstrated a benefit in shrimp production activities. Even though they are excluded from the farm, women help out in different ways. They work inside the house, mobilize resources from their social network, and cut spending in order to save for the family. Women walk a tightrope to maintain a balance between risk and security. They often prevent men from engaging in behavior that threatens to drain household resources and well-being. In households that have adopted commercial shrimp farming, women play a critical role in the management and control of the enterprise to minimize risk and loss from unnecessary expenditures. Fear of loss of household resources and money prompts women to follow shrimp production activities closely while fulfilling other responsibilities. Explaining the difference in the quality of care provided by women and men, a woman banker and shrimp investor in Long Toan said:

> Even though men do much of the work in shrimp farming, it is very important that we [wives] engage in that process. By the end of the day, when the men are exhausted, women need to fill in. The night is also a time when the shrimp are most vulnerable because fluctuation in water is much greater. So after work I would go directly to the farm, walk around the farm, and check the *nhá* (small net) to see if the shrimp are eating. Because the health condition of the shrimp can deteriorate rapidly once affected by bacteria, regular water monitoring is critical so that timely action can be taken. So while the men provide the physical labor, women are usually the one to detect these vulnerable moments more effectively.

Women display great creativity in maneuvering within their constrained spaces. The shift of productive resources to shrimp aquaculture has narrowed their access to resources and threatened their livelihoods. It is in the aftermath of crop failures that women's skills in subsistence security are revealed. Rain or shine, small incomes from growing vegetable beds, keeping a few cows and goats, raising fish in the pond, and fishing in the canals have enabled women to supply food for their families. These subsistence sources also provide minor cash incomes to support children attending school. Women also guard household resources by preventing men from risky undertakings. A forty-seven-year-old woman farmer in Cay Da explained: "My husband said that I have no guts [I dare not take risks]. I agree. But I do not give in. I reason with him that, without my 'lack of guts' you won't be able to pursue your adventure. If you pour [money/wealth] from high above and there is nothing to hold it up from below, it will leak in the bottom and nothing will be left. Women have to be thrifty and careful about money."

In households that have shifted to shrimp aquaculture, women's absence on shrimp farms belies the vital contribution they actually do make. A comparison of gender roles in shrimp aquaculture clearly shows that women's contribution is indispensable. Women are responsible for much of the logistical support for on-farm activities. As men spend time to prepare ponds, monitor water and feed, and guard the shrimp, women ensure timely financing that is needed to supply the farm with feed and chemicals, the cost of which can be extremely high for industrial farms. Indeed, much of women's contribution to shrimp farming takes place behind the scenes. A woman farmer from Cay Da explained how the allocation of work between husband and wife following the shrimp boom is far from equal: "While men guard and feed the shrimp, women have to take over other tasks. Women look after the rice paddies, arrange for finance and feed, and sell the shrimp. If the men take three, four shares [of the work], women have to shoulder five or six shares. Every woman has to do that much work. No one is free to play. Therefore, if any woman said she has lost her rights, it is she who deprives herself of the rights. She underestimates herself."

Mekong Delta women's agency is also manifested in their control over the informal credit networks that supply much needed capital for production not met by formal credit sources. Women mobilize assistance from their kin, neighbors, and acquaintances to secure finance that is needed for supplying feed and chemicals during shrimp production. Women's credit networks have helped offset bottleneck situations that could have caused many households to fail. Whether it is to apply for a new loan or renew old ones, women traverse this male domain because their "patience and humility" enable them to be flexible in daunting situations where masculine pride prevents "men from bowing" and begging for assistance.

Another area dominated by women is the marketing of shrimp both at home and local markets. In Duyen Hai and Cau Ngang, of the dozens of local collecting stations only a couple are run by men. For most households in Cay Da that engage in extensive shrimp farming, shrimp is collected according to semimonthly tides and sold to village traders. These households do not collect a large sum of money at once, but the harvest of shrimp that spreads over the year provides households with more regular incomes. In contrast, owners of large farms usually hire tractors to transport shrimp to the market or processing factories in Tra Vinh town. Men help to transport and protect the shrimp packed in heavy iced boxes from the farm to the market. Women negotiate the price with traders, monitor the weighing of the shrimp, and collect the money. In the post-harvest phase, women also fulfill a very important part of the production cycle, which is to settle payments for inputs purchased on credit during the production phase, such as industrial shrimp feed and chemicals, and to repay loans.

Conclusion: Sustainability and Gender in the Shrimp Farms

The shrimp boom has created fundamental changes in the ways households organize their production, and thus the roles of men and women. Male labor is channeled to shrimp farming, while women have to take on more responsibilities in agricultural production and reproductive tasks. However, changing resource use and management is not only explained by gender, but class as well. Although the marginalization of women from the land that has been shifted to shrimp aquaculture may suggest their absence in shrimp farming as an environmentally destructive enterprise, cross-household livelihood analysis clearly demonstrates how men's and women's relationships with the environment depend on household production strategies. Just as not all men are fully devoted to industrial and unsustainable shrimp farming, not every woman is bound by subsistence activities. Women from households that engage exclusively in industrial shrimp farming clearly contribute more to environmentally destructive activities compared with both women and men from poorer households who have never or can no longer engage in shrimp aquaculture.

From a different angle, women can be said to be more sensitive to household resources and thus the environment as compared with men. Women's tendency to avoid risks and their long-term perspectives contain elements of sustainability, reflected in their long-term strategies. They prevent men from spending household resources on drinking, cut expenses to minimize debts, and invest in children's education. In some instances, women even take the initiative to revitalize mangroves to protect family land from erosion. While these efforts are clearly the opposite of environmentally destructive actions, they are not necessarily a result of women's greater awareness of the need to protect the environment. Rather, women's risk-aversion strategies should be understood as motivated by their concern for the household's economic security. Thus, there is a need to distinguish between sustainability as a by-product of a household economic goal versus a deliberate strategy and to ask whether these goals can be complementary.

Most importantly, men's and women's actions are both largely constrained by the broader socioeconomic development environment. In Vietnam, the export growth model that currently dominates economic development is causing the exploitation of natural resources at a rate faster than the ability of nature to replenish itself. Impressive growth figures from exports of agroforestry and aquaculture products have been achieved in parallel with rapid decline of the natural resource pool, especially common property resources that have been critical to sustainable livelihoods for the local population, particularly the poor. Men and women from landless and land-poor households, especially widows and single women, have not only lost jobs in the agricultural sector but also access to the commons crucial for subsistence. Thus, the expansion of risky shrimp enterprises has resulted in the loss of mangroves, land degradation, water pollution, and it has also increased indebtedness and social disintegration. It is within the context of increasing risk and vulnerability that men and women engage in activities that can be both environmentally friendly and environmentally destructive, in both predictable and unexpected ways, as they struggle to protect household resources and strengthen their ability to buffer shocks.

In this chapter, I have attempted to show the complementarity of eco-feminist and feminist political ecological approaches in understanding the women-environment question. In particular, given the reemergence of environmental questions and concerns about global warming and climate change, feminist political ecology approaches offer a critical path to understanding the environmental impacts of continued expansion of neoliberal economic principles. While some, such as Leach (2007), have expressed disappointment at the loss of momentum of the environmental movement following the debates between ecofeminists and feminist ecological environmentalists, the case study outlined here notes that these discussions are still sorely needed. The need to treat environmental degradation as a feminist issue remains urgent, as development projects and economic policies continue to undermine women's and households' well-being.

Notes

1. Three main shrimp farming models are practiced in Tra Vinh: extensive, semi-intensive, and industrial. The extensive model has been most common in former mangrove areas, whereas the intensive or industrial model has only been practiced for a decade now. Industrial shrimp farming is highly risky, but promises greater profit, whereas the semi-intensive model requires less investment and is less risky but also

results in smaller incomes. (The difference in investment between the extensive and intensive models on a hectare of land is approximately US$7,000.) For the extensive model, apart from the initial cost of digging ponds, shrimp farmers use natural fries with some home-prepared or industrial feed when the shrimp is about two months old. The extensive model requires cleaning the pond only once in the beginning. Industrial farms, however, require large expenditures every step along the way, from pond preparation to chemicals, industrial feed, and medicines for the dense population of shrimp. Following the rise of industrial shrimp aquaculture, farmers started using fries that are artificially produced and industrial feed, making expenditure on farm inputs significantly higher than in the extensive model.

2. In 1993, the introduction of the Land Law recognized private ownership of land, giving owners five rights: to buy, sell, exchange, mortgage, and inherit land.

3. Farmers often refer to an excavator as a "Kobe," after the Japanese company that manufactures them (even though the excavator in photo 8.2 was made by Sumitomo).

4. Depending on its growth, a shrimp sheds skin twice a month. During this time, the shrimp becomes very sensitive and should be tended carefully until its shell becomes harder.

5. At the time of my fieldwork, only three of seven households in My Quy could sustain industrial shrimp farming. In Cay Da, three households who had attempted to adopt the industrial model without success had to shift back to the extensive model. The Long Thanh Industrial Zone had eighty households pursuing industrial shrimp farming, but only one-fourth at most were successful in a good year. However, it is difficult to state the number of industrial farms in each village given the flexibility in the ways farmers cope. The farming model adopted for one season depends on the outcome of the previous season. Farmers who have failed have to cut costs on the investment for the next season. For example, farmers may decide not to hire the Kobe excavator for pond cleaning, which usually costs a significant amount.

6. One công is equivalent to 500 square feet.

7. The "poor way" refers to shrimp farming that cannot follow the strict protocol of industrial shrimp farming. For instance, the shrimp fries are cast in the pond without undergoing any special cleansing process.

References

Agarwal, Bina. 1991. *Engendering the environment debate: Lessons from the Indian subcontinent.* Center for Advanced Study of International Development Paper No. 8. East Lansing: Michigan State University.

Bennholdt-Thomsen, Veronika, and Maria Mies. 1999. *The subsistent perspective: Beyond the globalised economy.* London: Zed Books.

Biehl, Janet. 1991. *Finding our way: Rethinking ecofeminist politics.* Boston: South End Press.

Boserup, Ester. 1970. *Women's role in economic development.* New York: St. Martin's Press.

Bryceson, Deborah Fahey. 1999. African rural labour, income diversification and livelihood approaches: A long-term development perspective. *Review of African Political Economy* 80:171–189.

Burton, Michael L., and Douglas R. White. 1984. Sexual division of labour in agriculture. *American Anthropologist* 86(4):568–583.

Davidson, Joan. 1989. Restoring women's link with nature. *Earthwatch* vol. 37. London: International Planned Parenthood Federation.

Douglas, Mary. 1975. *Implicit meaning*. London: Routledge.

Francis, Elizabeth. 2000. *Making a living: Changing livelihoods in rural Africa*. New York: Routledge.

Gaard, Greta. 1994. *Ecofeminism: Women, animals, nature*. Philadelphia, Pa.: Temple University Press.

Ho Tai, Hue-Tam. 2001. Faces of remembrance and forgetting. In *The country of memory: Remaking the past in late socialist Vietnam*, ed. Hue-Tam Ho Tai, 167–195. Berkeley: University of California Press.

Jackson, Cecile. 1993. Doing what comes naturally? Women and environment in development. *World Development* 21(12):1947–1963.

Leach, Melissa. 2007. Earth mother myths and other ecofeminist fables: How a strategic notion rose and fell. *Development and Change* 38(1):67–85.

Mies, Maria, and Vandana Shiva. 1993. *Ecofeminism*. Halifax, Nova Scotia: Fernwood Press.

Nguyen, Quang Khai. 2006. *Phong tục tập quán của người Việt: Tập tục và kiêng kị* [*Traditions and customs of Vietnamese: Traditions and taboos*]. Hanoi: NXB Lao Động-Xã Hội.

Rosaldo, Michelle Zimbalist. 1974. Woman, culture, and society: A theoretical overview. In *Women, culture and society*, eds. M. Z. Rosaldo and L. Lamphere. Stanford, Calif.: Stanford University Press.

Shiva, Vandana. 1989. *Staying alive: Women, ecology and development*. London: Zed Books.

Tinker, Irene, and Gale Summerfield. 1999. *Women's rights to house and land: China, Laos, Vietnam*. Boulder, Colo.: Lynne Rienner Publishers.

Tran Dinh Huou. 1991. Traditional families in Viet Nam and the influence of Confucianism. In *Sociological studies on the Vietnamese family*, ed. R. Liljestrom and Tuong Lai. Hanoi: Social Science Publishing House.

CHAPTER NINE

The Role of Gender in the Reduction of Fishing Effort in the Coastal Philippines

James F. Eder

A principal aim of coastal resource management (CRM) projects and related conservationist interventions is to reduce pressure on fish stocks by curtailing destructive fishing practices and establishing marine protected areas to allow fish stocks to recover. In the Philippines, the record of such projects has been mixed. One recent study of the nation's more than 400 marine protected areas concluded that only about 20–25 percent have successfully achieved their objectives (Pollnac et al. 2001, p. 694).

One important reason for project failure has been the lack of alternative income-generating activities for fishermen whose fishing incomes suffer due to CRM project measures and who are consequently reluctant to cooperate with project implementers and their goals. Repeatedly, CRM project managers and outside observers have concluded that CRM efforts require proportionately greater attention to livelihood issues than they have received in the past. Reflecting on the CRM project he studied in Saint Lucia, Yves Renard (2005, p. 175) observed that "dominant approaches in coastal resource management, in the Caribbean as in many other parts of the developing world, are concerned primarily with resource conservation, resource use control and conflict management. One of the lessons of this project is that local institutional arrangements need to give far greater attention to economic aspects, with a focus on poverty reduction and equity issues."

In the Philippines, the ambitious, US Agency for International Development–funded Coastal Resource Management Project (CRMP), which had one of its six learning sites at the same locale in which I conducted my own research, reached a similar conclusion. According to its completion report, among the major lessons learned from the project's experience was that CRM programs needed to directly address poverty issues: "The argument that CRM will in the long term provide greater economic benefits to resource users than current unsustainable practices is lame against the backdrop of hand-to-mouth poverty. Marginal fishermen who are asked to stop destructive fishing must be assured of livelihood assistance that will allow them to 'survive' low yields and income for as long as it takes fishery stocks and habitats to recover their productivity" (CRMP 2004, p. 111).

Indeed, one of the most effective measures to relieve pressure on fish stocks and better manage coastal resources may be to devote more effort and resources to developing new income sources and alternative livelihoods for coastal residents (White et al. 2005). Many CRM projects do feature an "alternative livelihood" component, but this component is often of a limited or showcase nature. At least in the Philippines, the particular economic activities proposed are wage work and intended primarily for women. The reasoning is understandable. Women in Philippine fishing communities badly need income-earning opportunities, and whatever CRM projects may offer women in this regard is intended to offset the income lost to men due to depletion of fish stocks or conservation-inspired restrictions on fishing activities. In practice, however, at least in my own observations, the additional household income afforded by alternative livelihood programs does not significantly reduce male fishing effort.

This chapter considers what form alternative livelihood programs for fishermen might more successfully take by examining the key role of women in getting new household enterprises started, in particular, enterprises that have the potential to mobilize and redirect the labor of male household members away from the fishery and into more sustainable economic activities. In brief, I argue that to better relieve fishing pressure in the Philippine coastal zone, CRM projects, microfinance programs, and other efforts to promote "alternative livelihoods" for fishermen should nurture such household enterprises rather than promote supplementary employment in the form of wage work to fishermen or to other individual members of those households. Such efforts can profitably build on the characteristic intrahousehold dynamics of Philippine fishing households, in particular, the frequent occupational multiplicity of those households and the key role of women in setting household economic agendas. In seeking insights from the new household livelihoods that women in some fishing households have developed on their own, I emphasize the importance of viewing fishing and possible alternative livelihoods for fishermen

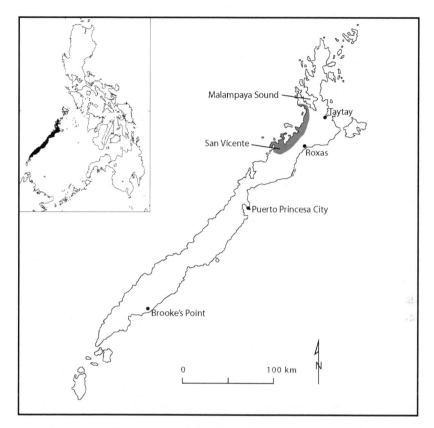

Figure 9.1. Map of Palawan Island, the Philippines. Map from Eder (2009)

in the wider context of Philippine coastal economies and ecosystems, where fishing is often found side by side with farming, fishermen and farmers regularly interact, and many individuals pursue both activities. At the same time and without intending to diminish the considerable role of women in the local fishing economy, my concern in this chapter is not with that role but, instead and more broadly, with the role of gender in a wider coastal economy.

The ethnographic setting for the chapter is San Vicente, a municipality of ten fishing and farming communities inhabited by about 20,000 people of mostly migrant origin. San Vicente is on the northwestern coast of Palawan Island, a major twentieth-century settler destination in the Philippines and still an important land frontier (see figure 9.1). Over the last thirty to forty years, San Vicente has suffered serious depletion of its fish stocks and other coastal resources due to settlement by migrant fisher-men from the Visayan Islands and elsewhere in the Philippines. Palawan still has some of the richest fishing grounds in the country, but migrants from longer and more densely inhabited regions of the nation have set in motion the same local cycles of coastal resource degradation that played out in earlier generations in their places of origin. Numerous government and NGO projects and programs are currently attempting to deal with the livelihood and resource management problems that have ensued.

Methods

I conducted fieldwork in San Vicente from January to April 2002 and subsequently made four follow-up visits, the most recent in 2008. During my first round of fieldwork, I primarily employed participant observation and informal interviewing. I began with courtesy calls on local municipal officials and get-acquainted visits to all ten communities, but as my field-work progressed I singled out four of them, each representing a particular aspect of San Vicente life, for more intensive study. For two of these latter communities, one where fishing predominated and the other where farm-ing predominated, I designed a short household survey and employed a local female research assistant to help me collect the survey data from a sample of households in each community purposively selected, with the assistance of community leaders, to represent occupational and socioeco-nomic variability. The survey included questions about the ages, educa-tional attainments, geographical origins, and occupations of household members and about ownership of farmland, fishing boats and equipment, and other productive assets. We eventually completed about eighty such surveys, representing 10–20 percent of the households in each community (see Eder 2009, pp. 22–30).

During the series of subsequent, follow-up visits, and following prelimi-nary analysis of my household-survey and other data, I gradually focused on several topics for more intensive study, including the role of gender in household decision-making about resource use, the topic explored here. As I began to learn about cases of household enterprise formation, both successful and unsuccessful, I further investigated each. Depending on happenstance and the arrangement that seemed most appropriate to each individual case, I sometimes interviewed the male and female coheads together and sometimes separately. At times I only interviewed one of the coheads or even relied on information from a close relative or friend. My interviewing on this topic remained largely informal, but I did seek answers to the same set of questions in each case, including the history of the enterprise, how the enterprise was capitalized, the respective roles of the two household coheads (both at the outset and at present), and how the growth of the enterprise had affected household livelihood reliance upon fishing.

As I sought details about successive cases, I began to look for similarities and differences between them, which in turn suggested further avenues of inquiry. At times, my inquiries led outward, as when I sought out the administrators of the several microfinance programs operating in San Vicente from which some women had borrowed money to start their enterprises, or when I visited with the managers of an ambitious CRM project in the municipality that included a modest "alternative livelihood" component for women. Throughout, I kept in mind that my own gender position inevitably influenced my access to data of all kinds, and particularly to the participant-observation and unstructured-interview data that I most valued. In this regard I was aided by my fluency in Tagalog, my prior field experience in the Palawan, and the considerable autonomy and forthrightness of rural Philippine women, all of which allowed me to discuss quite personal matters with them more freely than I might have otherwise.

Approaching Coastal Livelihoods

Livelihood studies have contributed much to our understanding of how individuals and households go about generating income. Several different livelihood frameworks are in use, but they agree on a need to understand assets and liabilities, strategies to deploy or exploit assets, and access or barriers to resources (Turner 2007, p. 390). Explicit attention to the fluidity and complexity of contemporary rural economic life has also helped to show the degree to which rural livelihoods generally are delocalized and increasingly divorced from farming and from the land (Rigg 2006). Instead, and not only in "farming" communities but also (as I will argue here) in "fishing" communities, livelihoods are constantly being reworked, as people adjust to changing local and global economic circumstances (Bouahom et al. 2004). Numerous local processes of livelihood diversification have taken form as rural households construct diverse portfolios of economic activities and social support capabilities in order to survive and hopefully to prosper (Ellis 1998).

Helpful for framing my analysis of coastal livelihoods is the sustainable livelihood approach, presently employed in South Africa and in various West African countries to align fisheries policy with wider poverty reduction efforts in the coastal zone. The approach combines a conceptual framework with a set of operational principles to guide integrated coastal management away from a bureaucratic, conservation-focused approach to a people-centered "sustainable development" approach (Allison and Horemans 2006; Glavovic 2006; Glavovic and Boonzaier 2007). The basic elements of sustainable livelihood approach thinking include: (1) putting people's economic and social activities at the center of the analysis; (2) building on strengths, by emphasizing the resources, capabilities, and potential of poor people, rather than being preoccupied with barriers to or constraints on development; and (3) making micro-macro links that encourage explicit attention to mediating institutions, social relations, and government actions that link local livelihood-related issues to meso-level processes and wider concerns (Allison and Horemans 2006, p. 758; Glavovic and Boonzaier 2007, p. 4).

While my own thinking about coastal Philippine livelihoods falls generally within this people-centered and poverty-focused framework, two weaknesses of the sustainable livelihood approach are particularly relevant to my argument here. First, as an essentially managerial and structural approach, it gives insufficient attention to the crucial role of power and power relations in shaping rural livelihoods by determining how, for example, credit sources and marketing channels are accessed. Second, the approach's focus on "households" does not explicitly engage important livelihood differences between women and men or the role of gender in intrahousehold economic decision-making (Ellis 1998, pp. 23–25; Bennett 2005, p. 452; Allison and Horemans 2006, p. 764). The first of these shortcomings was the subject of my previous work (Eder 2008); the second—the approach's lack of attention to intrahousehold dynamics—is my focus here.

Gender and the Intrahousehold Dynamics of Coastal Philippine Livelihoods

Although a superficial look suggests a certain sameness to coastal Philippine communities—everywhere one goes, it seems, people are engaged in various combinations of fishing and farming—fishing and farming are broad and diverse categories. Fishermen and farmers vary in their ownership of land, fishing boats and gear, and other productive equipment. They also vary in their ethnic backgrounds. In the Palawan region, Cuyonon and Aguytanen (two important ethnolinguistic groups) tend to be agriculturally oriented, whereas Cebuanos, Boholanos, and other Visayans (peoples originating from the Visayan Island region of the central Philippines) tend to be fishing-oriented. Some fishermen deploy fishing nets from motorized boats; others fish by hook-and-line from small outrigger canoes. Similarly, some farmers grow irrigated rice on the coastal plain; others plant corn, root crops, and fruit trees on hillsides. Further, fishermen do not simply employ different gear nor do farmers simply plant different crops, for within each of these broad categories people use coastal resources and mobilize household labor in different ways.

That coastal zone livelihoods are diverse is a truism, but less well appreciated is that much livelihood diversity plays out within individual households. Most coastal households depend on multiple sources of income, whether their primary occupation is fishing or farming. Households in the coastal zone are accustomed to exploiting different economic activities simultaneously and in ways that involve a complex interdependence of the labor of the male and female coheads. While occupational multiplicity in coastal zone households is oft-reported (e.g., Nowak 2008; Porter et al. 2008), whether occupational multiplicity in rural communities generally is economically and socially healthy or is instead indicative of poverty and household vulnerability varies between and within locales depending on the motivation behind household economic diversification and the likely outcome of the process (Ellis 1998; Bouahom et al. 2004).

Writing of the development options for the coastal zones of Southeast Asia, Connor Bailey and Caroline Pomeroy (1996, p. 196) saw considerable virtue in the characteristic livelihood diversity of some coastal communities: "Fishing communities in Southeast Asia are dependent upon a complex coastal ecosystem, not simply any one component. Fishers and members of their families occupy multiple niches and utilize a diversity of resources. This occupational multiplicity provides coastal communities with a significant degree of economic and social stability."

In Palawan, Bailey and Pomeroy's view that household economies in the coastal zone are "based on a wide range of income sources that are widely distributed both temporally and spatially" and are "dependent not on a single resource but on a whole ecosystem" (1996, p. 195) does not apply equally to all households. Some households—particularly those of recent migrants—are entirely dependent on fishing and hence on a single diminishing resource. Nonetheless, Bailey and Pomeroy's emphasis is consistent with my own findings that occupational diversity is a socially and economically healthy phenomenon that takes advantage of the natural diversity found in tropical coastal zones.

In coastal Palawan households, for example, fishing and farming are often interdependent (Eder 2003). In those Cuyonon and Agutaynen households that primarily farm for a living, an adult male, often the male household head, may operate a small, nonmotorized outrigger and fish several nights a week with a hook and line, with the catch intended primarily for household consumption and secondarily for sale to neighbors. In many net-fishing-oriented Visayan households, fishing is seasonally alternated with farming. The southwest monsoon brings large waves and periodic storms to Palawan's west coast between June and December, and on many days fishermen are unable to venture out. While some fishing households continue to fish all year and settle for reduced income during the southwest monsoon, many others seek alternate employment in the agricultural economy. Some such "part-time farmers" own farms of their own, on which they plant and harvest one crop of rice each year on fields seasonally inundated by southwest monsoon rains. Others lack agricultural land and instead help harvest, on a share basis, in the fields of fulltime farmers.

Those coastal households that primarily fish and those that primarily farm also interact economically in various ways. One such interaction revolves around beach seining and hog raising: The numerous smaller fish caught by beach seiners are dried and sold to farmers, who grind them into fish meal and feed this to pigs. (Hogs are also raised, of course, in many fishing households, whether or not any household members engage in beach seining.) Beach seining poses a dilemma for coastal resource managers in part for this very reason. The activity is environmentally destructive because of the by-catch of juvenile fish and the damage to sea grass beds it entails. For these reasons it is nominally illegal, but beach seining enjoys considerable local tolerance because even those who do not engage in it may themselves benefit from its presence.

Fishing is also systemically linked with noncoastal livelihood activities, both in space and over time. Many "migrant fishermen" I encountered had not fished for a living in their places of origin but had instead farmed or done something else entirely. Such cases remind us that fishing households are not only tied to wider commodity systems through the marketing of their catch, but that fishing itself, as a livelihood option, is always located on a wider field of other livelihood options. Just as not all fisherfolk used to fish for a living, not all remain fishermen, as fishing no less than farming is also left in favor of other occupations, both within the lifetime of individuals and—importantly—across generations. The earlier-noted processes of livelihood diversification in contemporary rural communities are one important seedbed of such occupational movement over time. Economic activities that were once supplementary to farming or fishing in some households become primary, and men and women who were once "farmers" or "fishers" become something else altogether, as they travel what de Haan and Zoomers (2005, pp. 43–45) envisioned as "livelihood trajectories," the outcome of individual strategizing decisions embedded in historical repertoires and in social differentiation.

What is the role of women in coastal zone economic diversity and in household livelihood trajectories? The prominent role of women in daily economic and social life in Southeast Asia has been much commented on, and the observation that gender roles are relatively egalitarian is a frequent touchstone in the ethnographic literature on the region (Li 1998, p. 679). Certainly as regards the Philippines, a long and distinguished tradition of empirical research attests to the prominent role of women in the household economy, both by direct involvement in income-earning activities and as managers of household economic resources (e.g., Szanton 1972; Ello and Polo 1990; Castillo 1991; Rutten 1993; Israel-Sobritchea 1994; Ello 1995; Jefremovas 2000). More is at stake here, furthermore, than control over the family "purse strings"; egalitarianism in domestic relations and democratic consultation between spouses on matters of labor allocation and expenditure are frequent themes in the literature on Philippine households and gender relations (Chant and McIlwaine 1995, p. 7). Addressing household headship in the Philippines in particular, Ello (1995, p. 245) argued that "authority in the home, the Civil Law of the Philippines notwithstanding, is not solely vested in the husband-father; rather, it is one which he shares with his wife. Data on decision-making within the home, contribution of the woman to the 'care and organization of the household,' as well as the local communities' recognition that the woman has the power to revoke her husband's commitments, all suggest that the concept of a singular, male household head is indeed an illusion which is perpetuated only in law and in other formal institutions."

In addition to women's substantial role in household economic decision-making, married women are extensively involved in independent income-earning activities, both to "help the household" (the most commonly cited reason, visible in such frequently heard comments as "households today cannot get by on just one income") and so that they are less dependent on their husbands for their economic and social standing. Because households remain the basic units of production and consumption in the rural Philippines, the income-earning activities of married women must thus somehow be reconciled with those of their husbands if the household itself is to function as it should. Local understandings of this process center on a culturally emphasized need for a household's coheads to discuss and agree to a common household *plano* (plan) that effectively reconciles their separate economic activities by deciding such matters as which income will go to consumption, which will go to investment, what kind of investment will be chosen, and so on. In coastal Philippine communities, women play a crucial and often a lead role in developing and implementing these plans—and hence in reorienting the economic activities of the household in new and potentially more remunerative directions (Eder 2006).

Whereas the income-earning activities of men in coastal Philippine communities mostly involve fishing (sometimes in combination with farming, as I discussed previously), women may pursue a wide variety of income-earning activities in addition to their housekeeping and childrearing responsibilities. Although fish capture, with the exception of beach seining, is a male activity, as elsewhere in Southeast Asia women have considerable local knowledge about coastal resources generally and are extensively involved in preparing fish for market and in other aspects of the fisheries supply chain (see Choo et al. 2008). Of greater relevance to this chapter, however, are the numerous other income-earning activities that coastal women may pursue. Although women with supplementary economic activities often deprecatingly minimize their importance and refer to them as their "sidelines," the income they contribute to household budgets is often substantial. In addition to beach seining and drying and marketing fish, the sidelines of women in coastal Philippine communities I studied include farming; storekeeping and other buy-and-sell activities; making and selling roof thatch, prepared meals, or snacks; providing daycare for preschool children; and serving as a pastor or Avon cosmetics dealer.

These economic activities of women differ importantly, however, in their implications for male fishing effort, as the following seven examples illustrate. The case studies all concern married women who work outside the home, in some of the many ways that wives in the coastal Philippines contribute to household income. Some of these ways may cause their fishermen husbands to reorient their own productive labor, whereas others will not. An important element in all of these cases, however, is the consensual basis of the new livelihood activities and the associated willingness of a household's coheads to negotiate and redefine gender roles.

Case Studies

Shirley and Rachel are two of the many women in coastal Philippine communities who work for daily wages in small marine products enterprises. Shirley dries fish on a piecework basis for a local marine products company (see figure 9.2). She is paid by the number of trays of drying fish she can set out on the company's beachfront drying racks in the course of a day. Rachel works in a small bottled-sardine factory established as one of several alternative livelihood initiatives under the CRMP in San Vicente. The factory employs ten to fifteen local women on an irregular basis, depending on the availability of a sufficient supply of sardines to make factory operation profitable.

The remaining women are self-employed. Alma operates a small store, and Winnie works as an Avon cosmetics representative. These are both one-person operations that are not likely to employ other household members. Most interesting for my purposes here are the efforts of three women, Sylvia, Amelita, and Flor, who are self-employed in activities that had or have the potential to grow and to employ the labor of their husbands as well.

Sylvia operates a small restaurant that she opened after borrowing money from a microfinance program to buy pots, pans, and plates. She had observed that due to its importance as a local center for marketing fresh and dried fish for residents of other fishing communities, her community attracted many visitors during the course of the day. Most arrived and left by boat. Those who lacked relatives there had nowhere to eat lunch except at several dining stalls in the small public market in a town a kilometer away. Sylvia saw a business opportunity here. At least some of the growing number of people who visited her community each day needed to buy lunch, and they would save the additional gasoline expense of traveling to the marketplace by eating at her restaurant. When I last visited, Sylvia's Canteen was thriving. There were still slow days, but recently business had been so good that she had hired a second kitchen worker. Her main concern was the high cost of the fresh pork and beef she needed to buy at the town market each day to prepare the food she offered her customers. Sylvia's latest plan was to convince her husband, Tirso, who had spent his entire adult life as a fisherman, to stop fishing and to instead raise pigs, so that she would have her own close-at-hand source of pork for her restaurant. "He's still thinking about it," she laughed, when I asked what she thought Tirso would do. But if it did happen, this is one example of the kind of enterprise that would reduce fishing effort and therefore contribute to coastal sustainability in the longer term.

Amelita once supplemented her husband Ramon's fishing income by buying and selling clothes at a time when none were sold locally. She took orders from neighbors for various clothing items, and when she had enough orders to justify a trip, she traveled by bus to a neighboring

Figure 9.2. A woman drying fish for sale. Photo by the author

municipality and bought the items there, marking up the price upon her return to recover her expenses and turn a profit. Eventually, however, their community grew large enough that someone opened a dry goods store, and Amelita could no longer attract customers to her buy-and-sell enterprise. About the same time, Ramon's fishing catch entered a prolonged period of decline, and their household began to suffer economically. Accordingly, Amelita took up hog raising. After several years her enterprise grew, but her very success made them increasingly concerned about costs of the needed feed. Discouraged about the profitability of fishing and with Amelita's encouragement, Ramon began to cultivate sweet potato and manioc on a part-time basis to help feed their pigs. When I last saw him, he had given up fishing altogether in favor of fulltime farming.

Flor and Benjamin today operate a successful household candy-making enterprise. Another life-long fisherman discouraged by the profitability of fishing—on some nights, he said, he could not even recover the cost of the gasoline for his boat engine—Benjamin attended a short vocational course on candy-making sponsored by the provincial government. Meanwhile Flor, who had previously dried fish for a marine products company, secured a microfinance loan to purchase the needed equipment, and their candy-making enterprise was born. Today, Flor handles candy deliveries and sales to a network of small local stores, and three times a week Benjamin makes the candy at home. He still fishes once or twice a week, but their candy business, which now employs an older child as well, makes the larger contribution to household income and has the added benefit of making it easier for Flor and Benjamin to share the care of their youngest child. I subsequently learned of a similar candy-making business in another part of Palawan where the wife made the candy and the husband handled deliveries.

These and other such cases suggest that economic diversification through household enterprise development, while not a panacea, may have a more beneficial effect on coastal economies and resources than the provision of alternative livelihoods that offer employment to individual members of households but do not change a household's primary subsistence strategy. Household enterprise development may be particularly beneficial to coastal communities such as those in San Vicente, where fishing is largely the domain of men and most newly proposed livelihood activities are for women. Periodic employment in one of San Vicente's two sardine factories may be important to some local women, but such work does not constitute an alternative livelihood so much as it does a supplementary one. To the degree that the husbands of these factory-working women continue to fish as before, such supplementary employment does little to relieve exploitation pressures on coastal resources. In contrast, where the supplementary economic activities of women become genuine household enterprises harnessing women's labor, technical skills, and economic planning abilities in ways that employ men and relieve exploitative pressures on fish stocks, coastal livelihoods may become more sustainable.

Gender and Sustainable Development Interventions in Coastal Communities

If the path to reducing the fishing effort of men runs, in part, through the economic activities of women, how might this finding be useful to CRM policy-makers and project implementers? Not all fishing households can raise hogs or open a restaurant. Programs to reduce fishing effort must work at a macro level to promote alternative economic activities that could work for large numbers of households. This is difficult terrain. The reality of many coastal areas in the Philippines is that alternative economic activities sufficiently remunerative to reduce pressure on coastal resources are hard to come by (see White et al. 2005, pp. 275–291).

The case studies considered here nevertheless suggest several ways that sustainable development interventions intended to relieve pressure on coastal fisheries might be better designed. First, some of the fisheries and aquaculture development assistance that has traditionally been targeted at men might usefully be redirected toward women, in the interest of fostering more progressive (and more sustainable) household and family enterprises (Choo et al. 2008, p. 178). This suggestion is consistent with Rigg's (2006, pp. 196–197) more general call for a "reskilling" of rural farmers (rather than further investment in smallholder agriculture) as the best means of promoting pro-poor growth and building productive and sustainable rural economies in areas where livelihoods are increasingly delocalized and de-linked from agricultural resources. The same argument, I believe, applies to fishing: People's efforts to reduce or to leave it on their own terms—and particularly women's efforts—need better support.

Second, although it is widely known that lack of credit is a significant constraint on livelihood diversification and household enterprise development (Ellis 1998, p. 26), microfinance programs are needed that are less aligned with the goals of the state and the political rationality of neoliberalism and more aligned with the goals and needs of individual women if the development of household enterprises is to be better fostered (Elmhirst and Resurreccion 2008, p. 17). Much has been written about the short-comings of microfinance programs in the Philippines and elsewhere, but in brief, women who participate in these programs hoping to develop economically viable household enterprises need larger loan amounts, longer payback times, and more flexible payback terms than most such programs currently allow (Milgram 2001; Milgram 2005). At present, the typical requirement that repayment installments begin within several weeks following a microfinance loan means that such loans most readily benefit women with existing small businesses, because they already have some regular income with which to make their payments.

Again, because not everyone can raise pigs or open a restaurant, women need assistance not just for production but to develop new or expanded markets. They may also need childcare, skills training, and other kinds of support to help ensure that they can actually do the work for which they borrow funds (Lynn Milgram, personal communication). If the providers of microfinance loans are unable or unwilling to provide such broader assistance, then (as Benjamin and Flor's candy-making business suggests) this is an appropriate partnership role for government agencies and NGOS.

In view of the emphasis I place in this chapter on gender roles and relationships, I should add here that to argue for greater attention in microfinance programs to what women want and need should not be taken to imply that what men want and need is not also important, if such programs are to better foster development of household enterprises that draw in male members. I have in mind here the oft-made observation that "fishing" in coastal communities is not just an economic activity but an entire way of life. Despite its hardships, fishing may bring considerable affective satisfactions to those who pursue it, and, perhaps particularly for men, it may be bound up with a person's sense of identity and self-worth. Although I did not specifically study the matter, my impression is that fishing men and women vary widely in their cultural and psychological preparedness to leave the fishing way of life behind, should other economic opportunities arise. Advantages of greater emphasis on household enterprise development hence include the element of self-selection involved and the fact that in the beginning, such enterprises are necessarily supplemental to fishing (and indeed, may remain that way), giving men a chance to reduce fishing effort gradually on their own terms. Comments I heard from men such as "I don't fish as often as before, but I'm still a fisherman at heart" and "I'm not a fisherman anymore but I still go fishing at times for the fun of it" help capture the personal tone of these new emerging lifeways.

To be sure, the record of efforts to promote rural nonfarming (and non-fishing) livelihood and enterprise development is mixed. Some have called it a "bargain basement sector" and are dubious of its long-term potential (see Ellis 1998, p. 26). Others believe that with appropriate outside support, household and other small enterprises have much to contribute to rural economic growth (e.g., Rice 2004, pp. 61–63). From the perspective that the emphasis on gender in neoliberal development programs is only a ploy to "marketize" women (Bennett 2005, p. 453), household enterprises have the considerable virtue of enabling women to resist unreliable or poorly remunerated wage work and instead to generate income in or near their homes and—in the absence of a redefinition of household gender roles—to more easily multitask.

Of course, to better capitalize on the entrepreneurial skills of women and set new household enterprises in motion in ways that draw in male members and reduce fishing effort, numerous extrahousehold conditions also need attention, including the goodness of fit of the new economic activities with available resources, credit and marketing channels, and the wider political economy (Eder 2008). From a livelihood perspective, changing the economic environment of fishing-dependent communities along the lines suggested here could dramatically affect the ability of women to actively support economic and social transformations that can alter the lives of both women and men (Bennett 2005, p. 453).

My observations that the household-level entrepreneurial activities of women may eventually redirect the labor of male household members in more sustainable directions also relate to broader scholarly concerns about gender, livelihood, and resource use. First and returning to what Rigg (2006, p. 189) aptly characterized as the "progressive disembodying of rural livelihoods from rural spaces," several of the household enterprises I observed entailed a considerable amount of mobility, much of it by women (see Elmhirst and Resurreccion 2008, p. 17). While mobility outside of local communities is most visibly associated with urban wage work, seasonal migration strategies, and the like, a more local movement of women within and between local communities or nearby urban centers (whether or not related to specific livelihood activities) may be part of the answer to the question of where women *get* their ideas for household enterprises or other entrepreneurial activities.

This was not a topic I specifically studied, and women's ideas in these realms likely come from a variety of extrahousehold sources, including kin, neighbors, and friends; work groups; and memberships in cooperatives, microfinance organizations, and church groups. But I believe that how women come to know about the opportunities that are present and develop ideas for new ones is significantly influenced by what they see and hear as they go about their own increasingly mobile lives, in settings where men—due to their farming- or fishing-based livelihoods—may be relative homebodies. That men and women may engage differently with migration and with multilocal livelihoods points to the fact that an appreciation of gender is essential to an adequate understanding of the complex and changing relationships between rural people and natural resources (Elmhirst 2008, p. 56).

A second area of broad scholarly concern to which my observations relate is what Elmhirst and Resurreccion (2008, p. 17) termed the reluctance of conservation and development organizations to address the "messy politics" of gender equality in their efforts to incorporate women into their projects. For my purposes here, I have called attention to how the economic efforts of some entrepreneurial women may lead them to call upon the labor of their husbands. But women, including women in rural communities, are scarcely a homogenous group with undifferentiated interests (Elmhirst and Resurreccion 2008, p. 17), and entrepreneurial women needing or able to employ others may also call upon the labor of other women. These women may be neighbors or close relatives, but that does not mean that they will be well treated or well paid. While again not a topic I specifically studied, the strategizing economic activities of women that give rise to incipient household enterprises unfold within, and may in turn precipitate, local processes of social differentiation, suggesting that the study of such enterprises might provide a valuable window on how class and gender intersect at the micro level in rural communities today.

Concluding Remarks

Examining the role of gender in the fisheries sector in West Africa, Bennett (2005, p. 452) observed that the "failure of policy makers and resource managers to fully engage with the issue of gender in the sector has resulted in a large resource (namely, the relationship between men and women) being underused and undervalued." Following this line of reasoning here has led me to look favorably on rural household enterprises (or at least certain kinds of them) and to agree with Brian Crawford (2002, pp. 17–18) that greater efforts should be made to "harness the considerable economic skills and energies of women to put households to work." In valorizing household-based employment over wage employment, however, I am acutely aware that large numbers of rural Southeast Asians, including many women, have reached the opposite conclusion and left behind what they perceive to be drudgery and unproductive household-based employment in favor of wage jobs, often quite beyond local communities and rural economies. While I do not believe that this observation vitiates my core argument here, that successful female-led household enterprises may reduce male fishing effort and help place fishing on a more sustainable basis, it does suggest that we need to understand how best to contextualize the prospects for and appeal of such enterprises, given the present economic, social, and cultural realities of coastal communities, within and beyond the Philippines.

Acknowledgments

Research in Palawan from January to April 2002 was supported by a Fulbright research award and a sabbatical leave from Arizona State University. I am grateful to the Council for the International Exchange of Scholars, the Philippine American Educational Foundation, and to Arizona State University for this assistance. During June 2003, additional comparative research in Palawan was made possible by an A. T. Steele Travel Grant from Arizona State University's Center for Asian Studies, for which I am similarly grateful. For their assistance during fieldwork, I thank Meng Amihan, Regino Balafiño, Jovita Borres, Boy Magallanes, and Lilibeth Uapal. I also thank Lynn Milgram for her helpful suggestions concerning an earlier version of the manuscript.

References

Allison, Edward H., and Benoit Horemans. 2006. Putting the principles of the sustainable livelihoods approach into fisheries development policies and practice. *Marine Policy* 30:757–766.

Bailey, Conner, and Caroline Pomeroy. 1996. Resource dependency and development options in coastal Southeast Asia. *Society and Natural Resources* 9:191–199.

Bennett, Elizabeth. 2005. Gender, fisheries, and development. *Marine Policy* 29:451–459.

Bouahom, Bounthong, Linkham Douangsavanh, and Jonathan Rigg. 2004. Building sustainable livelihoods in Laos: Untangling farm from non-farm, progress from distress. *Geoforum* 35:607–619.

Castillo, Gelia T. 1991. Family and household: The microworld of the Filipino. In *SA 21: Selected Readings*, ed. Department of Sociology-Anthropology, 244–250. Quezon City, Philippines: Office of Research and Publications, Ateneo de Manila University.

Chant, Sylvia, and Cathy McIlwaine. 1995. *Women of a lesser cost: Female labour, foreign exchange, and Philippine development.* Quezon City, Philippines: Ateneo de Manila University Press.

Choo, Poh Sze, Barbara S. Nowak, Kyoko Kusakabe, and Meryl J. Williams. 2008. Gender and fisheries. *Development* 51:176–179.

Coastal Resource Management Project (CRMP). 2004. *Completion report: The Coastal Resource Management Project, Philippines, 1996–2004.* Cebu City, Philippines: Coastal Resource Management Project of the Department of Environment and Natural Resources.

Crawford, Brian. 2002. *Seaweed farming: An alternative livelihood for small-scale fishers?* Working Paper, Coastal Resources Center. Providence: University of Rhode Island.

de Haan, Leo, and Annelies Zoomers. 2005. Exploring the frontiers of livelihoods research. *Development and Change* 36:27–47.

Eder, James F. 2003. Of fishers and farmers: Ethnicity and resource use in coastal Palawan. *Philippine Quarterly of Culture and Society* 31:207–225.

Eder, James F. 2006. Gender and household economic planning in the rural Philippines. *Journal of Southeast Asian Studies* 37:397–413.

Eder, James F. 2008. Alternative livelihoods for the Philippine coastal zone: Lessons from Palawan. Paper presented at the Eighth International Conference on Philippine Studies (ICOPHIL 08), Quezon City, Philippines, 23–26 July.

Eder, James F. 2009. *Migrants to the coasts: Resource management, livelihood, and global change in the rural Philippines.* Belmont, Calif.: Wadsworth Cengage Learning.

Ellis, Frank. 1998. Household strategies and rural livelihood diversification. *Journal of Development Studies* 35:1–38.

Ello, Jeanne Frances I. 1995. Who heads the household? Women in households in the Philippines. In *The Filipino woman in focus: A book of readings*, ed. Amaryllis T. Torres, 235–254. Quezon City, Philippines: University of the Philippines Press.

Ello, Jeanne Frances I., and Jaime B. Polo. 1990. *Fishers, traders, farmers, wives: The life stories of ten women in a fishing village.* Quezon City, Philippines: Institute of Philippine Culture, Ateneo de Manila University.

Elmhirst, Rebecca. 2008. Multi-local livelihoods, natural resource management and gender in upland Indonesia. In *Gender and natural resource management: Livelihoods, mobility and interventions*, eds. Bernadette P. Resurreccion and Rebecca Elmhirst, 55–69. London: Earthscan.

Elmhirst, Rebecca, and Bernadette P. Resurreccion. 2008. Gender, environment and natural resource management. In *Gender and natural resource management: Livelihoods, mobility and interventions*, eds. Bernadette P. Resurreccion and Rebecca Elmhirst, 10–23. London: Earthscan.

Glavovic, Bruce C. 2006. The evolution of coastal management in South Africa: Why blood is thicker than water. *Ocean and Coastal Management* 49:889–904.

Glavovic, Bruce C., and Saskia Boonzaier. 2007. Confronting coastal poverty: Building sustainable coastal livelihoods in South Africa. *Ocean and Coastal Management* 50:1–23.

Israel-Sobritchea, Carolyn. 1994. Gender roles and economic change in a fishing community in Central Visayas. In *Fishers of the Visayas*, eds. Iwao Ushijima and Cynthia Neri Zayas, 279–303. Visayas Maritime Anthropological Studies I, 1991–1993. Quezon City, Philippines: College of Social Sciences and Philosophy, University of the Philippines.

Jefremovas, Villia. 2000. Women are good with money: The impact of cash cropping on class relations and gender ideology in northern Luzon, the Philippines. In *Women farmers and commercial ventures: Increasing food security in developing countries*, ed. Anita Spring, 131–150. Boulder, Colo.: Lynne Rienner.

Li, Tania Murray. 1998. Working separately but eating together: Personhood, property, and power in conjugal relations. *American Ethnologist* 25:675–694.

Milgram, B. Lynne. 2001. Operationalizing microfinance: Women and craftwork in Ifugao, upland Philippines. *Human Organization* 60:212–224.

Milgram, B. Lynne. 2005. From margin to mainstream: Microfinance, women's work and social change in the Philippines. *Urban Anthropology and Studies of Cultural Systems and World Economic Development* 34:45–84.

Nowak, Barbara S. 2008. Environmental degradation and its gendered impact on coastal livelihood options among Btsisi' households of Peninsular Malaysia. *Development* 51:186–192.

Pollnac, Richard B., Brian R. Crawford, and Maharlina L. G. Gorospe. 2001. Discovering factors that influence the success of community-based marine protected areas in the Visayas, Philippines. *Ocean and Coastal Management* 44:683–710.

Porter, Marilyn, Rosemarie Mwaipopo, Richard Fastine, and Max Mzuma. 2008. Globalization and women in coastal communities in Tanzania. *Development* 51:193–198.

Renard, Yves. 2005. The sea is our garden: Coastal resource management and local governance in the Caribbean. In *Reducing poverty and sustaining the environment: The politics of local engagement*, eds. Stephen Bass, Hannah Reid, David Satterthwaite, and Paul Steele, 152–179. London: Earthscan.

Rice, Robert. 2004. The contribution of household and small manufacturing establishments to the rural economy. In *The Indonesian rural economy: Mobility, work and enterprise*, ed. Thomas R. Leinback, 61–100. Singapore: Institute of Southeast Asian Studies.

Rigg, Jonathan. 2006. Land, farming, livelihoods, and poverty: Rethinking the links in the rural South. *World Development* 34:180–202.

Rutten, Rosanne. 1993. *Artisans and entrepreneurs in the rural Philippines*. Quezon City, Philippines: New Day Publishers.

Szanton, Maria Cristina Blanc. 1972. *A right to survive: Subsistence marketing in a lowland Philippine town*. University Park: Pennsylvania State University Press.

Turner, Sarah. 2007. Trading old textiles: The selective diversification of highland livelihoods in northern Vietnam. *Human Organization* 66:389–404.

White, A. T., P. Christie, H. D'Agnes, K Lowry, and N. Milne. 2005. Designing ICM projects for sustainability: Lessons from the Philippines and Indonesia. *Ocean and Coastal Management* 48:271–296.

CHAPTER TEN

Contested Livelihoods

Gender, Fisheries, and Resistance
in Northwestern Mexico

María Luz Cruz-Torres

In October 2004, fishermen and women shrimp traders from southern Sinaloa coastal communities organized a protest to demand the end of a moratorium imposed on shrimp harvesting and consumption (Zapién 2004). The Health Department in Mazatlán had implemented the moratorium as a quick response to hundreds of people who had become ill or "intoxicated" after consuming wild shrimp caught in one of the most important lagoon systems in the region. The protestors pressed for local health authorities to conduct studies to determine the exact causes of the intoxication so they could take specific measures to stop the spreading of the illness, rather than a blanket ban on all shrimp. Another concern of the protestors was that as a result of the moratorium people had stopped consuming shrimp, thus negatively impacting those households whose livelihoods depended on fishing and marketing of this product.

The most powerful motivation for the fishermen and traders to protest together in collective action was to secure their livelihoods. As one of the shrimp traders in the protest despaired, "We are dying of hunger, no one has approached or brought us rice or beans. It's clear that the government is not going to take care of our children" (Paredes 2004, p. 16B). Those protesting felt that the government was not responding to their demands in a timely manner, but instead continued to threaten their livelihoods. Because of their collective action to press government authorities to conduct more studies, the local health department discovered that a bacterium (*Vibrio parahaemolyticus*) in the lagoon caused the illness. As expected, the government banned people from fishing or selling shrimp from this lagoon, thus having tremendous repercussions for the local economy.

Despite the negative outcome, women shrimp traders still regard their participation in the protests and marches as one of the most rewarding experiences in their lives. As one trader, Catalina, once told me, "I did not know that I was capable of protesting and marching in front of the Health Department. It was a good experience because we all shared the same concerns and because local authorities paid attention to us." Although this was Catalina's first experience with collective action, it is not necessarily true for many other people in southern Sinaloa. Indeed, struggles and conflicts over gaining access to and control over natural resources as well as their resulting collective political activism and grassroots social movements have permeated the history of this region (Rubio Ruelas and Hirata Galindo 1985; Ortega Noriega 1993; Padilla 1993; Verdugo Quintero 1997; García Ramírez and Gutiérrez 2004). Studies on the sources and outcomes of these social and political conflicts reveal that they have often revolved around the sustainability of resources, communities, and people whose livelihoods are linked to such resources (see McGoodwin 1987; Lobato González 1988). However, much of this analysis has lacked a gender dimension and thus has failed to show how and why these struggles and conflicts are gendered.

In this chapter I examine how gender interacts with local norms regarding natural resource use and state policies that dictate the allocation of such resources. My goal is to unravel how conflicts over access unfold and how people gain agency in the process of claiming access rights. I focus on the *camaroneras* (women shrimp traders) of southern Sinaloa to illustrate the way in which some of these conflicts are gendered and have given rise to local collective action, which has in turn been defined by gender.

I first give a brief and general overview of the main theoretical approaches that guide my research, followed by the methodology and an overview of the communities where this study was conducted. Second, I provide a portrait of women's work as shrimp traders in the context of their past and current struggles. Finally, I discuss the implications of women's resistance for the long-term sustainability of their livelihoods, communities, and fishing resources.

Feminist Political Ecology and Grassroots Social Movements: A Theoretical Framework

This study is framed within a feminist political ecology approach that merges the fields of political ecology, feminist anthropology, and social movement theory. I use this approach to better understand the gender dimensions of natural resource use and the grassroots social movements that emerge while contesting state and local policies and social norms. This approach also allows us to address issues such as women's exclusion from access to and participation in the management process of natural resources. According to Velázquez (2003), the examination of the factors that shape the access to the use and control of natural resources can shed light into the many dimensions of the relationships between men and women with their natural environment. This in turn can lead to a much better understanding of the ways in which people create their own paths to sustainability. Moreover, because political ecology is concerned with issues of power and agency in the access to natural resources, it is an appropriate approach for understanding women's struggles for inclusion within the Mexican shrimp industry.

Many anthropologists have addressed the relationship between people and natural resources in Third World countries from a political ecology perspective (e.g., Sheridan 1988; Edelman 1995; Stonich 1995; Dodds 1998; Gezon 1999; Escobar and Paulson 2004; Walsh 2004). Feminist scholars in particular have examined social and cultural differences in resource access and allocation by incorporating a gender perspective within their analysis of political ecology. For example, in her research conducted in rural Madagascar, Gezon (2002, p. 686) found gender differences in access to and control over land, as well as differences among women, in that those who are married or belong to extended family networks had the most access to land.

Rocheleau, Thomas-Slayter, and Wangari (1996, p. 4) noted that "feminist political ecology treats gender as a critical variable in shaping resource access and control, interacting with class, caste, race, culture, and ethnicity to shape processes of ecological change, the struggle of men and women to sustain ecologically viable livelihoods, and the prospects of any community for sustainable development." Such scholarship in feminist political ecology has documented the gendered dynamics of natural resource use and allocation (Gezon 2002); the role of gendered environmental practices in giving meanings to landscapes (Paulson 2003); methods for assessing gendered knowledge and empowerment (Fortmann 1996); the gender relations of production and survival strategies (Rocheleau, Ross, and Morrobel 1996); the relationships among gender, social capital, and natural resource management (Shields et al. 1996); and the formation of women grassroots environmental movements (Brú-Bistuer 1996; Campbell and the Women's Group of Xapuri 1996; Miller et al. 1996; Wastl-Walter 1996).

This chapter builds on this work by analyzing how gender interacts with class and culture to affect the struggles and experiences of rural women in gaining access to the use of fishing resources in northwestern Mexico. Such intersectionality, although complex, is an imperative dynamic to integrate here because it provides a more accurate portrayal of the issues at stake regarding the various dimensions of sustainability. I describe how women with very limited economic capital and political power undertook collective action and organized a grassroots social movement in order to gain access to and inclusion in shrimp fisheries; such a totally women-organized movement in Mexico has not been studied before with any depth.

Many feminist scholars have focused their research on the role of gender in the rise and fall of collective action and social movements in Latin America (Safa 1990; Schild 1994; Bennett 1995; Stephen 1997; Adams 2002; Simonian 2006; McCallum 2007). Their studies highlight some key points: Gender rather than class is often the basis for collective action; social networks play an important role in the evolution of the movements; women resist and accommodate their identities to dominant gender ideologies; women activists often abandon activism after their movement ends; identity politics are tied to local notions of race and class; neighborhood organizations voice women's struggles and identities; class and gender determine how women choose to protest; women engage in collective action when their livelihoods are endangered; and women's political action should be contextualized within local and global processes. Campbell and the Women's Group of Xapuri (1996), for example, showed that despite the fact that Brazilian women play an active role in the management of extractive reserves, their participation in the rubber tappers social movement has not been fully acknowledged nor recognized. These findings have special relevance to my study: Mexican women have been marginalized, as neither their social movement nor their participation within the fishing industry has been acknowledged or documented to date.

Mexican feminist scholars have addressed the relationship between gender and natural resources, although not from the perspective of political ecology or social movement theory. However, their findings are relevant to this chapter inasmuch as they reiterate that gendered environmental practices shape women's access to natural resources and that women often face barriers in gaining access to those resources (see Toscano 2001; Soares Moraes 2003; Castañeda Camey and Flores Medrano 2004; Vázquez-García and Montes-Estrada 2006). The work of Vázquez-García and Montes-Estrada (2006) in two fishing communities in the state of Veracruz provided a starting point from which to begin analyzing the complex dynamic of the relationship between gender and natural resource allocation and utilization in Mexican coastal communities. They noted that "the lack of attention to gender issues in fishery management has resulted in policy interventions that fail to promote sustainable livelihoods for women, their families, and communities" (Vázquez-García and Montes-Estrada 2006, p. 3, citing Bennett 2004). Similarly, my previous research conducted along Mexico's northwest coast also showed that women play an active role in fishing communities, most notably in the shrimp fisheries, which is often ignored (Cruz-Torres 2001; Cruz-Torres 2004a; Cruz-Torres 2004b). According to Neis (2005), this lack of attention to women in fisheries is because most policies and programs are not gender-neutral but rather gender-blind. In this regard, this chapter highlights the need to include gender when enacting programs and policies designed to ensure the sustainability of fishing resources, given that the livelihoods of the people whose survival is solely tied to their access to these resources is also at stake.

Methods and Research Sites

This study was conducted in the southern region of the Sinaloa state in northwestern Mexico (see figure 10.1). Between 2004 and 2010, I conducted anthropological ethnographic fieldwork in eight coastal communities. The information in this chapter comes from oral interviews, participant observation, and archival research. I first conducted preliminary research in the summer of 2004 through a socioeconomic survey designed to gather basic demographic and household information for shrimp traders in Mazatlán. Simultaneously, I conducted participant observation among this group. I interviewed thirty active and twenty retired shrimp traders, and I relied on family and economic networks among shrimp traders for contacting and interviewing retired shrimp traders. I also interviewed alumni of the Autonomous University of Sinaloa at Mazatlán who played a crucial role in the shrimp traders movement, and local authorities and representatives of workers organizations. I conducted archival research at the Archivo Histórico in Mazatlán in order to reconstruct the history of the shrimp traders movements, their struggles, and their portrayal in the local media.

The communities where I conducted my research differ in size, number of inhabitants, and degree of urbanization. Mazatlán, for instance, is the largest city and the most important port in southern Sinaloa. Tourism, fishing, and agriculture constitute the three most important industries in

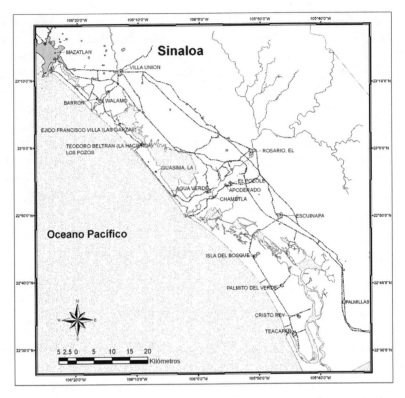

Figure 10.1. Map of southern Sinaloa, Mexico. Map by Israel Castro Leal

the region. Outside of Mazatlán, however, the great majority of the households I studied obtained their livelihoods from fishing and agriculture. Traditionally, fishing and agriculture were both considered male occupations, but this is rapidly changing as more women are also procuring a livelihood this way. The high incidence of female-headed households in the region is another reason why women seek work outside their homes. Globalization and neoliberalism can also be partially blamed for these changes, because they have contributed to an increase in the reliance on agriculture- and fishing-based export commodities. An increasing demand for the production of export commodities has also led to an increasing demand for a steady supply of laborers, especially in the agricultural sector. Processing plants now built in many rural communities hire women to work as packers in the production line or during the planting and harvesting of mangoes and chili peppers (Cruz-Torres 2004a).

In coastal communities, women also perform various roles in the fishing industry. Although some fish in the lagoons and estuaries around their communities, most are involved in the downstream marketing and processing of shrimp. Very frequently shrimp marketing is done informally, with women selling shrimp within their own communities or traveling to marketplaces in nearby towns. Rural women often network with urban women to learn valuable information about local and international shrimp prices, the yield of a given fishing season, and good places to sell their product. Particularly relevant for the present study is the fact that women have historically played an important role as shrimp traders in this region.

The Women Shrimp Traders of Southern Sinaloa

Overall, research on women traders has usually highlighted the role of trading in the informal sector of the economy. Fish trading in Third World coastal communities is considered both a microenterprise and a form of self-employment that affords women mobility and the opportunity to create multiple roles for themselves (Hall-Arber 1988; Overa 1993; Volkman 1994; Hapke 2001). For example, studies in Ghana found that women fish traders, known locally as "fish mammies," perform a variety of roles, including wholesaler, market trader, large-scale processor, and creditor (Overa 1993; Hapke 2001). Research has also shown that women's trading activities are crucial to household survival in coastal areas and that fish trading provides the only income for many households (Hapke 2001). Research on Latin American women fish traders, although scarcer, has generally confirmed that women in coastal communities market fish to help support their households (Pereira 2002). My previous research in northwestern Mexico has supported these accounts (Cruz-Torres 2001; Cruz-Torres 2004a).

Shrimp trading provides women in southern Sinaloa with a steady income. However, their work as shrimp traders has most often been permeated by political, social, and economic conflicts. Perhaps the largest obstacle women struggled to overcome was to gain legal rights to the marketing of shrimp. Traditionally the rights to exploit and market shrimp were allocated to fishing cooperatives. Women were not encouraged or allowed to join cooperatives because traditional gender norms dictated that women should not fish. Many men also found they could not join a cooperative, and thus became "free" fishermen. Their work, thus, was considered illegal because they did not belong to a fishing cooperative.

Figure 10.2. A shrimp trader at work. Photo by the author

Men who caught or sold shrimp illegally were punished with physical violence, fines, confiscation of their fishing gear, and incarceration. A resistance strategy based on a new pattern in the gender division of labor emerged within households in which men would go out fishing while women would sell the shrimp. Because Mexican social norms discourage maltreatment of women by men in the public sphere, women saw this as an opportunity to pursue a livelihood as shrimp traders. However, because the shrimp they sold was caught by *pescadores libres*, their work was also considered illegal.

Although there are no data showing how many women became shrimp traders in southern Sinaloa, there seems to be a consensus that the number of women increased during the mid-1980s as the direct result of the Mexican economic crisis and the austerity measures implemented by the Mexican government. Women's work as shrimp traders can be divided into three stages: In the first stage (from the late 1970s to the early 1980s), they began the incursion into the activity; in the second stage (around the mid-1980s), they took over a single street in Mazatlán for selling their shrimp (see figure 10.2); and in the third stage (from the late 1980s to early 1990s), they organized into a union.

Procuring a Livelihood:
Making a Living in the Informal Economy

Very little information is available about women's work as shrimp traders during the first stage, but Doña Lucrecia, a seventy-two-year-old shrimp trader, recalls that she and other women started selling shrimp in their rural communities, mostly from their houses, for economic reasons. Many women, like Doña Lucrecia, were single mothers with a pressing need to support their children and without any other available economic opportunities. She and other women knew free fishermen who were willing to sell them shrimp on credit. Soon, very tight social and economic networks emerged between the women and the free fishermen, enabling both to secure a day-to-day livelihood in the midst of turmoil and local and regional struggles over the legal rights to shrimp. Cemented by reciprocity and mutual trust, these networks gave rise to solidarity, which in time transformed into collective action. Because the livelihoods of both were linked, they protected and supported each other against the fishing cooperatives, local authorities, and state policies.

In time, as more women became shrimp traders in their rural communities, selling shrimp became more competitive and more dangerous because fishing cooperatives hired officers from the Mexican Army or Marines to guard the shrimp. The local police arrested, jailed, and often physically beat many free fishermen and shrimp traders. For instance, in October 1985 the local police in the town of Escuinapa arrested and assaulted a woman traveling by bus who was carrying a shrimp bucket. This "humble woman," according to the outraged press, "with a baby in her arms was brutally beaten" (Denuncian arbitrariedades 1985).

Other women, fearing for their lives and livelihoods, decided that it was time for them to expand their activities to other places, where they could be safer and where they could find new clients. They began traveling to Mazatlán on a daily basis, where there was already a great demand for wild shrimp. Going to Mazatlán became a very time-consuming and labor-intensive endeavor, because it required traveling by bus every day. It took women from two to three hours to get to Mazatlán, which meant they had to leave their homes between 5:00 or 6:00 a.m. Once in Mazatlán, they often tried to sell their shrimp in the local market, but other vendors pushed them away. Women then became street peddlers selling their shrimp door to door and walking long distances every day. "We walked all over Mazatlán," recalls Doña Lucrecia, "with a shrimp bucket on the head and one in hand. We went to the *colonias*. We walked for so many hours until our feet hurt so badly."

Many women agreed that this was very hard work, much harder than selling within their own communities. Long working hours combined with cold winters and very hot and humid summers, the uncertainty of not knowing if they were going to be able to sell the shrimp, and the long journeys back and forth from their communities every day were very difficult to bear. Moreover, the move to Mazatlán did not free them from the harassment of local authorities and fishing cooperatives. On the contrary, they were continuously bothered and persecuted. Many times their shrimp was confiscated and taken away, leaving them without money to even buy a bus ticket to go back home. They worked in total seclusion while trying to evade the authorities.

Because of all these constraints, many women quit. Those who stayed did so because they had no other options, as many were single mothers and sole breadwinners. These women quickly found creative ways to resist local authorities and state policies that mistreated, punished, and criminalized them. Many did so by confronting the local authorities, demanding to be left alone and to be allowed to work. Others, when caught selling shrimp by the cooperatives or fishery officials, threw it away or poured gasoline over it to prevent others from eating or selling it. Once in Mazatlán, women expanded their social networks to include fishermen, restaurant owners, and street and market vendors who advised them when the authorities were nearby, giving them time to hide the shrimp.

Eventually, the women who stayed working in Mazatlán developed relationships with other shrimp traders from rural communities who supplied them with wild estuarine shrimp. Encouraged by a new-found solidarity, both groups of women united against the local authorities and fishing cooperatives. These women faced the additional challenge of finding creative ways of evading local authorities and using innovative tactics while transporting their shrimp to Mazatlán. One way was by wearing a long, loose dress to hide the shrimp bucket underneath. Another way was to hire a private bus to transport the shrimp to Mazatlán at night. This bus ride, which came to be known as La Corrida, required that the driver knew how to evade the surveillance system implemented by the government and fishing cooperatives along southern Sinaloa's main highways. Women were also helped by market vendors who allowed them to sell shrimp near their market spaces.

Over time, the Mazatlán women got tired of walking along the hidden colonias and organized themselves to take over a permanent place on the street. In this way, women took over one of the busiest streets in Mazatlán, set up shop, and stepped into the public sphere. As they became more visible, their work also became more scrutinized, making them more susceptible to harassment and persecution by municipal authorities, the Mazatlán middle class, and fishing officials.

Out in the Street:
Engendering Public Space in Mazatlán

When one looks at travel brochures or web pages highlighting the tourist attractions of Mazatlán, one finds information about ecotourism, gift shops, restaurants, nightlife, and hotels. One also finds out that women shrimp traders are included among these "attractions." Working people all over Mazatlán as well as nearby towns and rural communities are aware of their contribution to the fishing sector and the local economy. Yet, for local fishing authorities and the government, they are nearly invisible. When I started my research, I found a complete lack of statistical or written information about them. In reviewing some fifty years of local newspapers at the Mazatlán Historical Archives, I found the newspapers focused on the work of women shrimp traders only when they were caught by officers of the National Fisheries Commission selling shrimp during the off-season, an act punishable by a fine, jail time, or both. The newspapers usually portrayed these women as criminals, as if they were the ones doing the actual poaching, without explaining that they actually bought the shrimp from suppliers. Only one male journalist, writing in 1984, defended them publicly from the way local authorities treated and labeled them as a "social problem." His argument highlighted the importance of women's work as shrimp traders, and praised them for making wild shrimp available to Mazaltecos, who no longer needed to leave the city to find fresh shrimp. He also stressed the many obstacles women faced to bring the shrimp to Mazatlán (Al rojo vivo 1984).

However, this journalist was the exception. For the most part, newspapers sided with local authorities and fishing cooperatives to keep women out of the streets. Susie Porter (2003), a historian writing about the use of public space during the Porfirian era in Mexico City, noted how class and gender influenced the use of public space in Mexico City. Women street vendors in Mexico City were marginalized and banned from working on the streets because of their class and their gender. Ironically, many years later, during the late 1980s, women in southern Sinaloa experienced similar circumstances after they took over one of the city's streets. However, unlike the women in Mexico City, who were marginalized based on notions of femininity such as sexual morality and honor created by the middle and upper classes, Sinaloan women were marginalized in terms of the nature of their work, which was considered illegal by the state and local authorities. Women became rivals of the state because they defied and resisted its policies regulating the allocation of shrimp resources and the use of public space in Mazatlán. Local authorities and fishing cooperatives tried very hard to ban them from selling shrimp in the street by demeaning their work and questioning its legality. One way authorities used to determine whether the shrimp women sold was caught by a member of a fishing cooperative was by asking women to present an invoice (*factura*) showing who the vendor was. In most instances women were unable to provide an invoice because either they bought the shrimp from free fishermen or from cooperative fishermen who sold it to them without notifying their cooperatives. Their work as street vendors was also considered illegal because they did not pay the daily fee required for the use of public space.

It is unclear why women decided to take over the Aquiles Serdán, one of the largest streets in Mazatlán, other than women wanted a permanent place to sell their shrimp instead of having to go from door to door. When I asked traders why this street was chosen, I was given several responses. One was that it is a very busy and centralized street, which makes it easier for them to attract more clients. Another response was that it is near the main market and that there are other businesses established along the street, which also makes it easier to attract clients. At first, only a few women set up a shop in the Aquiles Serdán. Soon others followed until forty women came by every day to sell their shrimp. Most of the women knew each other, and some were even family. Since all shared the same legal situation and the same economic needs, they developed a strong network based on *confianza* (mutual trust) and reciprocity. This helped them deal with the marginalization, harassment, and persecution they faced in the hands of the local authority.

For example, in 1985 the local police violently removed the camaroneras along with other street vendors from the Aquiles Serdán. This happened after the Mazatlán Chamber of Commerce complained to municipal authorities that the street vendors did not pay taxes and economically competed with local businesses (La policía desalojó 1985). Women returned to the street, but a year later local business owners met with the mayor of Mazatlán and asked him to remove them. Their argument was that the camaroneras portrayed a negative image of womanhood and brought poverty to the city's landscape. They also argued that shrimp traders were a health hazard because they lacked proper equipment to hygienically process, store, and market their shrimp. Finally, they also claimed that the camaroneras interfered with the aesthetics of the city because they made the street look dirty and ugly (Las Camaroneras 1986; Basura y aguas 1987).

Women responded vigorously in defense of their livelihoods. Consequently, they used various forms of resistance to empower and legitimate themselves as women, mothers, and workers. At times, they resisted local authorities by ignoring them and by returning to the street to continue with their daily work. Occasionally, they took collective action against the authorities, as in 1986, when a group of about one hundred women marched along the Aquiles Serdán demanding respect. While doing so, women relied on their gender and class to assert their roles and identities as workers and mothers. Women described their situation, saying that "We have the right to work and to earn a living. What can we do if we need to support our children? We need to eat" (No nos iremos 1987). The many times women applied for a legal permit to sell shrimp were unsuccessful; they were always denied because the shrimp they sold were caught illegally. They contested this policy by arguing that the fishermen who caught the shrimp illegally should be the ones punished, not them. As one woman pointed out, "They take the shrimp away from us, they chase us down the street, but the Fisheries Office allows others to shrimp illegally in the estuaries or to buy the shrimp at the docks without harassing them because it has already been arranged" (Las camaroneras 1986).

The situation for women shrimp traders became worse in 1987, when the Department of Social Action equated them with pornography by announcing that pornographic posters would be banned from the city's movie theatres, as the camaroneras would be banned from selling shrimp in the street (Siguen vendiendo camarón 1987). Women resisted by refusing to leave their street, asserting once again their identities as working mothers and workers. As Matilde Rojas, a shrimp trader, asserted when interviewed by a journalist, "For sure we are not going to allow the Fisheries Office or Social Action to take us away from the place where 100 families make their living; and it if wasn't for us, many people would not eat shrimp because we sell it cheaper than the market vendors" (Siguen vendiendo camarón 1987). But despite their resistance, and seeing that their situation was not improving, the camaroneras decided to take a different step and form a union. They hoped that this union would help them to gain greater political and economic power to continue facing local authorities, business people, and fishing cooperatives.

Women and Collective Action:
The Shrimp Traders Union of Mazatlán

One hot afternoon while I was conducting participant observation, Cristina, one of the shrimp traders and owner of a small seafood restaurant located across the women's shrimp market, asked me, "Who do you want to talk to? What do you want to know?" I watched her as she prepared an order of *camarones fritos* (fried shrimp) for a client that had just arrived. I told her that I wanted to learn more about how women organized their union. She did not hesitate and asked me to talk to Sofía, for it was she who had taken the first steps to organize the women.

Sofía and I talked about her early life in a small rural community in southern Sinaloa, her migration to the US–Mexican border region, and her work in a maquiladora where she gained experience as a labor organizer. After leaving the border, Sofía returned to Mazatlán and began to buy and sell shrimp on her own. At first, she supplied shrimp to the women already working on the Aquiles Serdán who were still struggling to become legitimate workers. Sofía soon began to develop social and economic ties with these women, who invited her to join them as a shrimp trader herself. A few months later, with help from university students, the camaroneras organized their own union. Because of her previous experience, Sofía became its official president and was instrumental in getting it notarized.

Once the union became legal, women hoped that their work and lives would be easier without the constant harassment and threats from local authorities and business people. The women were still harassed, but this time by the members of the Mazatlán fishing cooperatives, who saw them as economic rivals and tried, by all means necessary, to curtail their livelihoods. For example, in June 1989 the Regional Federation of Fishing Cooperatives handed a written petition to President Carlos Salinas de Gortari asking him to pressure local fishing authorities to "truly act against the shrimp traders who were selling wild ocean shrimp" (Federación Regional 1989).

Despite their unionization, local authorities still challenged their presence. The women were allowed to set up their open street market but were required to pay a daily fee of US$80 for space. When the fee increased to US$100, women refused to pay, arguing that the same local authorities responsible for collecting their fees still harassed them, even when they paid the same as other street vendors. At one point in 1989, officers of the Fisheries Department and local business owners tried to convince local authorities to resettle the women in another place. They believed that the camaroneras should work in an enclosed place instead of on the street. They also believed that the women's work continued to cause traffic jams and aesthetic and hygienic problems (Medrano 1989).

None of the attempts to resettle the camaroneras succeeded. Women fought back, and once again with students' support organized a sleepover on the street to protest how local authorities treated them. This action was successful and the camaroneras were left alone, but the municipal authorities and the Fisheries Office still wanted to be able to control them. The authorities did not recognize the legality of the women's union and planned new strategies for organizing them. Their plans coincided with the beginnings of the development of a shrimp aquaculture industry in the region; therefore, they conceived the idea of having the women sell only cultured shrimp because it could be tracked to determine its legality (Ramírez Osuna 1989). In that way, they believed that camaroneras would stop competing with the local fishing cooperatives for wild shrimp. A new union was formed with the support of the Institutional Revolutionary Party and local authorities.

According to Sofía, the Institutional Revolutionary Party slowly co-opted the women, who then began to withdraw from the old union and join the new one instead. The new union elected a new board and began to develop new rules designed to keep the street clean and to bring order and peace to the women's work (see figure 10.3). Shortly after, the street shrimp market was reorganized with the support of the local business community, who even provided the camaroneras with beach umbrellas to protect their products from the sun. The fishing cooperatives have also recognized the legality of their union and began to cement economic and social ties with the camaroneras by providing them with shrimp.

Today, women have a steady supply of fresh shrimp on a daily basis, without having to go to the estuaries or lagoons to get it themselves. They can also buy shrimp on credit. They have access to credit through local moneylenders or can organize their own rotating and savings credit associations in order to save money. In addition, they are able to rely on each other for financial help and support.

It has been many years since women first struggled to gain legal rights to sell shrimp. For shrimp traders, collective action led to their empowerment as women, mothers, and workers. They feel very proud of their achievements and the fact that they can still depend on their livelihoods to support themselves and their families. Local authorities and the middle class no longer consider them a "social problem." They are now a symbol

Figure 10.3. Carmen and Rosa, two founding members of the Mazatlán Shrimp Traders Union. Photo by the author

of pride and icons of the local Mazatlán culture. Now buses loaded with tourists stop by their market so they can be photographed side by side with the camaroneras. Their lives and work have recently even become a commodity within the production and consumption of popular culture. In 2008, a *telenovela* (Mexican soap opera) about them aired on the local television station. Finally the camaroneras have earned their own space and place within the society and economy of southern Sinaloa.

Concluding Remarks

The use of a feminist political ecology approach to explain how gender influences and shapes access to natural resources, as in the case discussed here, gives us an insight into how people with less power must struggle to have their voices heard. Rocheleau, Thomas-Slayter, and Wangari (1996, p. 15) argued that "the increased involvement of women in environmental struggles and in political and social movements derives from the difficulty they face in ensuring the survival of their families in the face of ecological and economic crises." This approach also gives us perspective regarding the manner in which women choose to deal with issues affecting their daily lives and well-being, such as environmental degradation and competition over scarcer resources.

The camaroneras understand that shrimp is a very fragile natural resource and that it could take just a few changes in the weather or in state policies for them to lose their livelihoods. They understand how the global economy works, as they have friends who work packing shrimp in Mazatlán processing plants destined for global markets. They also understand the difficult economic situation that their country is facing. They read about it daily in local newspapers, and they know that this is why many of their family members migrate to the United States in search of work. What they do not know is how much longer they will be able to sustain their current livelihoods. As Olivia told me, "Years ago we could make a living from shrimp trading, we could support our families. Not anymore. Now shrimp is becoming scarcer."

Women are well aware that their work as shrimp traders may not be a sustainable activity because it could contribute to the demise of wild stocks of shrimp. However, their main priority is to make a living from selling shrimp to support themselves and their families. Thus, for most women, the sustainability of the shrimp resources is closely tied to their abilities to make a living from it. Women think of their role in the marketing of shrimp as just another link in the overall production chain, making it harder for them to understand why they alone should be blamed for the illegal shrimp trade. As one woman explained, "The rope always breaks at the thinnest part," meaning that while they are harassed and their shrimp is confiscated, government authorities allow others to freely trade illegally caught shrimp (Las Camaroneras 1986).

As this case study demonstrates, tracing a path to sustainability in the southern Sinaloa region should be a top priority. However, sustainability should not solely focus on the protection and conservation of natural resources, but also on the social and human dimensions of their use and exploitation. This means that assuring the sustainability of the shrimp fisheries involves not only taking measures to protect the shrimp or its habitat, but taking steps to secure human sustainability as well to guarantee the livelihoods and well-being of those who depend on these resources for their basic survival. In this regard, a feminist political approach such as the one I outlined here can be useful not only in assessing the quality of the relationship between humans and the environment, but also in pointing out what is missing in this relationship. Gender has been one of those variables missing in natural resource management policies in Mexico for a long time.

One positive sign is that the Secretariat for the Environment and Natural Resources recently recognized that a gender analysis must be crucial in the path to sustainability by issuing a report entitled "Towards Gender Equity and Environmental Sustainability Program 2007–2012." Its main purpose is to mainstream and institutionalize a gender analysis in Mexico's public policies (SEMARNAT 2008). My research on the Sinaloan shrimp traders contributes to these goals by explaining the differential roles of women in coastal communities and in fisheries. It is my hope that a better understanding of the experiences of women shrimp traders can add a more human dimension to management policies currently guiding the sustainable development of shrimp fisheries in southern Sinaloa. These policies could greatly benefit from mainstreaming a gender analysis that includes input from women shrimp traders regarding their knowledge about shrimp, other fishing resources, coastal ecosystems, trading skills, and work ethics. Similarly their experiences with grassroots movements and labor unionization could greatly pave the way for other women seeking to improve their working conditions in other sectors of the fishing industry. After all, the fact that women shrimp traders were able to create a union from nothing and sustain their livelihoods for so long should testify to their persistence, resistance skills, and ability to create their own space within a strongly male-dominated fishing industry.

Acknowledgments

I thank the University of California at Riverside, UC-MEXUS, Arizona State University, and the Wenner-Gren Foundation (grant no. 7777) for providing the financial support to carry out the research on which this chapter is based. I want to express my gratitude to my colleagues at the Autonomous University of Sinaloa in Mazatlán for all their support and encouragement throughout the many stages of my fieldwork. I am forever indebted to the many women shrimp traders of southern Sinaloa for their good sense of humor, friendship, and cooperation during my fieldwork. A different short version of this chapter was previously published in *Signs: Journal of Women in Culture and Society*, volume 37, 3 (Spring 2012).

References

Adams, Jacqueline. 2002. Gender and social movement decline: Shantytown women and the prodemocracy movement in Pinochet's Chile. *Journal of Contemporary Ethnography* 31(3):285–322.

Al Rojo Vivo las Changueras. 1984. *Noroeste,* 2 de noviembre, 4c.

Basura y aguas negras proliferan en el centro y playas de la ciudad. 1987. *Noroeste,* 18 de agosto.

Bennett, Elizabeth. 2004. Gender, fisheries and development. *Marine Policy* 29(5):451–459.

Bennett, Vivienne. 1995. Gender, class, and water: Women and the politics of water service in Monterrey, Mexico. *Latin American Perspectives* 22(2):76–99.

Brú-Bistuer, Fosepa. 1996. Spanish women against industrial waste: A gender perspective on environmental grassroots movements. In *Feminist political ecology: Global issues and local experiences,* eds. Dianne Rocheleau, Barbara Thomas-Slayter, and Esther Wangari, 105–124. New York: Routledge.

Campbell, Connie, and the Women's Group of Xapuri. 1996. Out on the front lines but still struggling: Women in the rubber tapper's defense of the forest in Xapuri, Acre, Brazil. In *Feminist political ecology: Global issues and local experiences,* eds. Dianne Rocheleau, Barbara Thomas-Slayter, and Esther Wangari, 27–61. New York: Routledge.

Castañeda Camey, Itzá, and Guadalupe M. Flores Medrano. 2004. *Mujeres y hombres que aran el mar y el desierto, Reserva de la Biosfera.* Unpublished manuscript, El Vizcaíno, México.

Cruz-Torres, María L. 2001. Local-level responses to environmental degradation in northwestern Mexico. *Journal of Anthropological Research* 57(2):111–136.

Cruz-Torres, María L. 2004a. *Lives of dust and water: An anthropology of change and resistance in northwestern Mexico.* Tucson: University of Arizona Press.

Cruz-Torres, María L. 2004b. Street of the shrimp ladies. *Yemaya* 17:2–4.

Denuncian arbitrariedades y abusos de la policía destacamentada en Escuinapa. 1985. *Noroeste,* 3 de octubre, 7C.

Dodds, David. 1998. Lobster in the rainforest: The political ecology of Miskito wage labor and agricultural deforestation. *Journal of Political Ecology* 5:83–108.

Edelman, Marc. 1995. Rethinking the hamburger thesis: Deforestation and the crisis of Central America's beef exports. In *The social causes of environmental destruction in Latin America,* eds. Michael Painter and William H. Durham, 25–62. Ann Arbor: University of Michigan Press.

Escobar, Arturo, and Susan Paulson. 2004. The emergence of collective ethnic identities and alternative political ecologies in the Colombian Pacific rainforest. In *Political ecology across spaces, scales, and social groups,* eds. Susan Paulson and Lisa Gezon, 257–277. New Brunswick, N.J.: Rutgers University Press.

Federación Regional de Sociedades Cooperativas de la Industria Pesquera de la Ciudad y Puerto de Mazatlán. 1989. A la Opinión Pública. *Noroeste,* 16 de junio.

Fortmann, Louise. 1996. Gendered knowledge: Rights and space in two Zimbabwe villages. In *Feminist political ecology: Global issues and local experiences,* eds. Dianne Rocheleau, Barbara Thomas-Slayter, and Esther Wangari, 211–223. New York: Routledge.

García Ramírez, Guadalupe, and Jesús R. Gutiérrez. 2004. *Partidos políticos y movimientos sociales en Sinaloa, 1929–1940.* Culiacán: Universidad Autónoma de Sinaloa.

Gezon, Lisa. 1999. Of shrimps and spirit possession: Toward a political ecology of resource management in northern Madagascar. *American Anthropologist* 101(1):58–67.

Gezon, Lisa. 2002. Marriage, kin, and compensation: A socio-political ecology of gender in Ankarana, Madagascar. *Anthropological Quarterly* 75(4):675–706.

Hall-Arber, M. 1988. *Women fish traders of Guet Ndar, Senegal: The significance of small-scale earnings.* PhD diss., Brandeis University.

Hapke, Holly. 2001. Petty traders, gender, and development in a south Indian fishery. *Economic Geography* 77(3):225–249.

La policía desalojó a los vendedores de la Aquiles Serdán. 1985. *Noroeste*, 28 de diciembre, 3A.

Las Camaroneras de la Serdán sí que arriesgan todo. 1986. *Noroeste*, 17 de febrero, 1A.

Lobato González, P. 1988. *Estudio socioeconómico del cultivo de camarón realizado por Sociedades Cooperativas en México.* Mexico City: Secretaría de Pesca, Dirección General de Acuacultura.

McCallum, Cecilia 2007. Women out of place? A micro-historical perspective on the Black feminist movement in Salvador da Bahía, Brazil. *Journal of Latin American Studies* 39:55–80.

McGoodwin, R. 1987. Mexico's conflictual inshore Pacific fisheries: Problem analysis and policy recommendations. *Human Organization* 46(3):221–232.

Medrano, César. 1989. Las Changueras también serán reubicadas. *Noroeste*, 14 de septiembre.

Miller, Vernice, Moya Hallstein, and Susan Quass. 1996. Feminist politics and environmental justice: Women's community activism in West Harlem, New York. In *Feminist political ecology: Global issues and local experiences*, eds. Dianne Rocheleau, Barbara Thomas-Slayter, and Esther Wangari, 62–85. New York: Routledge.

Neis, Barbara. 2005. Introduction. In *Changing tides: Gender, fisheries and globalization*, eds. Barbara Neis, Marian Binkley, Siri Gerrard, and María Cristina Maneschy. 1–13. Halifax, Nova Scotia: Fernwood Publishing.

"No nos iremos: mientras paguemos no podrán desalojarnos" dicen vendedoras. 1987. *Noroeste*, 16 de marzo.

Ortega Noriega, Sergio. 1993. *Un ensayo de historia regional: El Noroeste de México, 1530–1880.* México, D.F.: Universidad Nacional Autónoma de México.

Overa, R. 1993. Wives and traders: Women's careers in Ghanaian canoe fisheries. *Maritime Anthropological Studies* 6(1):110–135.

Padilla, Francisco. 1993. *Lo que el tiempo no se llevó: Los conflictos agrarios en el sur de Sinaloa durante el período Cardenista, 1935–1940.* Culiacán: Universidad Autónoma de Sinaloa.

Paredes, J. L. 2004. Llegan a acuerdo SS y vendedoras. *Noroeste*, 5 de octubre, 16B.

Paulson, Susan. 2003. Gendered practices and landscapes in the Andes: The shape of asymmetrical exchanges. *Human Organization* 62(3):242–254.

Pereira, Graciela. 2002. *Informe preliminar de la segunda reunión de puntos focales de la Red Latinoamericana de las mujeres del sector pesquero-acuícola.* Montevideo, Uruguay: Red Latinoamericana de las Mujeres del Sector Pesquero-Acuícola.

Porter, Susie. 2003. *Working women in Mexico City*. Tucson: University of Arizona Press.

Ramírez Osuna, Francisco. 1989. Organizarán a las changueras, obtendrán el camarón de las Granjas Acuícolas y a buen Precio: SEPESCA. *Noroeste*, 25 de julio.

Rocheleau, Dianne, Barbara Thomas-Slayter, and Esther Wangari, eds. 1996. *Feminist political ecology: Global issues and local experiences*. New York: Routledge.

Rocheleau, Dianne, Laurie Ross, and Julio Morrobel. 1996. From forest gardens to tree farms: Women, men, and timber in Zambrana-Chacuey, Dominican Republic. In *Feminist political ecology: Global issues and local experiences*, eds. Dianne Rocheleau, Barbara Thomas-Slayter, and Esther Wangari, 224–250. New York: Routledge.

Rubio Ruelas, Baldemar, and Jaime F. Hirata Galindo. 1985. El movimiento campesino y las invasiones de tierras en Sinaloa durante 1976. In *Movimientos sociales en el Noroeste de México*, ed. Rubén Burgos Mejía, 67–83. Culiacán: Universidad Autónoma de Sinaloa.

Safa, Helen Icken. 1990. Women's social movements in Latin America. *Gender and Society* 4(3):354–369.

Schild, Veronica. 1994. Recasting "popular" movements: Gender and political learning in neighborhood organizations in Chile. *Latin American Perspectives* 21(2):59–80.

Secretaría del Medio Ambiente y Recursos Naturales (SEMARNAT). 2008. Programa "Hacia la Igualdad de Género y la Sustentabilidad Ambiental, 2007–2012." México, D.F.: Secretaría del Medio Ambiente y Recursos Naturales.

Sheridan, Thomas. 1988. *Where the dove calls: The political ecology of a corporate peasant community in northwestern Mexico*. Tucson: University of Arizona Press.

Shields, M. Dale, Cornelia Butler Flora, Barbara Thomas-Slayter, and Gladys Buenavista. 1996. Developing and dismantling social capital: Gender and resource management in the Philippines. In *Feminist political ecology: Global issues and local experiences*, eds. Dianne Rocheleau, Barbara Thomas-Slayter, and Esther Wangari, 155–179. New York: Routledge.

Siguen vendiendo camarón en las calles, pese al anuncio official, no fueron retiradas las changueras. 1987. *Noroeste*, 10 de marzo.

Simonian, Ligia T. L. 2006. Political organization among indigenous women of the Brazilian state of Roraima: Constraints and prospects. In *Social movements: An anthropological reader*, ed. June Nash, 285–303. Malden, Mass.: Blackwell Publishing.

Soares Moraes, Denise. 2003. Género y ambiente: Una aproximación a las relaciones socioambientales en dos comunidades de la Llanura Costera del Municipio de Loreto, Baja California Sur, México. *La Ventana* 17:140–187.

Stephen, Lynn. 1997. *Women and social movements in Latin America: Power from below*. Austin: University of Texas Press.

Stonich, Susan. 1995. The environmental quality and social justice implications of shrimp mariculture development in Honduras. *Human Ecology* 23(2):143–168.

Toscano, Ana Luisa. 2001. *Hacia la equidad de género: La conservación y desarrollo de humedales costeros en Bahía Santa María*. Guaymas, Sonora: Conservación Internacional.

Vázquez-García, Verónica, and María Montes-Estrada. 2006. Gender, subsistence fishing and economic change: A comparative study in southern Veracruz, Mexico. *International Journal of Sociology of Food and Agriculture* 14(1):1–17.

Velázquez, Margarita. 2003. Hacia la construcción de la sustentabilidad social: ambiente, relaciones de género y unidades domésticas. In *Género y medio ambiente*, ed. E. Tuñón. México, D.F.: Colegio de la Frontera Sur.

Verdugo Quintero, J. 1997. *Historia de Sinaloa*. Vol. I. Culiacán: Gobierno del Estado de Sinaloa.

Volkman T. A. 1994. Our garden is the sea: Contingency and improvisation in Mandar women's work. *American Ethnologist* 21(3):564–585.

Walsh, Casey. 2004. Aguas broncas: The regional political ecology of water conflict in the Mexico–U.S. borderlands. *Journal of Political Ecology* 11:43–58.

Wastl-Walter, Doris. 1996. Protecting the environment against state policy in Austria: From women's participation in protest to new voices in Parliament. In *Feminist political ecology: Global issues and local experiences*, eds. Dianne Rocheleau, Barbara Thomas-Slayter, and Esther Wangari, 86–104. New York: Routledge.

Zapién, Raquel. 2004. Vendedoras de camarón protestan ante Secretaría de Salud. *El Debate*, 5 de octubre, 3A.

PART FOUR

Conclusion

CHAPTER ELEVEN

Why Gender Matters, Why Women Matter

Lisa Gezon

As noted in the introduction to this book, it is timely to acknowledge gender as it pertains to sustainability, particularly in macro-level issues such as global warming and globalization, where the voices of women (or any actual people) are often ignored in studies of deforestation, soil degradation, sanitation, or other more immediate livelihood issues. While anthropologists have long identified the effects of globalization on people (e.g., Tsing 1993; Ong 1999) and have begun identifying on-the-ground effects of global warming (Strauss and Orlove 2003; Baer and Singer 2008; Crate and Nuttall 2009), gender dimensions of globalization, particularly regarding environmental sustainability, have received less attention (but see Padilla et al. 2007; Gunewardena and Kingsolver 2008).

Since the dawn of the discipline, anthropologists have recognized that people do not live in undifferentiated communities. Classic studies of marriage and kinship noted differences based on lineage and age categories, for example. Feminist scholars in the 1970s introduced new ways of analyzing gender as one of the main sources of differentiation and a critical basis for stratification within communities (Rosaldo and Lamphere 1974; Reiner 1975). Scholars such as Karen Sacks (1974) pointed out that gender difference provides a framework for assigning access to and control over important social and physical resources. The recognition of women's considerable contributions to subsistence, combined with their relative lack of political status, spurred criticism across the social sciences of Western economic development projects, where women's contributions had been ignored and their participation in projects not sought (Boserup 1970).

Unfortunately, the criticism of ignoring women in development projects has not resulted in a transformation of the field of development studies. The critique has had to be continually reintroduced, as the introduction points out so well in its tracing of the emergence of multiple and sequential women/gender and development paradigms. This book provides a contemporary iteration of the well-worn but necessary call for the inclusion of gender in analyses of development and sustainability. Not only does this volume put out a reminder to heed gender, it also engages in contemporary theoretical and topical discussions that push gender and sustainability scholarship to a new level. In this concluding chapter, I discuss the relevance of gender and sustainability to globalization, considering the relationship between local and global spaces. I also address why emphasis has been placed on focusing on women per se in a discussion of gender relations, particularly considering the dual patterns of women's vulnerability to ecological and economic downturns and of their proactive adaptations to it.

Globalization and Sustainability

Anthropologists have deconstructed the purported tendency of globalization to bring about homogeneous cultural and economic change (Hannerz 1989; Appadurai 1990). The widening gap between the rich and poor lays the framework for radically different experiences of and responses to new forms of global flows of information and capital. James Ferguson (2006) referred to the idea of "global shadows" in identifying spaces on the margins of the system, where people can only dream about having gainful employment in a country with a developed transportation, communication, and social services infrastructure. The lack of these resources have led to countless localized adaptations, manifest in a fusion of political, economic, and cultural strategies (Comaroff and Comaroff 1993).

These processes of globalization have effects on the environment, as well as on people. Almost without exception these changes have resulted in environmental degradation. The very concept of sustainability, however, implies that this end is not inevitable. To discuss sustainability is to imagine a world where change does not compromise the ability of future generations to meet their resource needs. This is a discussion of hope for both human and environmental well-being. It calls attention to the need to engage proactively in order to bring this into being and to shape the outcome of globally influenced local processes. It recognizes the agency of policy-makers, local people acting on them, and scholars like ourselves calling for measures to bring social and environmental sustainability into being. It is in this context that understanding gender relations on the ground becomes a critical link to potential outcomes of interventions.

Levels of Analysis and Method

Throughout her work, Anna Tsing (1993, 2000, 2005) has noted that what we refer to as global is not a top-down project but is coproduced across scales. Her concept of "friction" captures this sense: "As a metaphorical image, friction reminds us that heterogeneous and unequal encounters can lead to new arrangements of culture and power" (Tsing 2005, p. 5). Global and national institutions, such as national governments, the World Bank, or the US Agency for International Development, do not unilaterally shape the conditions in which local people act. What happens on the ground also shapes the context in which global policies are negotiated (Scott 1998; Goldman 2005).

Therefore, when investigating these issues, specific, localized contexts of interaction need to be a key focus of analysis; looking only at globalization from a bird's-eye view would be insufficient. This requires analyzing and deconstructing communities to identify social differentiation at many levels, with gender being one of the most salient. Grounded in feminist theory, empirical studies have considered hierarchies between individuals in groups. Because of the variability of response to global processes, it is difficult to identify abstract, predictive relationships between, for example, gender status and specific forms of resource management. Case studies involving both qualitative and quantitative data are valuable not only for revealing unique situations, but also for pointing to the various processes through which global and local processes coconstruct each other. The sustainability science model presented in the introduction calls for investigation into such factors as the determinants of human and environmental vulnerability, the effects of consumption and population growth on the environment, and the most effective incentive structures for encouraging sustainable action.

In-depth case studies indicate that local variation precludes narrow statements about relationships between these variables, but they do point to some patterns, and the cases elaborated in this volume suggest some important generalizations. First, women are particularly vulnerable to environmental change, and, second, women are also often in the forefront as agents of adaptation, both entrepreneurial and political. These cases point out the importance to sustainability of an analysis that focuses on gendered systems of access to and control over resources and that reveals the particular importance of women in specific cases. The cases also reveal some of the particular circumstances that either foster or impede empowerment for women.

Vulnerability to Negative Impacts of Change

Women in particular tend to be vulnerable to environmental degradation and related policy changes. This is in part because of their generally subordinate status, which gives them fewer resources and thus less of a buffer against detrimental forces. Women also frequently have primary responsibility for household reproduction, including care of dependents, which gives them a proportionately greater immediate need for resources. Providing for the household often entails responsibility for subsistence production or securing other sources of income. This was the case in many of the chapters in this volume. McElwee, for example, in her study of the bushmeat trade in Vietnam, noted that not being legally allowed to hunt common vermin from their subsistence fields interferes with women's ability to provide agricultural products for the household, for which they are responsible. Policies prohibiting the hunting of wildlife cause gender-differentiated hardships, with women's particular hardship being perhaps unanticipated by a policy ultimately concerned with endangered species. Singh's study acknowledges that women often suffer the consequences of severe deforestation, because it means they must travel further to get firewood and do not have access to certain forest products, such as medicinal plants. The Ecuadorian women in D'Amico's study experienced hardship under a government that turned to a pro-mining stance. In addition to losing a political voice, they were concerned that any environmental damage to the environment from mining would affect them first, as they were responsible for meeting children's immediate needs.

Vu, who studied shrimp farming in Vietnam, found that the turn to intensive production excluded women from high-return jobs because of the culturally prescribed division of labor and women's primary responsibility with subsistence farming and household maintenance. According to her study, women felt that a complementary relationship with men, one that balanced risk with fiscal conservativism, was necessary for a successful household. Nevertheless, women's crops were not as valuable, and the transition to aquaculture gave women access only to the lowest paying jobs. Thus, within households, aquaculture has tended to reinforce patriarchal norms. In Mexico, Cruz-Torres described how men fish for shrimp and women sell them on the streets in southern Sinaloa. Being part of the informal economy, the legitimacy of the women's activities was tenuous. In the mid-1980s, they were violently removed from the streets and forbidden from selling shrimp. Being more visible than the men who had actually caught them, they became an easy target for the authorities. This forced removal launched a long series of protests, where women underscored their need to feed their children.

In cases presented by Buechler, Drew, and Wutich, women's ability to provide for their households declined with environmental change, namely the growing scarcity of water. In Buechler's study of production in the US–Mexican border region, decreasing rainfall, influenced in part by local unsustainable land use policies, resulted in lowered production of fruit, which was the basis of women's informal economy of canning for money and exchange. Buechler noted that women's concerns were directly focused on their ability to continue to provide for their households. In Drew's study, both men and women suffered the impacts of a dam on the Bhagirathi Ganges River in India. But while men were often able to travel to find work elsewhere, women were left to care for the fields, animals, and dependents. Women were the ones to remain on the land and live within the constraints of environmental limitations. They were on the frontlines in experiencing the effects of resource degradation. Drew also noted how women were not only vulnerable economically, but also in terms of cultural identity. Notions of womanhood in general, domesticity, and women's role in showing respect for the supernatural were tied in with access to water from this river. Wutich's study of water scarcity in a squatter settlement in Cochabamba, Bolivia, also revealed that women are often on the frontlines of water provisioning, whereas men tend to be in charge of macro-level water management. Because of their proximity to subsistence use of water for cooking and cleaning, water scarcity hits women first, even though they do not formally have the authority to intervene in decision-making about water.

These studies in different parts of the world reveal a similar pattern: Women are often in charge of meeting basic household needs and are directly dependent on a healthy local resource base for doing so. This includes access to basic subsistence resources such as land and water, as well as commercial products such as fruit and shrimp. This means that women are often the first and hardest hit by environmental degradation. Sustainable futures thus should rely on an understanding of the nature of socially differentiated vulnerability, with particular attention to women's needs.

Changing Gender Relations, Increasing Women's Agency

Just as women tend to be particularly vulnerable to change, they are also critical agents of adaptation to that very change. Women's flexibility in adapting to change results in part from their generally subordinate status, which gives them less to lose in terms of power, prestige, and wealth. It also stems from the very factor that makes them more vulnerable: the imperative to meet primary subsistence needs and care for all household members. These chapters illustrated ways in which women respond to change through entrepreneurial as well as political risk-taking.

Eder's study suggested that women's entrepreneurial undertakings in the Philippines are critical in adjusting to more sustainable and less intensive fishing practices by providing alternative sources of income that can engage the men who would otherwise be fishing. Vu found that women engage in informal credit networks to finance shrimp production. In so doing, they shelter the household from the risks that men take. D'Amico discussed women's efforts at showcasing sustainability through such entrepreneurial activities as craft-making and engagement in fair trade initiatives. Realizing their political and economic stake in sustainable land use practices (which meant working to keep mining activities out), women engaged with the global discourse of sustainability on its own terms. They were flexible in developing strategies that would reinforce their capacity to meet their households' needs. Buechler noted that women originally developed informal canning production for sale and exchange as an adaptation to government policy changes that reduced subsidies for farmers, along with reduced access to credit and crop insurance beginning in the late 1980s. A reduction of water has come since and threatens this adaptation to already-precarious circumstances. Wutich explained that when water became extremely scarce in urban Bolivia, women played a crucial role in emergency water distribution among the most vulnerable in the community. Men's managerial roles were undermined as women, with their more intimate knowledge of individuals and their needs, began making more decisions.

In a focus on the political, D'Amico, Drew, Cruz-Torres, and Singh all discussed how women become involved in public struggles for livelihoods and more sustainable ecological conditions as a result of their frontline positions. Women protested mining operations (D'Amico), dams (Drew), and a moratorium on catching shrimp (Cruz-Torres) gave voice to alternative conceptions of development. For example, Singh reported how women in Orissa, India, inserted their voices in discussions of community forestry and began proactively protecting their forest resources, in many cases with greater success than men had found.

Women are thus important to sustainability discussions because of their tendency to be on the quiet but cutting edge of change. Women's strategies are critical in defining local adaptations to outside pressures—pressures in conjunction with globalization or the movement of global capital and the regulation thereof through such policies as structural adjustment. As Vu noted, it is important not to essentialize women's relationship to sustainability and assume that women will necessarily support the most sustainable options. They will, however, tend to support solutions that enable themselves and their households to survive, whether they are sustainable or not, and for that alone they must be acknowledged.

Why Gender? Why Women?

What began as women's studies, with an explicit focus on women, evolved into gender studies because of the need to understand systems of meaning and the relatedness of the elements within the system (Moore 1999). A gender focus rests on the recognition that women, for example, do not exist as an independent category, but rather in relation to other gendered categories. People become "women" in symbolic and practical opposition to "men" and sometimes other gendered categories that defy the binary gender differentiation so often assumed (Nanda 1998). Several of the studies in this volume illustrate the type of analysis that places women and men into a system of meanings and practical responsibilities. Buechler, Eder, and Vu, for example, pointed out that gender work complementarities exist within a household and the implications for that partnership for sustainable use of resources. McElwee showed how gender ideologies shape the bushmeat economy, as taboos against women hunting shape the production end, whereas cultural ideals of masculinity and prestige shape the market demand.

A focus on women has tended to remain in gender studies, however, despite criticisms that doing so merely replicates essentialist binary frames for understanding gender differentiation. Instead of positing any kind of universal womanhood or of focusing on women in an analytical vacuum, however, the best contemporary studies that focus on women examine their existence within gendered systems, as the chapters here have done. The need to emphasize women per se within these gendered systems remains because of their often-neglected, marked status. The gender category associated most commonly with female sexual anatomy nearly always holds a lower social status and is systematically overlooked in studies that do not explicitly analyze gender. In the chapters in this volume, women tend to holder lower status, and this lower status is clearly important for understanding use and management of resources.

For example, Vu, McElwee, and Drew identified gender ideologies that shape women's relationship with the resources in question. Vu noted that women are considered polluting to shrimp aquaculture, and this has practical implications for women's employability and access to the wealth associated with it. McElwee found that taboos restrict women's involvement in bushmeat hunting, a prestigious and lucrative activity. Drew reported that women's lack of mobility is marked by their lower levels of education and tendency to speak only regional dialects. Women's understanding is highly situated. They master local cultural forms of knowledge that also mark them as less prestigious and afford them fewer opportunities for wealth and power. In D'Amico's analysis, women have less freedom of movement than men, and this became clear when some men hassled their wives for leaving the home to participate in women's associations. While their voices were formally recognized, they had informal pressures not to become too involved.

One of the important insights of third-wave feminism was that gender does not consist of homogeneous categories. Factors such as race, class, and age shape experiences, becoming a source of differentiation among women or men (Lorde 1984; Anzaldúa 1990). This is an important caution for studies of gender and sustainability (Elmhirst and Resurreccion 2008). As Eder noted, even within rural communities, women do not form a uniform group. In his case, successful entrepreneurial Filipino women hire people to work for them and do not always treat them well, even if they are kin or neighbors. Women are not identical in their access to power, prestige, and wealth. Any gender category needs to be contextualized, considering such factors as rural and urban divides, ethnic identities, alternative sexualities, alternative household arrangements, marital status, and connectedness to social networks through kin, among others. To go even further, we must be cautious with regard to the generalizations that women are particularly vulnerable and innovative. Although case studies from many places in the world corroborate these findings, there will certainly be general cases and specific individuals within every case that do not conform. These exceptions should be acknowledged in carefully nuanced studies.

Fostering and Impeding Agency

While recognizing the variable and historically contextualized nature of globalization (Gunewardena and Kingsolver 2008), the case studies in this volume make it possible to trace some general conditions that either impede or foster women's empowerment to effect positive change for their own livelihoods and for the health of the physical environment upon which they depend. In her seminal analysis of factors that contribute to women's subordination, Karen Sacks (1974) recognized the importance of both ownership (or access to property) and the status of social adulthood. She identified several criteria for analyzing women's social status, including involvement in extradomestic decision-making, the ability to hold public office, and personal autonomy (to divorce, to socialize, to self-represent, and to organize in mutual aid associations).

Applying these criteria to an analysis of gender and sustainability reveals several important factors that foster or impede women's agency, while enhancing or threatening environmental sustainability. The first of these is that resources and livelihoods are threatened when women do not have access to subsistence resources that they rely upon for survival. In many places, women rely on primary resources such as firewood (Singh) or water (Wutich, Drew). When they lose access due to environmental degradation, sustainability is already threatened. When they lose access for political reasons, such as when the women of Bolivia were not involved in decision-making about water allocation (Wutich), then both livelihoods and sustainability are threatened. This leads to a second generalization: When women are excluded from decision-making about resources that they directly depend on, the sustainability of those resources will be threatened.

In addition, sustainability and livelihoods are enhanced when women have the right and the opportunity to organize socially and politically around issues critical to their basic subsistence needs. Many of the authors, including D'Amico, Wutich, Drew, Cruz-Torres, and Singh, identified the importance of women's collective political voices. There are many reasons for women's increased voice in political matters, including traditional cultural recognition of the importance of women's contributions. In addition, women's political involvement can increase when their input is explicitly sought and when, as Drew noted, their constraints to participation (such as domestic labor requirements) are recognized. When there is little to no traditional recognition of women's voices, and when no outside agent seeks it, women who are able to organize together often find their voice themselves (in Cruz-Torres' chapter, for example). Having political voice and economic opportunities often goes hand-in-hand, as income reinforces autonomy in many cases. Several factors contribute to shifts in access to resources and economic opportunities, which can lead to political change as well. First, a traditional division of labor can provide a framework for opportunities for innovation for women. In Buechler's study, for example, what began as an activity primarily in the private sphere of gift-giving (canning fruit) became an economic staple to the household as men's agricultural activities lost viability. Likewise, when men's economic opportunities shift, often related to environmental change (such as men emigrating to find work), women find opportunities for creative innovation.

Finally, initiatives coming from the outside can foster agency by providing opportunities, for example, for credit. Many successful microcredit projects have successfully targeted women (Yunus 2003), and access to financial opportunities is often associated with positive adaptation to changing environments. Although many entrepreneurial activities lead to resource degradation, several case studies, including those by D'Amico, Eder, and Vu, suggested that access to credit can contribute not only to livelihoods but to sustainability, especially when they provide opportunities that relieve pressure from local resources (Eder), engage in sustainable practices (Vu), or utilize renewable materials or services to increase incomes (Buechler, D'Amico), and in so doing, may relieve some of the need for scarce local resources.

In sum, then, several factors appear to foster both women's agency and environmental sustainability: access to subsistence resources that women control the acquisition and use of; participation in decision-making about those subsistence resources; access to political and social networks for collective action; and access to financial resources and services.

Concluding Remarks:
Gender, Sustainability, and Globalization

Why link gender and sustainability? Sustainability is specifically concerned with responsible management, and gendered systems shape access to and management of resources. Individuals think, make decisions, and act as members of social groups. Gender is a particularly salient category, as it emically and etically shapes relationships among people and between people and the material environment. It is particularly important to pay attention to women, first, because they tend to be ignored, and, second, because they are often the primary resource users, as well as being adept at flexible adaptations. Those qualities put them in a potential position to lead sustainability efforts.

Women do not inherently value the environment more than men, and they do not always follow paths that lead to resource sustainability. Like humans in general, they are instrumental in doing what it takes to survive. The association between women and the environment is not arbitrary or merely romantic, however. To the extent that women are responsible for household reproduction, including the long-term care of individuals, they tend to pay attention to issues of sustainability, taking care not to contaminate or destroy what they know they will need in the future. Without romanticizing women, we can still acknowledge the value in noticing what women, in conjunction with others, are doing to plan for the long-term availability of resources, taking care to remember that women are not all alike.

Each of the cases in this book suggests particular kinds of policy recommendations that could not be arrived at without a nuanced understanding of gender relations in those particular contexts. In general, appropriate policies will be based on careful analysis of local processes, considering the extent to which women rely on local resources for subsistence, gendered divisions of labor, and ideologies about gendered rights and responsibilities. Interventions will seek to include women's participation in managing the resources they rely upon and to strengthen the basis upon which women can organize among themselves. Changes in political access or financial opportunities will build upon existing practices, recognizing opportunities as well as constraints, with the understanding that too much innovation will jeopardize efforts at change (Kottak 1990).

These cases illustrate that local dynamics are not just shaped by but they also shape global processes. Gendered actions on the ground lay the framework within which the "global" is articulated and enacted. Communities survive the often devastating effects of global processes (including capital flows and government policies meant to facilitate them) in part through women's engagements in informal economies. Women actively protest unlivable conditions, forcing those at higher levels of authority to pay attention to their demands, even if they are not necessarily or even often successful in immediately changing courses of action. Women's entrepreneurial initiatives may actually encourage more sustainable livelihoods to take root. As these cases illustrate, ignoring women's interests and involvements would lead to naïve understandings and shortsighted interventions that would ultimately fail to address critical issues of local sustainability effectively.

Local actions thus bring into being what we call the "global." This way of understanding global processes empowers hopes for sustainability, because it points out that local actions make a difference. A gender lens helps us understand the meaningful social and cultural contexts within which individuals make decisions. In other words, paying attention to gender makes sustainability a more attainable goal.

References

Anzaldúa, Gloria, ed. 1990. *Making face, making soul: Creative and critical perspectives by women of color.* San Francisco, Calif.: Aunt Lute Foundation Books.

Appadurai, Arjun. 1990. Disjuncture and difference in the global cultural economy. *Public Culture* 2(2):1–24.

Baer, Hans, and Merrill Singer. 2008. *Global warming and the political ecology of health: Emerging crises and systemic solutions.* San Francisco, Calif.: Left Coast Press.

Boserup, Ester. 1970. *Woman's role in economic development.* New York: St. Martin's Press.

Comaroff, Jean, and John Comaroff. 1993. *Modernity and its malcontents: Ritual and power in postcolonial Africa.* Chicago: University of Chicago Press.

Crate, Susan A., and Mark Nuttall. 2009. *Anthropology and climate change: From encounters to actions.* San Francisco, Calif.: Left Coast Press.

Elmhirst, Rebecca, and Bernadette P. Resurreccion. 2008. Gender, environment and natural resource management. In *Gender and natural resource management: Livelihoods, mobility and interventions,* eds. Bernadette P. Resurreccion and Rebecca Elmhirst, 10–23. London: Earthscan.

Ferguson, James. 2006. *Global shadows: Africa in the neoliberal world order.* Durham, N.C.: Duke University Press.

Goldman, Michael. 2005. *Imperial nature: The World Bank and struggles for social justice in the age of globalization.* New Haven, Conn.: Yale University Press.

Gunewardena, Nandini, and Ann Kingsolver, eds. 2008. *The gender of globalization: Women navigating cultural and economic marginalities.* Santa Fe, N.M.: School for Advanced Research Press.

Hannerz, Ulf. 1989. Notes on the global ecumene. In *The anthropology of globalization: A reader,* eds. Jonathan Issa and Renate Rosaldo, 37–45. Malden, Mass.: Blackwell Publishers.

Kottak, Conrad Phillip. 1990. Culture and "economic development." *American Anthropologist* 92(3):723–731.

Lorde, Audre. 1984. *Sister outsider.* Freedom, Calif.: The Crossing Press.

Moore, Henrietta, ed. 1999. *Anthropological theory today.* Malden, Mass.: Polity Press.

Nanda, Serena. 1998. *Neither man nor woman: The Hijras of India.* Belmont, Calif.: Wadsworth Publishing.

Ong, Aihwa. 1999. *Flexible citizenship: The cultural logics of transnationality.* Durham, N.C.: Duke University Press.

Padilla, Mark, Jennifer S. Hirsch, Miguel Munoz-Laboy, Robert E. Sember, and Richard G. Parker, eds. 2007. *Love and globalization: Transformations of intimacy in the contemporary world.* Nashville, Tenn.: Vanderbilt University Press.

Reiner, Rayna, ed. 1975. *Toward an anthropology of women.* New York: Monthly Review Press.

Rosaldo, Michelle, and Louise Lamphere, eds. 1974. *Women, culture, and society.* Stanford, Calif.: Stanford University Press.

Sacks, Karen. 1974. Engels revisited: Women, the organization of production, and private property. In *Women, culture, and society,* eds. Michelle Rosaldo and Louise Lamphere, 207–222. Stanford, Calif.: Stanford University Press.

Scott, James. 1998. *Seeing like a state: How certain schemes to improve the human condition have failed.* New Haven, Conn.: Yale University Press.

Strauss, Sarah, and Benjamin S. Orlove. 2003. *Weather, climate, culture.* Oxford, U.K.: Berg Publishers.

Tsing, Anna. 1993. *In the realm of the diamond queen.* Princeton, N.J.: Princeton University Press.

Tsing, Anna. 2000. The global situation. *Cultural Anthropology* 15(3):327–360.

Tsing, Anna. 2005. *Friction: An ethnography of global connection.* Princeton, N.J.: Princeton University Press.

Yunus, Muhammed. 2003. *Banker to the poor: Micro-lending and the battle against world poverty.* New York: Public Affairs Books.

About the Contributors

Stephanie Buechler obtained a PhD in sociology from Binghamton University. Dr. Buechler is a research associate and lecturer with the School of Geography and Development at the University of Arizona. Prior to working at the university, she was a researcher with the International Water Management Institute in Hyderabad, India, and Irapuato, Mexico. Her research has focused on gender, migration, agriculture, water, climate change, and, most recently, cities and innovative strategies to address the urban heat island effect.

María L. Cruz-Torres is an associate professor in the School of Transborder Studies at Arizona State University. She holds a PhD in anthropology from Rutgers, The State University of New Jersey. Her research interests include political ecology; the impact of globalization upon local communities and households; gender and globalization; gender, sustainability, and the environment; and the environmental and social aspects of natural resource management.

Linda D'Amico earned a PhD in anthropology from Indiana University, Bloomington. She lived and worked in Latin America for almost twenty years. Currently, she is a professor at Winona State University in Minnesota, where she teaches in the Global Studies and Women's and Gender Studies Departments. She is also affiliated with Facultad Latinoamericana de Ciencias Sociales, Ecuador. Her current research interests include gendered environmentalism, integrated natural resource management, and community media.

Georgina Drew is a PhD candidate in the Department of Anthropology at the University of North Carolina, Chapel Hill. She has graduate degrees in anthropology and international relations and documentary arts training from Duke University's Center for Documentary Studies. Her research interests include human-nature relations, sustainability, gendered dynamics of natural resource management, and organizational development. Before beginning doctoral studies, she worked with NGOs in the United States and abroad.

JAMES EDER received a PhD in anthropology from the University of California, Santa Barbara, and is currently a professor of anthropology in the School of Human Evolution and Social Change at Arizona State University. His research interests concern the indigenous and migrant inhabitants of Palawan Island in the Philippines and include the subsistence economy of indigenous forest dwellers; economic change and social differentiation in frontier farming communities; and livelihood, resource management, and global change in the coastal zone.

LISA L. GEZON has a PhD in anthropology from the University of Michigan and is currently a professor in the Department of Anthropology at the University of West Georgia. Her primary research area has been Madagascar on many facets of humans and their relationship to the material environment. Her most recent book (2012) analyzes the locally produced drug, khat, from environmental, political, economic, and health perspectives.

PAMELA MCELWEE is an assistant professor in the Department of Human Ecology at Rutgers, The State University of New Jersey. She obtained her PhD in anthropology and forestry and environmental studies at Yale University. Her research focuses on global environmental problems, broadly defined, with specific expertise in biodiversity conservation and climate change. She has conducted research on these issues in Vietnam since 1996, with a focus on ethnographic and household-level analysis of environmental decision-making and resource use combined with an examination of global institutional practices and norms that influence environmental policy.

NEERA SINGH is an assistant professor in the Faculty of Forestry at the University of Toronto. She has an interdisciplinary PhD in resource development from Michigan State University. Her research focuses on community forestry, democratization of forest governance, and commodification of nature. Prior to her academic career, she worked for a decade in India on environmental conservation and community rights. She is the founder of Vasundhara, a leading NGO in Orissa that works on environmental conservation and sustainable livelihoods.

HONG ANH VU received her PhD in 2011 from the Department of Anthropology at Syracuse University. Her dissertation research in a coastal province of Vietnam's Mekong Delta focused on the impact of globalization and neoliberal policies on rural livelihoods, particularly as a result of intensified shrimp farming, and her future projects will be exploring the impact of changing land rights and water availability on women in the delta.

AMBER WUTICH received her PhD in cultural anthropology from the University of Florida. She is currently on the faculty of Arizona State University's School of Human Evolution and Social Change. Her research explores the limits of human adaptability using theories of culture, ecology, and economy. She has examined how resource insecurity affects human well-being, vulnerability, and resilience in urban environments in Bolivia, Mexico, and the United States.

Index